Flavors of Cape Cod

School's out for the cranberry harvest.

Cranberry picking on what is now Beaton's Bog, Spring Hill.

Martha Blake
Green Briar Jam Kitchen

"Tis a wonderful thing
to sweeten the world
which is in a jam
and needs preserving."
T. W. Burgess

FLAVORS
of
CAPE COD

A
gathering
of new
and favorite
old Cape Cod
recipes
including
Indian Pudding,
Sea Clam Pie,
Baked Beans,
Potato Bargain,
and numerous other
taste-tempting treats
presented with
historical facts and
old photographs.

Rosemary ~ Herb of Remembrance

Cape Kitchen

I sing of the sturdy old black iron stove
   with its trimming of bright nickel metal,
the wooden-armed clothes drier hanging above,
   the bright colored braided rug grandmother wove
and the hum of the simmering kettle.
   The smell of the baking of brown crusty bread
and the pies as they cooled on the sill.
   The plate in the corner where pussy was fed,
the chair with its cushions of gay turkey red
   and the cookie jar Gram used to fill.
The potted geraniums always in bloom,
   the red checkered cloth spread for tea.
The crisp white curtains, the sunshiny room,
   the glass spoon holder, the old corn broom
and the special treats Gram saved for me.

Joyce Tomlinson

Copyright 1987 ©
Fifth Printing
Thornton W. Burgess Society, Inc.
6 Discovery Hill Road
East Sandwich, Cape Cod, Massachusetts

TABLE OF CONTENTS

Acknowledgments

Sincere gratitude is expressed to all who contributed in any way to the production and publication of this unique cook book. We especially appreciate the willingness of our many good cooks who shared their favorite recipes in the interest of this book.

* * * * * * * * *

"Hide not your talents,
   they for use were made.
What's a sundial
   in the shade??"

Poor Richard's Almanac, 1750

* * * * * * * * *

COMMITTEE
  Pamela Anderson
  Patricia Bryant
  Dorothy Clark
  Rosanna Cullity
  Florence Eaton
  Georgia O'N. Flagg
  Janet Grigg
  Helen Hayward
  Jacqueline Jacobsen
  Penelope Lovell
  Laura Maleady
  Nancy Siebert
  Nancy E. Titcomb
  Mary Williams

DESIGN
  Donald Clark
PHOTOGRAPHY
  Edward Robinson
  John Cullity
CONSULTANT
  John Carafoli
DECORATIVE ART
  Shirley G. Cross
  Carolyn J. Mosher
  Michael DiPersio
HISTORIAN
  Russell A. Lovell
TYPISTS
  Mary Legwin
  Hazel Packer
  Sarah ter Horst

Foreword

The taste of the foods of Cape Cod is multitudinous and varied, from the succulent native products found on land and sea to the offerings of people that lived here early and others who arrived later on these shores.

Cape Cod has long been known for the corn meal, Indian pudding and game which were staples of the Wampanoags, first inhabitants of this narrow land who aided the Pilgrims in the early 1600s as they carved out settlements in the wilderness. The Pilgrims in turn introduced the natives to stew, baked beans and dumplings. Both races enjoyed the delicious meals developed from offerings of the sea as well. As the generations continued, ancestors of the present day inhabitants developed recipes which ingeniously used the potato, the turnip and codfish (sometimes called Cape Cod turkey) to brighten the somewhat limited menus of the day. Nuts and berries were a staple, especially cranberries when sugar became more readily available.

New tastes were added in the 1700s when the Portuguese arrived in Provincetown. Kale soup, linguica and their distinctive breads added a welcome touch to local menus. Corn fritters, black-eyed peas and grits tickled the taste buds of the locals when blacks arrived from the south and Italians brought pasta and a multitude of ways to serve tomato and cheese.

When the 1800s brought Irish to Sandwich to work for the Boston and Sandwich Glass Company, they brought their recipes for mussel stew, breads and Irish coffee. Finnish folk emigrated, looking for a better life, bringing their recipes for smoked and pickled fish as well as cardamon coffee bread. Jewish folk brought borscht, bagels and their special chicken soup. When the Greeks arrived, stuffed grape leaves, moussaka and baklava tickled the taste buds of the populace. The French introduced Cape Codders to their mouthwatering pastries and the Germans brought along sauerbraten and strudel. Swedish folk introduced recipes for rice porridge and lutfisk (dried codfish).

In the 1900s colonies of Lithuanians settled on the Cape adding favorite foods like kopustu (cabbage and homemade sausage). Polish arrived in goodly numbers with the conscription in the old country, bringing with them recipes for kielbasa (sausage) and golomki (stuffed cabbage). The Scottish heritage is strong here too and puff pastry turnovers, shortbreads and scones have increased the number of flavors on this peninsula. Armenians arrived also adding chicken rice pilaf and paklava to the feast.

In more recent years, there has been an influx of Mexicans, Chinese, Vietnamese, Cambodians, Central Americans and others seeking a new homeland and bringing with them a wealth of new food offerings to tempt Cape Cod taste buds. No doubt new flavors will continue to be added as long as America continues to be a haven.

Space does not permit the Thornton Burgess Society to include recipes for all these taste treats in one book. However, in honor of the Town of Sandwich's 350th birthday, members and friends present here a representative collection from the wealth of tasty foods available. It is our hope that these recipes will not only give you an idea of the variety available, but also tickle YOUR taste buds.

— *Marion Vuilleumier*

Green Briar Nature Center
and Jam Kitchen

Appetizers

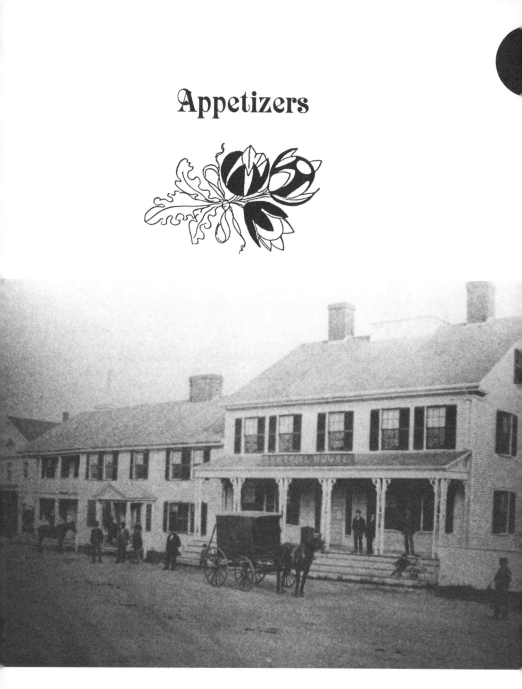

THE DANIEL WEBSTER INN

The Central House in Sandwich began as the Fessenden Parsonage and became the Fessenden Tavern, headquarters for Patriots in the American Revolution. Enlarged in 1830, its guest list included Daniel Webster, Frederick Tudor, Deming Jarves, Grover Cleveland and Joseph Jefferson. It was renamed the Daniel Webster Inn in 1915 and was consumed by fire in 1971. The present establishment is called the Dan'l Webster Inn.

SETTING THE TABLE

Cook books written in America after the Revolution provided not only "receipts" for the food but also advice to hostesses on how to arrange things on the table. Each diner had a plate, knife and fork, while glasses and drinks were on a sideboard.

The fork was in common use by 1770 but this was a 2-tine item which was for holding food while it was cut, not for eating. The knife was broad, slightly dished and round ended, and this was the implement for getting food to the mouth. About the 1830's the forks of 3 and 4 tines became available, and hostesses were advised that they should be used to eat with, but this was considered by many as a European affectation and was spurned. It took a whole generation to get Americans to eat with the fork, and that was in the left hand as still done in England today. Transferring the fork to the right hand for eating was a much later development and only in America.

There were no napkins until the 1820's or 1830's. People wiped their hands and mouths on the edge of the tablecloth, which was removed at the end of the main course. A dessert and wines were served on the bare table, with an emphasis on symmetrical placement of bottles and dishes. The ladies were expected to leave after one glass of wine, and to sit chatting in the parlor until the gentlemen joined them. Then the meal would close with hot tea in the parlor without further food. These guest meals typically began at two and lasted most of the afternoon.

In country houses the main meal was at noon and served in the kitchen without ceremony. If an evening party were called for, this would begin with tea at the end of the day followed by a more or less extensive supper, but served in the front rooms not in the kitchen. In city homes with a dining room, evening entertaining for guests would begin later and would consist of tea and cakes and fruit on the best dishes, to be followed at intervals with an iced pudding or ice cream, then candies and cookies throughout the evening.

America greatly welcomed the arrival of inexpensive glass made by the New England Glass Company or the Boston & Sandwich Glass Company, made cheaply in presses, so that even houses of modest means could have beautiful drinking glasses and table accessories.

BLACK OLIVE SPREAD

8 ounces of cream cheese
8 ounces of blue cheese
2 ounces butter
2 tablespoons chopped onion

1 can black olives, drained,
  minced
1 tablespoon lemon juice

Soften cream cheese and butter. Crumble blue cheese. Put cheeses in food processor or blender and mix until smooth. Add rest of ingredients and process until only small pieces of olives are visible. Form into ball. Chill. Serve with thin crackers.

Mary Williams

BOURSIN

8 ounces softened cream cheese
½ teaspoon garlic powder
½ teaspoon dried dill weed
½ teaspoon celery salt

1 tablespoon lemon juice
½ teaspoon dried basil
½ teaspoon minced parsley
¼ teaspoon ground pepper

Beat all ingredients until smooth and chill. Garnish with extra parsley and serve with crackers. Also great on roast beef sandwiches!

Sara Titcomb

CHEESE AND BACON CRISPS

½ cup soft butter
¼ teaspoon salt
1 teaspoon Worcestershire
  sauce
1½ cup flour

½ pound sharp cheddar cheese
  grated
dash of hot liquid pepper
¼ cup crisp bacon crumbled
¼ teaspoon dry mustard

Mix well butter, cheese, salt and pepper, and Worcestershire sauce. Add bacon bits, flour and mustard and mix again. Shape into two rolls 1 inch in diameter. Wrap in waxed paper and chill overnight. Cut into 1/8 inch slices and bake on greased cookie sheet in preheated 375° oven for 6 minutes or until brown. May be served hot or cold. Chilled rolls may be kept in refrigerator for several days before baking.

Jeanne Kelly
(Owner of Sandy Neck Motel)

CUP-A-CUP-A-CUP

1 cup grated sweet onion
1 cup mayonnaise

1 cup grated cheddar cheese
paprika

Mix all ingredients, except paprika, well and put in a small baking dish. Sprinkle with paprika and bake in a 350° oven for 30 minutes. Serve hot with crackers.

JEZEBEL

10 ounce jar of pineapple or
  apricot preserves
10 ounce jar of apple jelly

2 tablespoons mustard powder
2 to 4 tablespoons horseradish
large block of cream cheese

Mix all ingredients except cream cheese. To serve, pour mixture over cream cheese on serving dish and surround with crackers. Sauce can be stored in refrigerator for up to 2 weeks.

Violet White

Appetizers

KILLER DIP

1 part mozzarella cheese
  (shredded)
3 cherry peppers (chopped)

3 parts sharp cheddar cheese
  (shredded)
10 shakes of oregano

Place all ingredients in baking dish. Bake 1 hour at 250° F.

This is a wonderful, zesty dip to be used with thick chips. It has a pizza-like flavor and is very popular with young people. Great for a card game!

PIZZA DIP

8 ounce package softened
  cream cheese
12 ounce bottle chili sauce
½ cup chopped onion

2 2-ounce cans sliced black olives
2-cup bag shredded mozzarella
  cheese

On large glass plate the size of a pizza pan spread ingredients in layers (cheese first, then chili, onions, olives and cheese). Serve with Mexican chips.

Laurie Crigler

ROQUEFORT SPREAD

½ cup Roquefort cheese
2 teaspoons lemon juice
1 teaspoon chopped chives

¼ cup fresh parsley
2 tablespoons heavy cream
2 tablespoons virgin olive oil

Mix thoroughly all ingredients in blender or food processor and use as spread on crackers. Also can be used on cooked vegetables or baked potatoes.

TOMATO - CHEESE CANAPÉS

2 tablespoons soft butter
2 cups shredded sharp cheese
8 slices sandwich bread

2 tablespoons Worcestershire
  sauce
4 tablespoons chili sauce

Butter cookie sheet. Combine all ingredients except bread. Spread combined ingredients on slices of sandwich bread. Place on cookie sheet and cut into squares or rectangles. Bake in a 425° preheated oven until bubbly and slightly brown, about 5 to 10 minutes. These canapés can be made in advance and frozen before cooking.

Margaret Clark

The Sandwich Glass Museum is housed in what was originally termed a "spite barn". In 1813 the disgruntled owner, a member of the Old Parish Church, reputedly gave vent to his anger at the new Calvinist group meeting directly next door by stirring up his livestock during their meetings. The barn was subsequently moved to its current location opposite the Town Hall and was used as a shop, residence, and finally in 1907 was acquired by the Sandwich Historical Society. Many additions later the "spite barn" has become the world-renowned Sandwich Glass Museum.

BRESELTINI

small eye of round roast beef
1 cup grated Parmesan cheese
fresh mushrooms
2 tablespoons vegetable oil

2 cups bread crumbs
1 onion
celery

Have butcher slice roast lengthwise in long, very thin slices. Finely chop mushrooms, celery and onion and mix with Parmesan cheese and bread crumbs. Add vegetable oil. Lay out beef slices and spread each evenly with stuffing mixture. Roll beef slices and skewer with a toothpick. If rolls are long, cut into pieces about 1½ inches in length. Place on baking sheet and bake in pre-heated 350° oven for about 15 minutes. Tastes best when served hot from the oven.

A tasty, filling party hors d'oeuvre, which has been a special favorite of the teenagers at our family gatherings. The recipe has an Italian origin.

Joan DiPersio

CHICKEN LIVER PATÉ

1 cup butter
1 medium onion sliced
½ teaspoon paprika
1/8 teaspoon black pepper

1 pound chicken livers
½ teaspoon curry powder
1/8 teaspoon salt
dash of garlic powder

Melt butter in saucepan. Cook chicken livers, onions and seasonings in butter over medium heat until onions are soft. Blend in blender or processor until smooth. Pour into 4 cup mold. Refrigerate at least 8 hours or overnight. Unmold and serve.

Sandi Simpson

DILL IN THE ROUND

2 cups mayonnaise
2 cups sour cream
2 tablespoons minced onion flakes
2 tablespoons minced parsley
2 tablespoons dry dill weed

1 tablespoon finely chopped
celery
1 tablespoon Accent seasoning
1 package chipped dried beef
1 pound round rye loaf

Day before using, mix all ingredients together except bread and refrigerate. For serving, hollow out rye bread, reserving pieces for dipping. Pour dip into hollowed bread and serve with rye pieces.

GLAZED HAM BALLS

1 pound ground ham
½ pound fresh pork
¾ cup bread crumbs

2 eggs — beaten slightly
½ cup milk
2 tablespoons chopped onions

GLAZE:

1 cup crushed pineapple
⅓ cup brown sugar

1 tablespoon vinegar
2 tablespoons mustard

Combine ham, pork, bread crumbs, eggs, milk and chopped onions — shape into 1½" balls — makes about 18. Place in shallow baking pan. Combine pineapple, sugar, vinegar and mustard and spoon over ham balls. Bake at 350° for 45 minutes, basting often.

Nan Higgins

LIVER PATE STRAWBERRIES

1 pound liverwurst
1 teaspoon horseradish
1 cup bread crumbs
red food color
8 ounces whipped cream cheese

2 or 3 tablespoons excellent
  mustard (preferably Dutch-
  French-German)
parsley

Add food color to bread crumbs until color reaches that of a strawberry. Use electric mixer to combine all other ingredients. Form mixture into strawberry shaped pieces, (sizes should vary). Roll in red bread crumbs and tuck a piece of parsley in top to resemble real thing.

Colorful and fun for parties. No one ever eats strawberry hors d'ouevres!

Sarah ter Horst

CLAMS CASINO I

6 to 8 large quahaugs
1 clove garlic
¼ pound butter or margarine
4 to 6 slices bacon

¼ pound salt pork
1 cup fresh parsley chopped
1½ cups bread crumbs

Scrub quahaugs in cold water and steam until open. Save clam juice for another use and grind meat using coarse cutter. Fry salt pork and add finely chopped garlic clove. Sauté until golden brown. Add ground quahaugs and ¼ pound butter and sauté 5 to 6 minutes. Add parsley and simmer 4 to 5 additional minutes. Add bread crumbs gradually until mixture is crumbly. If too dry, add more butter. Fill cleaned quahaug shells with the mixture and top with 2 to 3 small pieces of bacon. Place under broiler until bacon is crisp.

Arthur Bukovich

CLAMS CASINO II

12 large quahaugs
quahaug liquid
2 medium onions
1 inch piece bacon for
  each shell

8 slices toasted bread
1 teaspoon salt
2 tablespoons butter
garlic salt and black pepper
  to taste

Clean and remove bellies from quahaugs. Grind. Strain liquid and add enough water to make one cup of liquid. Break toasted bread into small pieces and cover with liquid. Chop onions and sauté in butter until softened. Mix clams, bread mixture, onions, and seasoning well. Stuff into greased shells. Place on cookie sheet and cover entire sheet with aluminum foil. Pre-heat oven to 325 degrees, then bake for 25 minutes. Sauté bacon pieces just enough to soften. Remove casinos when done and place piece of bacon on each. Place under broiler until bacon becomes crisp. Place on heated platter and serve immediately.

Muriel White

CLAM DIP

2 8-ounce packages cream cheese
grated rind of one lemon
1 can minced clams

1 small onion very finely minced
1 teaspoon Worcestershire sauce
lemon juice

Whip cream cheese until light and fluffy. Add minced onion, lemon rind, Worcestershire sauce. Whip until well blended. Drain clams. Discard liquid or use for other purposes. Whip clams into cheese mixture. Add enough lemon juice to bring to desired consistency. Flavor improves with standing.

STUFFED CLAMS

1½ cups ground clams
1¼ cups plain breadcrumbs
1¼ cups seasoned breadcrumbs
½ large onion, chopped
½ large pepper, chopped
2 tablespoons butter

2 tablespoons chopped parsley
½ cup clam broth
18 clam shells
1 lemon
paprika

Sauté onions and pepper in butter or margarine until soft. Mix all ingredients together. Stuff into clam shells. Put pat of butter on each clam and sprinkle with paprika. Squeeze a few drops of juice over each clam. Bake in pre-heated oven for 15 minutes at 350 degrees.

Evelyn Shernowit

HOT CRAB DISH

8 ounces cream cheese
1 tablespoon milk
6½ ounces crabmeat, flaked

2 tablespoons minced onion
1 teaspoon horseradish
salt, pepper, almonds

Blend well and spoon into ovenproof dish; top with almonds. Bake at 325 degrees for one hour. Serve with crackers.

Carolyn Plate

CRAB "Croustades"

Sheet of puff pastry
1 large onion
¼ teaspoon thyme
pepper to taste
¼ cup sour cream
3 tablespoons butter

1 can drained crabmeat
½ teaspoon salt
2 tablespoons flour
2 tablespoons sherry
  or dry white wine

Roll out a sheet of puff pastry to about 10″ by 10″. Using miniature muffin pans, press 2″ by 2″ squares into each muffin space. (Pastry will stick up like envelope flaps.) Heat butter, sauté onion, then add crabmeat and sauté 1 minute. Add thyme, salt, pepper and sprinkle with flour. Stir in sour cream until mixture thickens. Add sherry or white wine. Fill puff pastry with this mixture. Bake 15 minutes at 400°. After baking these can be cooled and frozen on a cookie sheet. They can be packed in freezer bags for later. If reheating, heat for 25 minutes at 325°.

Hazel Packer

GRAVLAX (Cured Salmon)

2 pounds fresh salmon
1 tablespoon salt
1 bunch fresh dill

1 tablespoon sugar
1½ tablespoons ground black
  pepper

SAUCE:

2 tablespoons Dijon mustard
2 tablespoons vinegar
1 tablespoon chopped fresh dill

1 tablespoon sugar
6 tablespoons oil

Filet fish and remove skin and all bones. Coat fish heavily with salt and sugar on both sides and wrap tightly in foil. Place on tray with another tray on top. Weight top tray and refrigerate for 24 hours. Spread dill and pepper over fish and refrigerate an additional 24 hours. Scrape off toppings and slice thin. Serve with mustard sauce.

For sauce: mix mustard, sugar and vinegar in a processor and gradually add oil and chopped dill.

The Brodericks
First Edition Restaurant

KIPPER PATÉ

2 3¼-ounce cans of kippered
  herring (drained)
1 slice firm white bread,
  crust removed
2 tablespoons onion, minced
4 teaspoons fresh lemon juice

¼ cup mayonnaise
2 tablespoons milk
2 tablespoons minced fresh dill
2 drops hot pepper sauce
baked toast rounds

Mix everything except toast in processor or blender. Chill at least 1 hour. Serve on baked toast rounds.

PICKLED OYSTERS

1 pint of fresh oysters, shelled
2 teaspoons lemon juice
½ teaspoon salt
¼ cup olive oil
2 cloves garlic, crushed

6 peppercorns
2 small hot green chili peppers
  seeded and cut in strips
½ cup mild vinegar

Add lemon juice and salt to oysters with their juice and bring to a boil. Drain oysters (reserving liquid) and fry in oil until edges curl. Remove and drain. Reduce temperature of oil and fry garlic and peppercorns until garlic colors. Combine oyster-lemon juice, fried oysters, garlic mix and add pepper strips and vinegar. Marinate and chill overnight.

SEVICHE

1 pound fillet of flounder or sole
lemon juice to cover fish
½ onion, chopped
1 clove garlic, pressed
3 tablespoons chopped parsley

3 tablespoons olive oil
2 canned green chilis, chopped
¼ teaspoon oregano
salt and pepper to taste
1 ripe avocado, diced

Cut fish fillets into small cubes. Place fish in a glass bowl and cover with lemon juice. Let stand in refrigerator for at least 8 hours or overnight. Add remaining ingredients, except avocado and refrigerate for an hour or so more. When ready to serve, stir in avocados and serve with toothpicks or on top of taco chips.

Jill Wyman

SMOKED SALMON CAVIAR

½ pound smoked salmon
½ cup chopped onion

2 hard boiled eggs
crackers

Combine all ingredients in a blender except crackers and process until the consistency or look of caviar. Chill and serve on crackers.

Joy Moore

ARTICHOKE HORS D'OEUVRES

2 jars marinated artichoke
  hearts
1 medium onion, chopped
1 clove garlic, crushed
4 eggs

1/8 teaspoon each pepper,
  tabasco sauce and oregano
¼ teaspoon salt
¼ cup fine bread crumbs
2 cups shredded cheddar cheese

Drain marinade from 1 jar artichokes, and sauté onion and garlic in it until soft. Chop rest of drained artichokes. Beat eggs. Add seasonings and crumbs to bowl. Stir in cheese and artichokes and onions. Grease 7x11 pan and spread mixture in it. Bake at 325° for 30 minutes or until set. Cool. Cut in pan. Yield: 5 dozen.

Dorothy Clark

BAKED ARTICHOKE SPREAD

1 cup HELLMAN's mayonnaise
1 cup grated cheddar cheese
1 tablespoon minced onion

dash Worcestershire sauce
1 can artichoke hearts (NOT
  marinated!)

Break up artichoke hearts a bit, and combine with remainder of ingredients. Bake 30 minutes at 350°. Cut into bite-sized pieces for serving.

Louise Hannegan

JILL'S GUACAMOLE

1 large ripe avocado (peeled and
  seeded)
3 teaspoons lemon juice
½ cup mayonnaise
½ package Taco seasoning

½ cup sour cream
½ can refried beans
1 scallion (chopped)
1 tomato (chopped)
grated cheese

Mash and mix well avocado, lemon juice and mayonnaise and chill. Mix Taco seasoning with sour cream and reserve. Spread refried beans on plate. Spread over them avocado mixture. Layer that with the sour cream mixture and top with chopped scallions, chopped tomato and grated cheese. Serve with Mexican chips.

Mrs. Ralph S. Thompson

Known as The Thornton Burgess Museum, the Deacon Eldred house, was built in the mid-1700s, on the probable site of a 1643 home. The first owner of record is Deacon Cornelius F. Eldred in the early 1800s. This home has an early connection with the Burgess Family as it was inherited by Thornton's Aunt Arabella Eldred Burgess.

IRISH PIZZA

1 can crescent refrigerator rolls
8 ounce container flavored dip
(clam or whatever you like)
chopped celery

8 ounce container cream cheese
grated carrot
chopped brocolli flowerets

On the day or night before, press crescent rolls into flat piece on cookie sheet. Cook according to can instructions and cool. Spread cream cheese on cooked dough and then flavored dip. Sprinkle with fresh raw vegetables and store in refrigerator until ready to serve.

You can vary the recipe by using any pretty fresh vegetables and changing the flavor of the dip. You might try to decorate to your own taste with olives or whatever is in the refrigerator at the time.

Sarah ter Horst

ITALIAN ANTIPASTO FROM MY GRANDMOTHER

½ cup catsup
¼ cup olive oil
½ cup sliced carrots (cooked)
1 clove garlic, grated
1 jar sweet onions
1 can sliced mushrooms

1 can anchovies
1 can small black olives (pitted)
½ cup chili sauce
¼ cup vinegar
1 can tuna drained
½ cup sliced celery (cooked)

Put chili sauce, anchovies, garlic, oil and vinegar in a medium saucepan. Heat to boiling. Boil for one minute. Add other ingredients in order named and bring to boil again. Remove from heat, cool, bottle. This will keep several weeks in the refrigerator.

Diane Morash

MUSHROOM HORS D'OEUVRES

1 package cream cheese (3 ounces)
¼ cup sour cream
chives (chopped)
parsley (chopped)

chopped raw mushrooms
French bread
butter

Sauté mushrooms in butter. Mix all ingredients together except bread. Butter one side of thin slices of bread and spread other side with mixture. Bake for 15 minutes at 375°.

Spread can be made with grated mozarella cheese and chopped cooked mushrooms.

RAW VEGETABLE DIP

1 cup salad oil
½ cup light corn syrup
4 tablespoons white vinegar
dash of paprika
½ teaspoon salt
3 ounces cream cheese

½ cup sugar
1 teaspoon dry mustard
1 teaspoon celery seeds
1 tablespoon lemon juice
1 onion cut into chunks

Put ingredients in blender in order listed. Blend until well mixed. Chill and serve with platter of raw vegetables.

Mary Thomas

PITKIN BON-BONS

PICKLED TOMATOES:

green tomatoes (golf ball size)   1 quart water
½ cup salt   2 cups vinegar
10 sprigs dill   garlic buds

FILLING:

1 cup sauerkraut   ¼ cup chopped sweet red pepper
pulp from tomatoes   (may substitute hot peppers)

Pack each quart jar with halved tomatoes and a bud of garlic. Bring the water, salt and vinegar to a boil, add dill and boil an additional 5 minutes. Pour this hot brine over tomatoes to cover. Cover jars and refrigerate 4 weeks. Makes 3 quarts. After 4 weeks, scoop the pulp out of the tomatoes and chop pulp with sauerkraut and pepper. Pack mixture into tomato shells and allow to marinate several hours before serving.

I'm sure they have a Polish name, but we called them "Pitkin Bon-Bons". These stuffed green tomato pickle treats were peddled by the pushcart vendors along Pitkin Avenue.

Jean A. Frank

SPINACH SQUARES

4 tablespoons butter   2 packages frozen spinach
3 eggs   (chopped and drained well)
1 cup flour   1 tablespoon chopped onion
1 cup milk   1 pound grated sharp cheddar
1 teaspoon salt   cheese
1 teaspoon baking powder

Melt butter in 9"x13"x2" baking pan. Beat eggs in large bowl. Add flour, milk, salt, baking powder, cheese, spinach and onion. Mix well. Spread in prepared pan. Bake in preheated 350° oven for 35 minutes. (May be frozen after baking and reheated to serve.) Cut in small squares and serve warm.

Nancy Siebert

YUMMY DIP

1 can of hearts of palm (sliced)   1 cup of mayonnaise
1 cup grated parmesan cheese

In a square baking dish, spread a canful of hearts of palm. Mix mayonnaise with cheese and spread on top of hearts of palm. Bake until brown. This recipe can be doubled in an oblong pan.

Marilyn Holland

The 1833 First Parish Unitarian Church replaced an earlier meeting house on the site, which had been used for such purpose since 1638. The 1800 building has undergone many alterations over the years including the rebuilding and raising of the steeple, and the major change of 1871 when the entire church was raised 10 feet to allow for the vestry and heating plant in the basement area. In more recent years the Gothic Revival building has been established as "Yesteryears Doll Museum."

ZUCCHINI APPETIZERS

3 cups zucchini, thinly sliced
  (unpared)
1 cup biscuit mix
½ cup onion, finely chopped
½ cup grated parmesan cheese
2 tablespoons parsley (chopped)

½ teaspoon seasoned salt
½ teaspoon dried marjoram or
  oregano leaves
dash pepper
½ cup vegetable oil
4 eggs lightly beaten

Beat eggs, add biscuit mix and mix. Add remaining ingredients and mix again. Spread on greased 13"x9"x2" pan. Bake about 25 minutes at 350° or until golden brown. Cut into squares and then triangles. These can be frozen.

Virginia Aitken

AMANDA'S PICKLED EGGS

2 cans sliced beets (1 pound each)
3 cups granulated sugar
1 quart cider vinegar

1 to 1½ dozen hard boiled eggs
  shelled

Heat vinegar to boiling and add sugar. Stir until dissolved. Set aside. Put beets in a 1 gallon glass container and add vinegar and sugar mixture. Then add eggs. Let set in refrigerator for at least 3 days before using.

Lorraine Lee

Beverages

The clipper "Peruvian" was wrecked off Truro in 1872, and among the materials cast ashore were crates of English dishes. This illustration is copied from a platter retrieved by the Captain of the Peaked Hill Bars Life-Saving Station, and passed down to a descendant now living in Spring Hill.

Wreck of the Annie Spindler at Provincetown — see next page.

RUM RUNNING

There was a prohibition in the United States against making, selling or importing alcoholic beverages, which went into effect June 16, 1920, and lasted until December 5, 1933. However a large number of persons including leaders in all walks of life still enjoyed having an occasional drink, with the results that (a) making moonshine flourished and (b) smuggling good liquor from Europe into the East Coast of the U.S. became highly organized. Freighters from Europe brought cargoes of cased liquor with papers for points in Africa or the West Indies, and stopped outside the 12-mile U.S. limit where they were called "rum row". From them, smaller vessels would move at night to points along the shore where work parties would meet them and store the cases in a friendly shed or barn, to be moved by truck to the consumption centers. This network required communication, trust and luck. The faster the sequence, the more profits. The Coast Guard knew about "rum row" but without radar could not easily catch the coastal vessels, which quickly graduated from sloops to motorboats to racy high-powered vessels which could outrun the Coast Guard cutters.

Cape Cod was widely used for rum-running because of its long empty beaches, skilled fishermen who also knew the terrain, and its long tradition of using whatever came ashore. A pattern of quiet collusion and acceptance was established in every town, which it was dangerous to breach. Eugene Morrow of Sandwich was a Selectman who went out for lobsters on November 19, 1927. Fragments of his motor dory washed up a month later, and it was widely believed that he had been murdered at sea, in retaliation for testimony against rum runners. Piracy and interception of liquor in transit were found, in parallel to today's drug traffic.

The Coast Guard station at Sandwich had no powerful intercept motor boats and a small budget, so it was easily by-passed in most rum-running operations. However it caught some disabled rum-runners and figured in several intercepts on land where informers provided tips that led to stopping trucks at the bridge or to making seizures on shore.

The "Annie Spindler" case is a fascinating example of how the law was allowed to defeat itself. She came ashore at Race Point in a storm in 1922 and was found to have a cargo of whiskey with correct papers from Yarmouth, Nova Scotia to the West Indies. The captain insisted that he had been driven into shore by the storm and the Coast Guard actually cooperated by keeping wreckers at bay and moving his cargo safely to Railroad Wharf, Provincetown, where a second vessel later picked it up with new papers for the West Indies. This same cargo was then run ashore near Plymouth.

SPICED BUTTERMILK

1 quart fresh buttermilk
½ teaspoon vanilla
dash of ground allspice

1-2 teaspoons sugar (to taste)
½ teaspoon ground cinnamon

In blender, whisk buttermilk, sugar, vanilla, cinnamon, and allspice until frothy. Chill thoroughly. Serve with grated nutmeg on top. Serves: 2-4.

Frances Laura Karnes

ICED SPICED CIDER

2 quarts rich apple cider
½ cup brown sugar
1 teaspoon allspice
12 whole cloves

2 2-inch sticks cinnamon, broken
in pieces
grated nutmeg

Make a spice bag from cheesecloth. Put in it the allspice, cinnamon pieces, and cloves. In a large saucepan simmer cider, sugar, and spice bag for about 10 minutes. Taste, and add more sugar if needed. Remove spice bag. Chill mixture. Serve over ice with a dash of nutmeg.

This is an old English recipe which is particularly good on a warm autumn evening.

Anne Maleady

MULLED CIDER

1 gallon cider
1 cup brown sugar
2 teaspoons whole cloves

2 teaspoons whole allspice
8 3-inch sticks of cinnamon
grated nutmeg

Heat cider, sugar, cloves, allspice and cinnamon and simmer 15 minutes. Serve hot in punch cups or mugs. Recipe can be divided to suit needs. Early American recipes call for steeping the sugar and spices for several days, poured into pewter cups and then heated by inserting a red hot poker into the cider. This imparts slightly different flavor and if you have a fireplace in which to heat the poker, this can be a nice way to serve an after-ski or skating party. Serves: 16-20.

Peter Maleady

BEACH PLUM CORDIAL

screw-top jar — quart size
beach plums

2 cups rum or vodka
2 cups sugar

Pour 2 cups rum or vodka into quart jar with tight fitting lid. Add 2 cups sugar and shake until dissolved. Fill jar with beach plums to top and store in cool dark place. Every few days jar should be turned gently. After about six to eight weeks cordial is completed and the contents can be strained and bottled. Liquid will be a clear dark red. Serves: 12.

Susi Lott

COFFEE

An old Cape Cod recipe proposes: "Put a coffeecup full into a pot that will hold 3 pints of water; add the white of one egg, or 2 or 3 clean eggshells, or a dried bit of fishskin of the size of a ninepence. Pour upon it boiling water and boil it 10 minutes. Let it stand 8 to 10 minutes where it will keep hot, but not boil; boiling coffee a great while makes it strong, but not so lively or agreeable." We don't suggest making it this way today!

23

EGG NOG

12 fresh eggs
1 pint cognac or bourbon
½ pint Jamaican rum (dark)
1 pint milk

½ pint heavy cream
12 tablespoons sugar
nutmeg or cinnamon

Separate eggs. Beat yolks, adding sugar until it is dissolved. Slowly add cognac or whiskey and dark rum, stirring constantly. Then stir in milk and cream. Let mixture stand. Later beat egg whites until stiff and fold them into batch. Keep refrigerated until ready to place in punch bowl. Add nutmeg or cinnamon to taste. Serves: 12.

Robert & Pat Maximoff

LAMB'S WOOL

4 large apples
1 quart strong ale
brown sugar to taste

¼ teaspoon ginger (each mug)
nutmeg

Put apples (whole, unpeeled) in a baking dish and roast in 400 degree oven until skins burst and apples are very soft. Peel and core apples placing one in each of 4 mugs. Gently heat ale until very hot and pour over apples. Add ¼ teaspoon of ginger to each and stir. Add brown sugar to taste. Top with dash of nutmeg. Serve very hot. Serves: 4.

This is an adaptation of a medieval English recipe used in this area as a holiday drink or a "warming" after winter sports. "Lambs Wool" is used in England as a traditional Shrove Tuesday punch bowl.

Jennie Amelia Thompson

FIRESIDE COFFEE MIX

2 cups instant hot chocolate
2 cups powdered non-dairy
  creamer
1½ teaspoons cinnamon

1 cup instant freeze-dried
  coffee
¾ teaspoon nutmeg
1 cup sugar

On medium speed with blender, blend chocolate, creamer, coffee and spices for 5 minutes. Stir in sugar by hand. To serve: Use 3 teaspoons per mug of hot water. If desired add whipped cream and/or liquor.

Mary Ann Bukovich

APRICOT MIST PUNCH
(non-alcoholic)

1 can apricot nectar (46 ounces)
1 can pineapple juice (46 ounce,
  unsweetened)
1 fresh pineapple

3 cans frozen limeade (6 ounce,
  thawed)
3 quarts ginger ale
4 oranges

Pour all liquid ingredients into punch bowl. A block of decorated ice is attractive if available. Garnish with slices of fresh fruit (orange and pineapple). Serves: 50.

Polly Leis

HOT CRANBERRY PUNCH
(non-alcoholic)

2 cups granulated sugar
1 cup water
1 cup lemon juice
4 cups cranberry juice

4 cups pineapple juice
½ teaspoon cinnamon
½ teaspoon ginger
lemon slices studded with cloves

Boil sugar and water over medium heat for 10 minutes. Add lemon, cranberry and pineapple juices and spices. Heat slowly until just boiling. Cool slightly; pour into warmed punch bowl. Garnish with lemon slices studded with cloves. Serves: 20 4-ounce servings.

This delicious punch has been enjoyed during the Victorian Christmas celebration at the Burgess Museum for years.

Green Briar Jam Kitchen

PINEAPPLE PUNCH
(non-alcoholic)

2 cups strong tea
6 ounces lemon juice
14 ounces orange juice
1 ounce lime juice
1 cup sugar

12 sprigs mint
1 pound can sliced pineapple
2 quarts ginger ale
2 quarts soda

In saucepan, combine the tea, fruit juices, sugar, and mint, and stir to mix. Cool in refrigerator. Before serving, strain mix into punch bowl, and add all pineapple, ginger ale, and soda over a block of ice. Serves: 30.

Margaret Breitzke

PLANTER'S PUNCH

fresh lime
maraschino cherry
orange slice
pineapple slice
sugar syrup (see note)

Meyers rum (dark Jamaica)
straw
measuring pitcher and
10-ounce glass

A planter's punch is based on an ancient formula: "one of sour, two of sweet, three of strong and four of weak." We interpret this as follows: In a measuring pitcher for each drink anticipated, mix one ounce of fresh lime juice, two ounces of sugar syrup, and three ounces of dark rum. Fill a tall 10-ounce glass with ice (this is the weak), and pour in six ounces of the 1-2-3; mix. Garnish with a cherry, a slice of orange, and a slice of pineapple. Some hosts have been known to float a teaspoon of 151-proof rum on top of this drink for added bouquet and effect, but this is not for the unwary. Serves: 1.

Note: Make up a batch of sugar syrup for general summer-time use. Heat together 2 cups of sugar in a pint of water. When dissolved, put it in a bottle or jar in the refrigerator. This makes about 3 cups of syrup and is convenient for iced tea or coffee.

Dodge MacKnight, Twentieth Century artist,
Sandwich resident, and benefactor of Sandwich Public Library

WHISKEY PUNCH

2 cups orange juice
1 cup lemon juice
½ cup sugar syrup
½ cup Curaçao or Triple Sec
block of ice

1.75 liter bottle of blended
  whiskey
2 quarts soda water
slices of orange or pineapple
cherries

Place a block of ice in large punch bowl. Add 16 ounces (2 cups) of orange juice and 8 ounces of lemon juice. Add 4 ounces of sugar syrup and 4 ounces of Curaçao or Triple Sec liqueur. Add a 1.75 liter bottle of blended whiskey (80 proof). Stir; let cool. When consumption is about to commence add two quarts of chilled soda. Garnish the punch with sliced fruit and cherries. Serves: 30.

Russ Lovell

HOT BUTTERED RUM

1 large jigger light rum
1 lump of sugar or equivalent

1 pat of butter

Coat inside of toddy mug with butter. Put sugar in mug; fill ⅜ full with boiling water. Stir gently. Serves: 1.

These are very pleasing but rather intoxicating cold weather drinks. They were considered by many to be the best cure for the common cold or the "grippe" until replaced by modern medicine. One drank the hot toddy, took to bed with lots of blankets and "sweat" it out.

SANGRIA WINE COOLER

3 oranges
3 lemons
3 limes
1 small can sliced or crushed
  pineapple

3 peaches or nectarines
sugar syrup
brandy
Rhine wine or chablis

In a big 4-quart saucepan place the fruit, all sliced thin, with seeds removed. Add a half cup of sugar syrup and a half cup of brandy. Stir and let marinate for an hour or so. Add 3 quarts or liters of chilled white wine and place in the refrigerator with a cover for several hours. When ready to serve, decant into a large pitcher without the fruit. Check for sweetness and add sugar syrup if desired. Pour over ice into cups or stemmed glasses.

Variations of this drink using only wine were much in use in Colonial days as a bracer.
Robert & Pat Maximoff

SPICED MINT TEA

1 cup water
2 teaspoons black tea
½ teaspoon allspice
¾ cup orange juice

1 cup sugar
2 spearmint or applemint leaves
6 tablespoons lemon juice
2 quarts boiling water

Boil sugar with one cup of water for 5 minutes or until sugar is thoroughly dissolved. Add tea, mint, allspice. Cover and let steep for 10 minutes. Strain. Add fruit juices, 2 quarts boiling water, and bring to boiling point. Serves: 12.

Marie Olander

TEA

In 1775 a Sandwich boy, John Nye, ran away and joined the Boston Tea Party and while the tea was being thrown overboard secured some and brought it home to his aged grandmother, Deborah Nye, who drank it in secret.

Breads & Baked Goods

DEXTER GRIST MILL

During the 19th century the ancient Dexter Grist Mill (left) was less needed because flour became available by railroad. The picturesque wooden water wheel was replaced by a more efficient steel turbine, and a second mill was built to do other work such as cutting marble slabs. Grinding corn meal here stopped in 1881, but was resumed when the mill was restored in 1961. Thornton W. Burgess toured the new mill and wrote a poem for it — see next page.

FOOD FOR THE COLONISTS

When the Pilgrims came to Plymouth, their tastes were based on the English diet, which featured roasted meat and fowl, with sauces and gravies, steamed suety puddings, fish, pastry pies, thick soups and stews, a variety of vegetables, cheese, fruit, bread and for drinks ale, beer, wines and strong waters such as brandy, Dutch gin and aqua vita. They brought seed of wheat, oats, rye and barley here to be planted, but found the Indian maize grew very well and quickly added it to their usual diet in many forms. They also quickly adopted American beans, squashes, pumpkins, berries and of course the fish, game and shellfish that were abundant. The worst time was in the spring and early summer when winter supplies were gone and the new crops not yet ripe. The Pilgrims became bored with lobsters, clams and water and wanted beer, bread, and beef as they had at home.

Trade with Europe and the West Indies and the Virginia Colony was quickly established. Persons on Cape Cod who imported arms, spirits or tobacco had to declare their receipts promptly to the Assistant Governor for the area, and pay duty, or face fines. Retail prices for imported goods were fixed by Colony law in 1646 as:

Spanish wine (sherry)	$3.40 per gallon
French wine	$1.70 per gallon
Strong water	$7.50 per gallon
Vegetable oil	$0.42 per gallon
Beer	$10.00 per hogshead
Tobacco	$0.42 per pound
Seasonal fishing by non-residents in Cape waters	$25.00 per season

(These prices are based on an estimated rate of 1980 $100. to a Pound Sterling.)

THE HONEST MILLER

Beside his open door he stands
And sees the world go by;
A ruddy glow is in his cheek
And laughter in his eye,
As if he found a golden key
In every bag of rye.

The dripping wheel below him chants,
The melody it caught
From limpid waters, brown and clear
In nature's temple taught;
And in the miller's very soul
Its harmony is wrought.

(Poem written by TWB in 1962 for the Sandwich Miller,
Mr. Vernon Prior)

ONION BAGELS

4-4½ cups flour	3 tablespoons sugar
2 packages active dry yeast	1 tablespoon salt
1½ cups warm water (110°)	¼ cup instant minced onion

In large mixer bowl combine 1½ cups of flour with yeast. Dissolve sugar and salt in warm water. Add this and minced onion to dry mixture and beat at low speed ½ minute, scraping sides of bowl constantly. Beat 3 minutes at high speed. By hand, stir in enough flour to make a moderately stiff dough. Turn onto lightly floured surface and knead 8-10 minutes or until smooth and elastic. Cover and let rest 15 minutes.

Cut into 12 portions (about 2½ ounces each); shape into smooth balls. Using a floured finger, punch and enlarge a hole in the center of each ball. Cover and let rise 20 minutes.

In a large kettle combine 1 gallon water and 1 tablespoon sugar and bring to a boil. Reduce to simmer; cook 4 or 5 bagels at a time for 7 minutes, turning them once. Drain on wire racks. Place on greased baking sheet. Bake at 375° for 30-35 minutes or until golden brown. Yield: 1 dozen.

Jeanne Stone

BROWN BREAD

1 cup sifted all-purpose flour	pinch of salt
1 cup rye meal (flour)	1 cup sour milk
1 cup graham meal (flour)	½ cup molasses
½ Indian meal (corn)	1 teaspoon baking soda
1 cup raisins (optional)	

Mix together the flours, all-purpose, rye, graham and Indian, baking soda and salt. Add sour milk and molasses. Pour into 2 greased coffee cans, filling three-quarters full. Steam in large kettle on rack, with the water half-way up the tins. Steam for 2½ hours.

Abigail Cullity

"The Olde Time Shop", owned by Walter and Rosanna Cullity in East Sandwich, was originally an ell on a 1700 cape home on Old County Road. It has been moved three times, and is a classic example of the economy with which Cape Codders value useful buildings.

CORN BREAD

1 cup sifted flour	3 teaspoons baking powder
2 tablespoons sugar	1 cup corn meal
1 cup melted vegetable	2 eggs
shortening	1 cup milk

Mix all ingredients together and place in greased 9"x9" pan. Bake in preheated oven at 400 degrees for 30 minutes.

Arlene Ellis

Tom and Arlene Ellis live in the Spring Hill area in an early Sandwich home known as "Locust Hill". The house has undergone many changes and additions since its start in 1727 as a single story, one room-deep home for Judah Allen and his bride.

SOUTHERN CORNBREAD

This is what oldtimers call "real cornbread", no flour, no sugar — made with stone-ground cornmeal. It is delicious.

1 cup stone-ground cornmeal	½ teaspoon baking soda
½ teaspoon salt	3 tablespoons butter
1 cup buttermilk	1 egg

Pre-heat oven to 400 degrees. Put butter in a heavy 8″ or 9″ iron skillet or quiche baking dish and place in oven while oven is heating. Meanwhile, combine all dry ingredients in a bowl. Beat egg in a separate bowl and add buttermilk. Pour melted butter in with the liquid ingredients. Add liquids to the dry ingredients and barely mix. Pour into the pre-heated pan and bake for 30 minutes. The secret to light cornbread is to stir it, never beat.

The Roberti Dairy Farm, which closed in the late 1970's was a wholesale and retail business with 45-50 cows and 20 young stock. The area of Sandwich known as "Canterbury Estates" is part of the 90 acres the Robertis used for growing corn, which was originally purchased from the King family who had the first deed to the property.

CRANBERRY FRITTERS

As an accompaniment to dinner or dessert — delicious either way.

1 can jellied cranberry sauce	¼ teaspoon salt
(17 ounce)	2 eggs, separated
¾ cup all-purpose flour, sifted	1 teaspoon shortening,
1 teaspoon lemon juice	melted
⅓ cup milk or water	extra flour

Cut the cranberry sauce into half-inch slices; then divide into halves crosswise, set aside. Beat egg whites until stiff and set aside. Sift flour and salt together. Make a hollow in the center and pour in well-beaten egg yolks, lemon juice, melted shortening and part of the milk or water. Beat until perfectly smooth. Add remaining milk or water and finally fold in stiffly beaten egg whites. Roll cranberry slices in the extra flour then dip in batter. Drop gently into deep hot fat (390 degrees). Cook until golden brown. Drain on paper towel or brown paper and dust with granulated sugar.

Use your favorite muffin mix to make a cranberry surprise: Place a tablespoon or so of muffin batter into the muffin tin, drop two or three small cubes of cut-up jellied cranberry sauce in, then top off the muffin batter as usual, covering the surprise.

Mae Foster

APPLE SOUR CREAM COFFEE CAKE

½ cup almonds or walnuts
   chopped
1½ cups sugar
2 eggs
2 cups flour
½ teaspoon salt
1 cup sour cream

2 teaspoons cinnamon
½ cup butter or margarine
1 teaspoon vanilla
1 teaspoon baking powder
1 teaspoon baking soda
3 apples, sliced

Mix almonds or walnuts, cinnamon, ½ cup sugar in bowl and set aside. Beat together until creamy butter, 1 cup sugar, eggs and vanilla. Add baking powder, salt and baking soda to flour and beat into butter mixture, alternating with sour cream. Spread half the batter into a well greased angel food cake pan. Layer in sliced apples and top them with half cinnamon mixture. Add remaining batter and finally top with balance of cinnamon mixture. Preheat oven to 350 degrees and bake for 40 minutes. Let cool; remove from pan after 30 minutes.

Lorraine Lee

Sour cream coffee cakes are popular in the area and Florence Hall and Betty Allen submitted similar recipes, but without apples.

AUNT ADDIE'S COFFEE CAKE

1 stick butter or margarine
8 ounce package cream cheese
1¼ cups sugar
2 eggs
2 cups sifted flour

1 teaspoon baking powder
½ teaspoon baking soda
¼ teaspoon salt
2 teaspoons vanilla
¼ cup milk

TOPPING MIXTURE:

⅔ cup brown sugar
3 teaspoons cinnamon

⅔ cup flour
¼ cup shortening, softened

Cream shortening, cream cheese and sugar. Add eggs and vanilla and beat until smooth. Mix flour, baking powder, baking soda and salt and add to creamed mixture alternating with milk. Grease and flour two 8" cake pans and preheat oven to 350°. Spread the heavy batter in the pans.

Topping: mix the brown sugar, flour, shortening and cinnamon together until crumbly. Scatter the crumbly topping on the coffee cakes and bake at 350° for 35-40 minutes. Cool on rack in the pans and sprinkle with confectioners' sugar when cooled.

This is an old recipe from a favorite aunt who "composed her own" recipes and never once measured anything. When I asked her portions this is what she gave me. She was quite a baker and in my opinion always had great success.

Marilyn McKechnie

The first Friends arrived in the Sandwich area in 1656 and held their meetings in private homes and, at times, in the woods. Christopher Hollow is probably the place Christopher Holder, the Friend preacher met with his group for worship.

The 1810 Quaker Meeting House just off Spring Hill Road is the third to be built on the site originally granted to the Friends by the Town of Sandwich in the 1670's, thus establishing the oldest continuous Quaker meeting in North America.

31

DELICIOUS DOUGHNUTS

2 tablespoons soft shortening
¾ cup sugar
4 egg yolks or 2 whole eggs
½ teaspoon mace
¼ teaspoon cinnamon

3½ cups all-purpose flour
4 teaspoons baking powder
1 teaspoon salt
½ teaspoon nutmeg
1 cup milk

Mix shortening, sugar and eggs together. Sift together flour, baking powder, salt, nutmeg, mace, cinnamon and stir into shortening mixture, alternating with milk. The dough will be very soft, but use as little additional flour as possible when rolling it out. Handle gently and as little as possible. Roll the dough out to ⅜" thick. Let it stand for 10 minutes before cutting and frying doughnuts. Cut with a 2½" or 3" cutter, lightly floured. Fry until brown in hot fat at 375 degrees, turning when first crack appears. Use a long handled fork to turn and lift. Drain on brown paper or paper towels. Frying time is about 1½ minutes. If sugar doughnuts are desired, place sugar and cinnamon mixture in a paper bag or plastic bag and add a few warm doughnuts at a time. Shack gently until they are covered.

JOHNNY CAKES

1 cup corn meal
1 teaspoon sugar
cream or milk to thin batter

pinch salt
1⅓ cups boiling water

Add boiling water (bubbles bursting) to corn meal, salt and sugar and mix thoroughly. Let stand 5 minutes to steam. Thin with cream or milk to consistency of mashed potatoes. Drop large tablespoonsful lightly onto hot greased griddle. Cook until brown (15 minutes or longer) then turn and cook 15 minutes longer. Serve piping hot.

Note: No one seems sure how the words "Johnny Cake" evolved. Some say it is a corruption of "journey cake" that early travelers in this country carried to sustain them. Others say it derives from the French Canadian "Jaune (yellow) cake". Whatever the background, it has endured through the years because it's good to eat!

APPLE PIE MUFFINS

1 cup whole wheat flour
1 cup all-purpose white flour
¼ teaspoon salt
¼ teaspoon cinnamon
1 medium apple, peeled, sliced fine
2 teaspoons baking powder

1 egg, beaten
¼ cup oil
¼ cup light molasses
1½ cups milk
½ cup raisins
grated peel of 1 orange

Mix dry ingredients. Beat egg; add oil, molasses, milk, and orange rind. Add liquids to dry ingredients and stir until just moistened. Add finely sliced apple and raisins, barely mixing. Fill well-greased muffin tins three-quarters full and bake at 400 degrees for 20 minutes. Baking Hint: Stir as little as possible for tender muffins.

Abigail Cullity

BLUEBERRY MUFFINS

2 cups all-purpose flour
3 tablespoons sugar
1 cup milk
2 eggs, beaten

½ teaspoon salt
3 teaspoons baking powder
3 tablespoons melted butter
1¾ cups blueberries

Sift flour, sugar, salt and baking powder together. Pour milk in gradually, beating well. Add butter and beat well. Add eggs and mix thoroughly. Fold in blueberries. Place batter in greased muffin tins filled over half full. Bake in preheated oven at 425 degrees for 20 minutes.

Variations on this basic blueberry muffin recipe: add grated rind of half a lemon to give muffins zip. Brush tops with melted butter and roll in cinnamon-sugar while still warm. Yield: Approx. 18 muffins.

CRANBERRY MUFFINS

1 cup cranberries
2 cups flour
¾ teaspoon salt
1 cup milk

½ cup sugar
4 teaspoons baking powder
1 egg, beaten
3 tablespoons melted butter

Put cranberries through food chopper; mix with half the sugar. Sift remaining sugar with dry ingredients. Combine beaten egg, milk and melted butter, and add to dry ingredients. Stir only until blended. Fold in sweetened cranberries. bake in buttered muffin pans in hot oven (425 degrees) about 25 minutes. Yield: 12 medium sized muffins.

Good cranberries bounce — or so it is said. The early settlers were quick to use the freely available cranberries they found growing wild in New England. By the early 1800's the cranberries were being cultivated in Massachusetts and New Jersey and the new cranberry industry had been founded. Cranberries freeze well and retain their high vitamin C content.

SWEET POTATO MUFFINS

½ stick butter or margarine
½ cup sugar
1 egg
⅔ cup canned sweet potatoes,
   drained and mashed well
½ cup milk
1 tablespoon cinnamon-sugar mix
   mix

¾ cup all-purpose flour
2 teaspoons baking powder
½ teaspoon salt
½ teaspoon cinnamon
¼ teaspoon nutmeg
4 tablespoons chopped nuts
   (pecans, walnuts or
   macadamia)

Cream butter and sugar well. Beat in egg and mashed sweet potato. Sift flour, baking powder, salt and spices together. Add dry ingredients to butter mixture alternately with the milk. Do not overmix. Mix only until blended. Add nuts, and spoon into greased muffin tins, filling them to the top. Sprinkle tops with sugar-cinnamon mix. Bake in pre-heated oven at 400 degrees for 25 minutes. Yield: 2 dozen.

T. K. Ankner

The Ankners own "Home for the Holidays, Ltd.", the gift shop at 154 Main Street in Sandwich. The lovely 1800 home, with its traditionally "sea-captain" high ceilings, was once owned by Theodore Kern, who was employed in the cutting shop, and later became superintendent at the Boston & Sandwich Glass Company.

MORNING GLORY MUFFINS
(CARROT PINEAPPLE)

2 cups sugar
3 eggs
2¼ cups all-purpose flour
1 teaspoon salt
2 cups flaked coconut
1 (8 ounce) can crushed
   pineapple (drained)

1½ cups vegetable oil
2 teaspoons vanilla
2½ teaspoons cinnamon
2 teaspoons baking soda
2 cups shredded carrots
1 cup chopped walnuts

Combine sugar, oil, eggs and vanilla in a large bowl and blend using a wooden spoon. Stir in flour, cinnamon, soda and salt and mix well. Fold in shredded carrots, coconut, pineapple and walnuts. Pour into greased cupcake tins about three quarters full. Bake at 350 degrees in a preheated oven for about 20 minutes. Remove from tins and cool on absorbent paper. The muffins are very moist.

Variation: For a great carrot cake, pour mixture into a 9x13 inch greased pan and bake 50 minutes at 350 degrees. Let cool in pan for 5 minutes and invert onto rack and let cool. Frost with cream cheese icing. Yield: 24 muffins.

Janet Grigg

These muffins are served to off-season guests at the Old Colony Motel on Route 6A in East Sandwich. The Motel was named after the Old Colony Railroad which brought supplies to Sandwich in the mid-1800's.

APRICOT NUT BREAD

1 cup dried apricots
2 tablespoons softened butter
¼ cup water
2 teaspoons baking powder
2 cups flour

1 cup sugar — 1 egg
1 teaspoon salt
½ cup orange juice
¼ teaspoon baking soda
½ cup chopped nuts

Cut the cup of dried apricots into quarter inch pieces and soak in warm water to cover for 30 minutes. Mix together sugar, butter, and egg, and stir in water and orange juice. Sift flour, baking powder, soda, and salt together. Drain apricots and mix with chopped nuts. Grease loaf pans (recipe makes 1 large loaf and two minis), line bottoms with waxed paper. Grease waxed paper and pour in batter. Let stand 20 minutes. Bake in preheated oven at 350 degrees for 55-65 minutes for full size loaf. Smaller tins require less time.

VanNessa

We are pleased to share with you a Christmas breakfast tradition of the Dillon clan. Just the fragrance of it baking brings scentimental visions of Christmas past but not forgotten, and we are warmed by the knowledge that family and friends join in a custom begun so long ago.

BEER BREAD

3 cups self-rising flour
3 tablespoons sugar
1½ tablespoons caraway seeds

1 egg
1 12-ounce can of beer (room
   temperature)

Mix all ingredients thoroughly. Put in greased 9"x5"x3" loaf pan and bake at 375 degrees in a preheated oven. Cooking time approximately 50-60 minutes (55 minutes is usually perfect). This is a winner!

Carl E. Anderson

BLUEBERRY QUICK BREAD

2 eggs
1 cup milk
3 cups all-purpose flour
4 teaspoons baking powder

1 cup sugar
3 tablespoons cooking oil
1 teaspoon salt
1½ cups fresh blueberries

Beat eggs; add sugar gradually, mixing thoroughly. Add milk and oil, then add dry ingredients, mixing until smooth. Fold in blueberries. Spread batter in greased and floured 9x5 inch loaf pan. Bake at 350 degrees in a pre-heated oven for about 60 minutes.

Note: It's easy to make and delicious to eat. The loaf has a nice texture and freezes beautifully.

Rainy Reagen

Blueberries sun-dry beautifully, usually in 7-10 days. The Indians dried blueberries to use as currents in pemmican, puddings and cakes.

DILL QUICK BREAD

2 cups all-purpose flour
1 teaspoon baking soda
1¼ to 1½ cups whole wheat
  flour
1½ cups buttermilk
2 tablespoons brown sugar

2 teaspoons salt
½ teaspoon baking powder
1 rounded teaspoon dried
  dill seed, crushed
3 tablespoons melted butter
1 egg yolk + teaspoon water

Sift together white flour, salt, baking soda and baking powder. Stir in whole wheat flour and dill seed. Mix buttermilk, butter and sugar, then add it to dry ingredients. The dough should be fairly stiff. If it isn't, add a bit more flour. There is no need to knead the dough, rather shape it into a round loaf and place in a buttered pie pan. Gash a cross on top of the loaf and brush it with an egg yolk beaten with a little water. Bake at 375 degress for 55 minutes and let cool thoroughly before slicing. Note: This recipe doubles very nicely.

Carol Colburn

DATE NUT BREAD

1 8-ounce package pitted dates
2 tablespoons margarine or butter
1 teaspoon salt
2 eggs, beaten
1 teaspoon baking soda

1½ cups boiling water
1¼ cups sugar
1 teaspoon vanilla
2¾ cups sifted all-purpose flour
¾ cups pecans, chopped

Cut dates in small pieces with scissors dipped in water. Add boiling water, shortening, sugar, salt and vanilla. Let cool slightly. Add beaten eggs. Sift dry ingredients and add to date mixture. Stir in chopped nuts. Pour into small greased pans and bake about 50 minutes in preheated 325 degree oven. It is better if ripened overnight and it keeps quite a while. Good for tiny sandwiches when sliced thin and spread with cream cheese.

Kay Adams

CHEESE BREAD

1 cup unbleached white flour
½ teaspoon baking soda
1 large egg
⅓ cup butter, melted
2 teaspoons each of dried herbs:
  basil, oregano, rosemary,
  dill weed

1 cup whole wheat pastry flour
2 teaspoons baking powder
⅔ cup plain yogurt
1 teaspoon Dijon mustard
2 5-ounce mild semi-soft cheese
  (gouda or edam)

Sift together flours, baking soda and baking powder. Prepare cheeses by spreading with mustard using pastry brush. Sprinkle all surfaces with dried herbs. Set aside. Beat egg, add yogurt and melted butter. Blend egg-yogurt mixture with flours and knead for a few minutes on lightly floured surface. Divide dough into two balls. Using one dough ball roll or pat out into an oblong shape on a lightly floured surface. Shape should be adapted to shape of cheese. Roll out to approximately one quarter inch thick. Place herbed cheese in center of dough and fold edges up and around cheese, forming it to cheese. Keep same thickness throughout. Repeat same procedure using second ball. Place on unbuttered baking sheets and bake in preheated oven at 350 degrees for 35-40 minutes or until lightly browned. Allow to cool thoroughly and slice from the center as you would a pie.   *Lynn Cullity*

Lynn and John Cullity have been instrumental in founding the Sandwich Conservation Trust, an organization in the forefront of the rapidly growing movement toward preserving open space in Sandwich. The town's most recent acquisition is the 86 acres of upland known as "Sam Nye's Mountain".

GRAPENUT BREAD

2 cups milk, scalded
1 cup grapenuts
1 teaspoon salt
3 cups all-purpose flour

4 teaspoons baking powder
½ cup sugar
1 egg, well beaten
3 tablespoons margarine, melted

Pour milk over grapenuts and let cool. Sift flour, salt, sugar, and baking powder together. Add egg and margarine to grapenut mixture. Add dry ingredients to liquid, mixing only enough to moisten. Turn into greased loaf pan and let stand 20 minutes. Preheat oven and bake at 350 degrees for 1 hour 20 minutes.

Variations: Add 1 cup chopped dried apricots. This bread makes excellent sandwiches with cream cheese and pineapple filling.   *Florence Eaton*

GRANMA McLAUGHLIN'S IRISH BREAD

5 to 6 scoops (tablespoons) soft
  shortening
¾ cup sugar
2 eggs
4 teaspoons baking powder

dash of salt
⅔ cups raisins
¾ cup whole milk
3 cups unbleached flour

Mix by hand . . . never over mix. Grease and flour a loaf pan and preheat oven to 450 degrees. Cream sugar and shortening, add eggs, mix in remaining ingredients, adding raisins after second cup of flour. It is a stiff batter. Bake at 450 degrees for 10 minutes, then reduce heat to 350 degrees; baking for about 25 minutes more (test with a toothpick).   *Kaethe O'Keefe Maguire*

This recipe was given me just after my marriage by my husband's grandmother. She had come over from Ireland as a young girl to marry her childhood sweetheart, who came over a few years before.

LEMON TEA BREAD

½ cup butter
grated rind of one lemon
1½ cups all-purpose flour
½ cup milk

1 cup sugar
2 eggs, beaten
1 teaspoon baking powder

SYRUP:

juice of one lemon

¼ cup sugar

Cream butter and sugar. Add grated lemon rind and mix thoroughly. Add beaten eggs and mix again. Sift together flour and baking powder and add to butter and eggs mixture alternately with the milk. Bake in a greased 9"x5"x3" loaf pan in a preheated oven at 375 degrees for 35 minutes. Combine the juice of one lemon and ¼ cup of sugar and pour it evenly over the top of the bread as soon as it is removed from the oven. Let cool in the pan 10 minutes then remove to rack and cool completely. Variation: ½ cup chopped walnuts may be added to the batter. Yield: 1 loaf.

Beth Barrett
Marilyn McKechnie

MINCEMEAT-PUMPKIN BREAD

3½ cups flour
1½ cups white sugar
2 tablespoons pumpkin pie spice
2 teaspoons baking soda
1 teaspoon salt
1½ cups brown sugar
4 eggs, slightly beaten

⅔ cup water
1 cup salad oil
2 cups canned pumpkin
9 ounce package dry mincemeat,
  crumbled
1 cup chopped walnuts

In a large bowl sift flour, sugar, spice, baking soda, and salt. Mix in brown sugar. Make a well in the center of bowl and add eggs, water, oil, and pumpkin. Beat at low speed 3 minutes. Stir in mincemeat and nuts. Bake in two greased 9"x5"x3" loaf pans (or 4 small pans) at 350 degrees for 55-65 minutes. Let cool and remove from pans. Extra loaves will freeze well. Yield: 2 loaves.

Dorothy Alvord

WINCHESTER NUT BREAD

¾ cup water
½ cup molasses
1 cup all-purpose flour
1½ teaspoons salt
2 cups whole wheat flour
1 teaspoon baking soda

½ cup brown sugar
¾ cup milk
2½ teaspoons baking powder
¾ cup broken nuts (walnuts or
  pecans)

Dissolve sugar in water, add molasses and milk. Sift flour, salt, baking powder and baking soda. Add whole wheat flour, unsifted. Mix all ingredients and add nuts. Bake in greased 9"x5"x3" pan for 2 hours at 275 degrees or until it tests done. The loaf will cut better if set aside for one day.

Elsa Gerling

Sandwich Town Hall, built in 1834, was originally designed to carry on town business on the second floor, while the first floor was rented out to shopkeepers. An addition in 1910 provided a stage for the upper level, which had also been used for banquets and dances. The white clapboard Greek Revival building, which was originally referred to as "the Town House set on the bog between Dillingham's shop and Fessenden's", has been declared a Landmark on the National Register of Historic Places.

APPLESAUCE OATMEAL QUICK BREAD

1 ¼ cups flour
1 ½ cups rolled oats
1 teaspoon baking soda
1 teaspoon cinnamon
⅓ cup butter or margarine
1 cup unsweetened applesauce
2 eggs

1 ¼ cups whole wheat flour
1 teaspoon baking powder
½ teaspoon salt
½ teaspoon nutmeg
⅔ cup brown sugar
1 cup currants

Sift dry ingredients together. Cream shortening and brown sugar, and beat in eggs and applesauce. Add dry ingredients and mix just until well blended. Fold in currants. Preheat oven to 350 degrees and bake in greased and floured 9"x5"x3" loaf pan for about one hour.

Peggy Wilson

RHUBARB BREAD

¾ cup honey
½ cup oil
1 egg
1 cup buttermilk
1 tablespoon baking soda

2 ½ cups whole wheat flour
1 teaspoon salt
1 ½ cups diced rhubarb
1 ½ teaspoons vanilla
½ cup nutmeats, finely chopped

TOPPING:

½ cup brown sugar
1 ½ tablespoon butter

1 teaspoon cinnamon

Preheat oven to 325°. Mix honey and oil; add egg and beat well. Dissolve soda in buttermilk; set aside. Sift flour and salt together; add to honey and oil mixture alternately with buttermilk. Stir in rhubarb, vanilla, and nuts. Pour into two greased bread pans. Combine topping ingredients and sprinkle over the batter. Bake 1 hour. Remove bread from pans and cool on wire rack.

Kathy and Stu Parsons

PARKER HOUSE ROLLS

2 cups scalded milk
½ yeast cake
¼ cup lukewarm water
6 cups all-purpose flour

¼ cup melted butter
2 tablespoons sugar
1 ¼ teaspoons salt

Dissolve yeast in water. When cooled to lukewarm mix scalded milk, two cups flour and yeast and beat well with beater. Let rise until spongy (approx. 3 hours). Add melted butter, sugar, salt and just enough flour to knead (approx. 4 cups). Knead 5 minutes. Let dough rest for 5 minutes and knead 2 minutes more. Let rise until doubled in size. Handle gently and roll lightly to ¼ inch thick. Cut into rounds with cookie cutter, dot with butter and fold over, pinching edges to seal. Place on baking sheets and let rise until double (approx. 2 hours). Bake in preheated oven at 350-400 degrees for 10 minutes or until delicately browned. Remove from oven and brush with butter if desired. Cool on rack.

SPOON ROLLS

1 package dry yeast
2 cups warm water
4 cups self-rising flour

1 egg, beaten
4 tablespoons sugar
¾ cup oil

Dissolve yeast in warm water; set aside. Beat egg in large bowl, add sugar and oil, mix well. Add water mixture then flour. Spoon into greased muffin pans filling about half full. Bake at 450 degrees until brown (approximately 15 minutes). Unused dough may be stored in the refrigerator for several days.

Eleanor Heckler

No Cape Cod recipe collection would be complete without the story of the fisherman who, tired of his wife Anna's cornmeal mush, added yeast and flour to it and proceeded to bake a loaf of bread muttering, "Anna-damn-er," thereby creating —

ANADAMA BREAD

¾ cup boiling water
½ cup yellow cornmeal
3 tablespoons, butter, softened
¼ cup light molasses
2¾ cups all-purpose flour, sifted

1½ teaspoons salt
1 package active dry yeast
¼ cup warm water (110-115°)
1 egg

Stir together boiling water, cornmeal, butter, molasses and salt. Set aside to cool. Dissolve yeast in ¼ cup warm water. Add yeast, egg, and only 1¼ cup flour to cornmeal mixture. Beat two minutes with electric mixer at medium speed. Stir in remaining flour a little at a time until batter is smooth. Grease 9"x5"x3" loaf pan and sprinkle with cornmeal. Spread batter evenly in pan; cover and let rise to 1" below top of the pan. Bake 50-55 minutes in 375 degree preheated oven. Crust will be dark brown. Remove from pan immediately and allow to cool on rack.

Variation: Although not in keeping with the legendary formula, a half cup of raisins adds a bit of interest to this bread, which is delicious toasted.

Vivian Storey

SHREDDED WHEAT BREAD

4 cakes of shredded wheat cakes
2 cups scalding hot water
1 cup molasses
2 tablespoons kosher salt

3 cakes yeast
½ cup warm water
2 cups warm milk
8 cups flour

Combine shredded wheat cakes with scalding water and let stand. When cool, add molasses and salt. Dissolve yeast in ½ cup warm water and add to shredded wheat mixture. Add all other ingredients and mix well. Let rise covered in a greased bowl until double in bulk. Punch down and separate into 2 loaves. Place into buttered bread tins and let rise. Bake in pre-heated oven at 325 degrees until golden brown. Brush top of loaves with butter before removing from the pans. Yield: 2 large loaves.

Christine Pope Gallagher

Mrs. Gallagher is a descendent of early settler Seth Pope, who built a home for his newly married son in 1699 sharing some of his farm acreage. The house, a half cape, has been expanded and added to many times over the ensuing years. It still stands on Tupper Road now a full colonial with a long span making it an unusual "five-quarter" house. The home is listed on the National Register of Historic Places.

HATALEIPA
(Finnish Rye Bread)

1 package dry yeast
2 tablespoons molasses
1 tablespoon oil, melted lard,
  melted butter or bacon
  drippings

1 cup warm water (105-
  115 degrees)
1 teaspoon salt
½ cup rye flour (dark or light)
1½ cups all-purpose flour

In mixing bowl, dissolve yeast in warm water. Add molasses and let stand 3-5 minutes until yeast foams. Stir in oil, salt, and rye flour. Stir in white flour, and beat 50 times. Cover baking sheet with parchment paper or grease the sheet generously. Turn dough out on sheet, spreading into a circle about 8" in diameter. Let rise 30 minutes. Preheat oven to 400 degrees. Bake 20 minutes or until center of loaf springs back when touched. Brush top with melted butter. Serve hot, cut into wedges and split horizontally.

Variation: Hataleipa with ham and cheese — Follow above recipe and turn dough out on sheet, spreading it into a circle about 10" in diameter. Let it rise 30 minutes. Press 1-2 cups cubed cooked ham into the dough and bake at 400 degrees for 15 minutes. Remove from oven and top with 1-2 cups of shredded or cubed Swiss, Monterey Jack or Cheddar cheese. Return bread to oven for 5-10 minutes until browned and cheese is melted. Cool 5 minutes; then cut in wedges to serve.

Fun to make, fun to serve, and a great Sunday night special.

Vicky T. Uminowicz

OATMEAL BREAD

2 cups rolled oats
1 tablespoon lard
1 cup molasses
1 cup warm water
4 tablespoons dry yeast

1 tablespoon salt
⅓ cup oil
4 cups boiling water
10 cups flour

Combine oats, salt, lard, oil, molasses and 4 cups of boiling water and let cool. Add yeast to cup of warm water and let proof. Mix all ingredients and add flour until dough is easy to handle. Knead for 10 minutes; place in greased bowl, turning once to grease the top. Let rise until double in bulk. Punch down and divide into 4 loaves; place in 9"x5"x3" greased loaf tins. Let rise until doubled. Bake in pre-heated oven at 350 degrees for 45 minutes. Yield: 4 loaves.

Oatmeal bread recipes were submitted by Mrs. Robert Gerling, Virginia Aitken, and Tim Cross. All were quite similar, and this one came with the following note:

This is the bread we baked in a stone oven at our wilderness camp in the Mahoosuc. We kneaded it on a piece of oilcloth, set it to rise in a greased bucket covered with a blanket and spent the day climbing. First man down built the fire, put the soup kettle on and shaped the biscuits in the bottom of the dutch oven and the two loaves in bread pans. Loaves went into the stone oven after heating one hour, 20 minutes after supper. They cooked while we slept scenting the air of the lean-to with a marvelous aroma. Tim Cross

PORTUGUESE SWEET BREAD

2 packages active dry yeast
¼ cup warm water
1 cup milk, scalded
¾ cup sugar
1 egg (for brushing
    bread)

1 teaspoon salt
3 eggs
½ cup butter
5½-6 cups flour, all-purpose
1 teaspoon sugar (for brushing
    bread)

Dissolve yeast in warm water in a large bowl. Scald milk and soften butter in milk while milk cools. Stir into yeast cooled milk mixture, salt, eggs, ¾ cup sugar, and three cups flour. Beat until smooth. Stir in enough remaining flour to make dough easy to handle. Turn the dough out on lightly floured surface and knead until smooth and elastic (about 5 minutes). Place in greased bowl, turning once to grease top, cover and let rise to double bulk in warm place (1½-2 hours). Punch down; divide in half. Shape into slightly flat round loaf and place in greased round layer cake pans 9″x1½″. Cover and let rise until double in bulk (about 1 hour). Beat one egg slightly and brush over top of loaves, sprinkle 1 teaspoon sugar over tops, and bake in pre-heated oven at 350 degrees until golden brown (35-45 minutes). Yield: 2 loaves.

Variation: Although not ethnically pure, about a cup of golden raisins, soaked in boiling water for about 3-5 minutes and well-drained, adds a bit of color to this lovely bread. A cup of candied fruit adds a festive note to one loaf while leaving the second plain.

Mrs. John F. Flagg

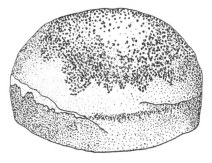

GINGERBREAD WAFFLES

2 cups sifted cake flour
2 teaspoons baking powder
1 teaspoon cinnamon
¾ cup light sour cream
1 egg, slightly beaten

¼ teaspoon soda
½ teaspoon salt
⅔ cup dark molasses
¼ cup milk
2 teaspoons ginger

Sift together flour, baking powder, soda, salt, sugar, and spices. Combine all liquids and add to flour mixture, beating until smooth. Bake in hot waffle iron and serve with whipped cream.

Diana Coppi's recipe
submitted by her daughter Eleanor

WHOLE WHEAT BREAD

The secret to making light whole wheat bread is to mix only half the flour with the yeast, sweetener and water or milk. Oil and salt retard the rising and should be added after the sponge is made. The first mixture is called a Sponge. There will be four risings.

STAGE ONE: Add 2 tablespoons yeast (or 2 packages) to 1 cup lukewarm water with 1 teaspoon honey. Let this sit until it rises (10 minutes). Meanwhile in a large bowl or bread mixer, add 5 cups warm water, ½ cup sweetener (honey, molasses or brown sugar), 2 cups dry milk powder (or 2 packages). Add yeast mixture, making sure the water and sweetener are not more than 105°. Add 8 cups whole wheat flour and beat 50 times. Cover and let rise in warm place for **1 hour.**

SECOND STAGE: Stir down. Add 2½ tablespoons salt. At this time, you may add 2 cups sunflower seeds (or 2 cups raisins). Use more sweetener if using raisins (¾ cup). Add ½ cup vegetable oil, about 8 cups whole wheat flour a little at a time. **Beat.** Add only enough flour so you can handle the dough. Put on floured board and knead until it doesn't stick to your hands. The longer the better, but don't add too much flour. Coat large bowl with 2 tablespoons oil and put ball of dough in and turn over. Cover and let rise for **50 minutes.** Punch down and turn over dough and let rise again for **40 minutes.**

Put dough on board, knead a couple of turns. Cut into 4 sections. Round each section, put on board. Cover and let sit for 5 minutes. Shape into loaves and put in greased pans. Cover and let rise for **30 minutes** more. Bake at 350° for about ¾ of 1 hour. Test by knocking loaf out of pan and tapping bottom of loaf. Should sound hollow.

I made whole wheat bread (bricks!) for one year before I found this recipe.

R. C.

Desserts – Cakes & Pies

Lady
berry pickers
in East
Sandwich.

Somebody's Grandma
Her back door led direct to the pantry where
the sugar cookies are — and here apple pies
are in the making.

WHY HE GOT NO PIE AT ALL

A small boy sat on the top of the fence,
And thought he was quite a bright fellow.
For he counted the days 'til Thanksgiving time,
And he counted the pumpkins yellow.

And he said as he sat in royal state
On top of the fence so high,
"A pumpkin pie most highly I rate,"
And he mused on the pleasures of by and by.

And now near at hand was Thanksgiving Day,
And the kitchen was all in a whirl.
And his mother was busy as busy could be,
Likewise his aunt and the servant girl.

To take a pie this small boy intended,
For what was one pie more or less?
No doubt his mother would be offended,
But who the culprit she'd never guess.

His chance soon came for a neighbor came in
To ask for the loan of the rolling pin;
And when none were looking or standing by,
This dreadful boy ran off with a pie.

The pie was hot and burned him so
And running so fast he stubbed his toe.
That over he fell, hot pie and all
And loudly did for his mother call.

She sadly looked at her pride and joy,
And separated pie from boy.
He cried very hard at having done wrong,
But he knew he'd cry more before very long.

Next day at dinner all wondered why,
This small boy was debarred from pie.
But his mother and he alone knew the reason,
And he thought their remarks quite out of season.

Anonymous

(found in an old hand written recipe book)

Blueberries, blackberries, whortleberries, huckleberries were sometimes referred to by early American cooks as "pie timber," and they do, in fact, make a great pie, as well as many other delicacies.

APPLE CAKE

2 cups sugar
4 eggs
1 cup oil
⅓ cup orange juice

2 cups sifted flour
3 teaspoons vanilla
3 teaspoons baking powder
5 baking apples

Preheat oven to 350 degrees. Grease and flour a 9" tube pan. Beat all ingredients except apples for 7 minutes at medium speed. Spread half the mixture in pan. Peel and slice apples about ¼ inch thick. Mix apples with 4 tablespoons sugar and 3 teaspoons cinnamon. Place half the apples on batter in pan. Repeat batter and apples on top. Bake for 1¼ hours or until done.

Marilyn McKechnie

BLUEBERRY CAKE

½ cup shortening
1 cup sugar
2 eggs
½ cup milk

1 teaspoon vanilla
1¾ cups sifted flour
1½ cups blueberries
2 teaspoons baking powder

Cream shortening and sugar; add eggs, one at a time, beating with electric mixer. Add vanilla to milk, mix alternately with flour, which has been sifted with baking powder. Fold in blueberries. Pour into 7"x10½" pan. Bake at 350 degrees until done.

Florence Taylor

CALLA LILIES SPONGE CAKES

3 egg yolks
1 cup sugar
½ teaspoon grated lemon rind
3 tablespoons lemon juice
1 teaspoon vanilla
½ cup boiling water

1-1/8 cups cake flour
2 teaspoons baking powder
3 egg whites
¼ teaspoon salt
whipping cream and orange peel

Beat egg yolks until light; add gradually sugar, beating constantly. Add grated lemon rind, lemon juice, vanilla and boiling water. Sift flour and baking powder three times. Add dry ingredients to yolk mixture and beat until well blended. Beat egg whites until stiff, with salt. Fold them into batter. Spoon batter into about thirteen or fourteen saucers — ungreased. (About two rounded tablespoons to a saucer.) Bake at 325° about 20 minutes, or until lightly browned. Remove cakes from saucers and fold, pinching together one side and fastening with toothpicks to form lily. This has to be done while warm. Toothpicks may be removed when cool. Fill center of lily with sweetened whipped cream. Cut strips of orange peel, add one to each lily to form stamen. Very pretty for a party. Serves: 12.

Alice Sears

CARROT CAKE

FOR CAKE:

1½ cups flour
1¼ cups sugar
1½ teaspoons baking soda
1½ teaspoons cinnamon
¼ teaspoon salt
2 4½ ounce jars baby food
   carrots (purée)

⅔ cup oil
2 eggs — slightly beaten
½ teaspoon vanilla
1 8-ounce can crushed pineapple
   (drained)
⅔ cup shredded coconut
½ cup chopped walnuts

FOR TOPPING:

3 ounces softened cream cheese
¼ cup butter, softened

½ teaspoon vanilla
2 cups confectioners' sugar

CAKE: In a large bowl, mix well, flour, sugar, baking soda, cinnamon and salt. Add carrots, oil, eggs and vanilla. Mix briskly by hand until well blended. Stir in pineapple, coconut and nuts. Bake in preheated oven 350 degrees for about 40-45 minutes in a 9" square pan. I grease and flour pan.

TOPPING: Mix cream cheese, butter and vanilla. Add sugar. Beat until smooth (I double recipe because I like lots of frosting.) EXCELLENT!

June Ashley

CARROT LAYER CAKE

2 cups salad oil
2 cups sugar
3 eggs
3 cups flour
1 teaspoon salt
2 cups grated carrots
1 10-ounce can crushed pineapple

1½ tablespoons each of: clove,
   cinnamon, ginger, nutmeg
   allspice
1½ tablespoons baking soda
1½ tablespoons baking powder
1 cup chopped walnuts
1 cup raisins

Mix oil, sugar, eggs. Add flour, salt, spices, baking soda, baking powder and mix. Add crushed pineapple; mix. Stir in walnuts and raisins. Pour into 3 9" greased, floured layer cake pans. Bake at 350 degrees for 30-35 minutes. When cool spread two layers with raspberry jam. Place one layer on top of second, top with third layer. Frost with cream cheese frosting.

Mary Ellen Pierce

NEW BEDFORD CRANBERRY NUT CAKE

1 cup shortening
1½ cups sugar
4 eggs
3 cups sifted flour
2½ teaspoons baking powder

½ teaspoon salt
½ cup milk
1 cup cranberries, chopped
1 cup pecans, chopped

Cream shortening and sugar thoroughly. Add eggs, one at a time, beating well after each addition. Sift flour, baking powder and salt. Add sifted ingredients to creamed mixture alternating with milk, blending well. Fold in cranberries and pecans. Spread in greased and floured 10" tube pan. Bake at 350 degrees for 1 hour. When cool simply sprinkle with confectioners' sugar.

Prize winning cake. New Bedford Standard Times 1966

Louise Martens

EGG PLANT CAKE

1 package yellow cake mix
(2-layer size)
1 package vanilla flavor instant
pudding
4 eggs
½ cup oil

2 cups peeled and grated eggplant
½ teaspoon nutmeg
¼ teaspoon cinnamon
1/8 teaspoon cloves
1/8 teaspoon salt

Combine all ingredients in large mixer bowl. Blend; then beat at medium speed for 4 minutes. Pour into greased and floured 10" fluted tube pan. Bake at 350° for 50-55 minutes or until cake springs back when pressed and cake pulls away from sides of pan. Do not underbake. Cool in pan 15 minutes. Remove from pan and finish cooling on rack. Sprinkle with confectioners' sugar if desired.

Olga Roberti

OLD FASHIONED
HOT WATER GINGERBREAD

2 cups sifted flour
1 teaspoon soda
½ teaspoon salt
½ teaspoon cloves
1 teaspoon ginger

½ cup shortening
½ cup sugar
1 cup molasses
1 cup boiling water

Cream shortening and sugar. Add molasses. Add dry sifted ingredients. Mix well and add cup of boiling water. Beat well; pour into greased 8" x 8" pan. Bake at 350 degrees for 35 to 40 minutes.

Grammy Phoebe

POPPY SEED CAKE

2⅔ cups sifted all purpose flour
1¼ teaspoons baking powder
1 teaspoons baking soda
½ teaspoon salt
1 cup unsalted butter

1¾ cups sugar
5 eggs — separated
1 cup buttermilk
⅓ cup poppy seeds
1 tablespoon grated lemon rind

Sift flour, soda, baking powder and salt together. Beat butter and 1½ cups sugar until fluffy. Beat in egg yolks one at a time. Add sifted dry ingredients, alternately with buttermilk, to egg yolks starting and ending with dry ingredients. Beat until smooth. Add poppy seeds and lemon rind. Beat egg whites until foamy. Gradually beat in remaining ¼ cup sugar until meringue forms soft peaks. Fold into batter until no white remains. Pour into prepared 10" bundt pan. Bake in pre-heated 325 degree oven for 55 minutes. With spatula loosen cake and invert on wire rack. Cool and sprinkle with confectioners' sugar before serving.

Nancy Titcomb

TOMATO SOUP CAKE

½ cup shortening
1 cup sugar
1 egg
2 cups sifted cake flour
2 teaspoons baking powder

¾ teaspoon baking soda
¾ teaspoon cinnamon
¾ teaspoon nutmeg
¾ teaspoon cloves
1 can tomato soup

FROSTING:

3 ounces softened cream cheese
¼ cup butter, softened

½ teaspoon vanilla
2 cups confectioners' sugar

Sift dry ingredients with flour. Cream shortening and sugar. Add egg. Add dry ingredients in mixer. Add soup. Last, add 1 cup of nuts if desired, by hand. Bake at 350 degrees for 25-30 minutes.

FROSTING: Mix cream cheese, butter and vanilla. Add sugar. Beat until smooth. Spread over cake when cool.

Ruth Stuart

Wedding cake from Home.

Plum Cake

5 lbs. of Flour, 5 lbs. of Butter 5 lbs. of Sugar, 60 eggs, 15 lbs. of Raisins 15 lbs. of Currants, 5 lbs. of Citron 2 oz. of nutmeg 1 oz. of Mace, 1 oz. of Cinnamon, 1 oz. of Ginger, ½ oz of Cloves, 5 wineglasses of Brandy, 2 teaspoonsfull of Saleratus.

P.F.C.

From an 1852 Receipt Book

MAPLE SYRUP FROSTING

2 cups maple syrup (real)   2 egg whites

Boil syrup to 238 degrees F. or until it can be formed into a soft ball when a little mixture is dropped in cold water. Remove from heat. Beat egg whites quickly until stiff. Pour hot syrup in a fine stream over the whites, beating constantly. Continue beating until mixture is stiff enough to spread. (One-half the recipe is really sufficient for a square 8″ or 9″ cake.)

SWEDISH APPLE PIE

6-8 apples
1 teaspoon sugar
1 teaspoon cinnamon
1 stick soft butter
1 egg

1 cup sugar
1 cup flour
pinch of salt
½ cup walnuts, chopped

Butter 9" or 10" pie plate. Fill with peeled and sliced apples. Sprinkle with sugar and cinnamon. For crust, which goes on top of apples, cream butter and 1 cup sugar. Add salt and egg. Add flour. Mix well and spread over apples. Sprinkle with chopped nuts. Bake at 350° for 45 minutes. Serves: 6.

Elizabeth T. Richards

CHOCOLATE ANGEL PIE

2 egg whites
1/8 teaspoon cream of tartar
½ teaspoon vanilla
1 package Baker's German
  sweet chocolate
3 tablespoons water

1 cup whipping cream
1/8 teaspoon salt
½ cup sugar
½ cup chopped walnuts
1 teaspoon vanilla

Beat egg whites with salt and cream of tartar until foamy. Add sugar, 2 tablespoons at a time, and beat well. Continue beating until stiff peaks are formed. Fold in ½ teaspoon vanilla and nuts. Spoon into lightly buttered 8" pie pan, building up the sides. Bake in slow 300° oven 50-55 minutes. Cool. Stir chocolate over low heat until melted, add the water. Cool, add 1 teaspoon vanilla and whipped cream and pile into meringue shell. Chill and serve.

Mrs. Oscar Hollander, Jr.

CHOCOLATE PIE

1 baked pie shell (either pastry
  or graham cracker)
1 8-ounce chocolate or sweet
  chocolate bar

18 large marshmallows
Scant ½ cup milk
½ pint heavy cream

Place chocolate, marshmallows, and milk in top of double boiler. Cook over simmering water until marshmallows and chocolate are melted. Cool. Whip heavy cream and fold into chocolate mixture when it has cooled. Pile into baked shell and chill until ready to serve.

Pam Anderson

"MELT IN YOUR MOUTH" CRANBERRY PIE

2 cups whole cranberries
1½ cups sugar
½ cup chopped walnuts

2 eggs
1 cup sifted flour
¾ cup melted margarine

Grease 10" pie plate, spread whole cranberries over the bottom. Sprinkle with ½ cup sugar and nuts. Beat eggs well. Add 1 cup sugar gradually and beat until mixed. Add flour and melted margarine to egg mixture. Beat well. Pour batter over top of cranberries. Bake in slow oven at 325° for 60 minutes or until crust is golden brown. Cut like pie and serve warm with ice cream. Serves: 6-8.

Barbara Maxwell

CRANBERRY-APPLE PIE

4 to 5 cups apples — sliced
1 cup cranberries — fresh
½ cup raisins
1 to 2 tablespoons lemon juice
¾ cup sugar or more to taste

2 tablespoons flour
½ teaspoon salt
2 tablespoons butter
pastry for 2 crust pie

Combine apples, cranberries and raisins and sprinkle with lemon juice. Combine sugar, flour and salt and toss with apple mixture. Put filling in unbaked pie shell and dot with butter. Top with pastry crust. Prick with fork to make vents for steam and brush crust with milk. Sprinkle with sugar if desired. Bake approximately 45 minutes or until crust is golden brown at 375°. Note: One cup of fresh or frozen blueberries can be substituted for the cranberries. Serves: 6-8.

MOTHER'S GRAHAM CRACKER CRUST CREAM PIE

⅓ cup flour
⅔ cup sugar
¼ teaspoon salt
2 cups milk, scalded
2 tablespoons butter

3 slightly beaten egg yolks
½ teaspoon vanilla
baked graham cracker
   crust, cooled

Mix flour, sugar and salt thoroughly. Add scalded milk to dry ingredients gradually, stirring constantly. Cook over hot water until thick, stirring often, about 15 minutes. Add butter and egg yolks. Cook 2 minutes longer. Cool and add vanilla. Pour into baked graham cracker crust. When cool, cover with meringue. Brown slightly in oven.

Substitutions:

Butterscotch Pie: Substitute 1 cup brown sugar for granulated.

Chocolate Pie: Increase sugar to 1 cup. Add 2 squares unsweetened chocolate to scalded milk and allow to melt.

Coconut Pie: Add 1 cup shredded coconut to cream pie and sprinkle ½ cup to cover top of pie.

Banana Pie: Slice 2 or 3 bananas and add to cream pie.   Emily Snyder

FROZEN LEMON PIE

¼ cup fine graham cracker
   crumbs
3 egg whites
¼ cup sugar
3 egg yolks

1 cup whipping cream
2 or 3 teaspoons grated lemon
   peel
¼ cup lemon juice

Sprinkle half the crumbs in well greased 9″ pie plate. Beat egg whites until frothy, add sugar and beat until stiff and glossy. Beat yolks until light and lemon color. Fold in egg whites, add lemon rind and juice. Beat cream until stiff. Fold into egg mixture. Pour into crumb-lined pie plate. Sprinkle with rest of crumbs and freeze to desired consistency.

Christine Pope Gallagher

SUGAR PIE

1¼ cups heavy cream
2½ cups light brown sugar
1 10″ unbaked pie shell

2 tablespoons flour
1 egg

Mix everything together. Pour in unbaked 10″ pie shell. Cook at 350° for 35 to 45 minutes.

Claudette Powers

LEMON SPONGE PIE

1 large cup sugar
1 tablespoon flour
pinch salt
butter — size of a walnut
1 unbaked pie shell

3 egg yolks, beaten well
juice and rind of a lemon
1 scant cup milk
3 egg whites, beaten

Sift sugar and flour into bowl. Cream in butter and salt. Mix in remaining ingredients and add beaten egg whites. Pour into unbaked pie shell. Bake at 425° for 10 minutes, then at least 30 minutes at 350°.

Doc McGee

PINEAPPLE PIE

1 can crushed pineapple, drained
1 cup sugar
1 cup water
3 eggs

2 tablespoons flour
salt
butter — size of a walnut
crust for 1 2-crust pie

Put pineapple, ¾ cup sugar and water on stove and bring to boil. Beat eggs and add flour, ¼ cup sugar and salt (which have been mixed together). Add to pineapple mixture by first adding a little hot pineapple to egg mixture. Cook until thickened. Cool slightly, then pour into pie crust and top with crust. Slit to let steam escape. Bake 400° until brown. Serves: 6.

Alice Sears

RASPBERRY REVEL MERINGUE PIE

SHELL:

4 egg whites
¼ teaspoon cream of tartar

1 cup sugar

FILLING:

2 packages (10 ounces each)
  frozen raspberries — thawed
3 tablespoons cornstarch
1 cup whipping cream
1 cup miniature marshmallows

1 package (8 ounce) cream cheese,
  softened
½ cup sugar
½ teaspoon vanilla

MERINGUE SHELL: Heat oven to 250°. Cover baking sheet with brown paper. Draw 8″ circle on brown paper. Beat egg whites and cream of tartar in small bowl until foamy. Beat in sugar, 1 tablespoon at a time. Continue beating until stiff and glossy, about 4 minutes. Spread half of meringue mixture in 8″ circle, building up sides. Drop remaining meringue by rounded teaspoonfuls on edge of circle, making small peaks. Bake 1½ hours. Turn off oven. Leave meringue in oven **with door closed** until cool — at least one hour.

FILLING: Mix raspberries and cornstarch in saucepan. Heat to boiling, stirring constantly. Boil and stir 1 minute. Cool. Beat whipping cream in chilled bowl until stiff. Blend cheese, sugar and vanilla. Fold cheese mixture and marshmallows into whipped cream. Spread ⅓ raspberry mixture in meringue shell. Spread ½ cheese mixture over raspberry layer. Repeat, using ½ of remaining raspberry mixture, remaining cheese mixture and top with remaining raspberry mixture. Refrigerate at least 2 hours, but no longer than 24 hours. Serves: 8-10

Barbara Howland

51

FAVORITE RHUBARB PIE

2 cups rhubarb, cut into small
   pieces
⅔ cup sugar
2 tablespoons flour

2 egg yolks
2 teaspoons water
salt, just a shake
1 unbaked pie shell

Mix together, vigorously, sugar, flour, egg yolks, water and salt. Add rhubarb and stir until well coated. Turn into unbaked pie shell. Put into preheated 400° oven for 20 minutes. Reduce heat to 350° and bake exactly 20 minutes more. Cool on a rack. Try it and LIVE!

Helen Clark

PHOEBE'S SOUR CREAM PIE

12 ounces cream cheese (room
   temperature)
2 eggs
½ cup sugar

½ generous pint sour cream
3 tablespoons sugar
½ teaspoon vanilla
1 unbaked graham cracker crust

Beat together softened cream cheese, eggs and sugar. Pour into shell and bake 20 minutes at 350°. Cool. For topping, mix sour cream, sugar and vanilla. Spread on cooled pie. Bake at 425° for 5 minutes. Cool. Store in refrigerator.

Phoebe Dunn

STRAWBERRY PIE

1 baked pie shell
4 cups fresh strawberries
1 cup sugar

3 tablespoons cornstarch
½ cup water
1 tablespoon butter

Crush 1 cup berries and put in a pot, add sugar, water and cornstarch. Cook until thick (like pudding). Remove from heat and add butter.* Cool slightly. Place remaining whole berries in pie shell. Pour cooked berries over this. Refrigerate until ready to serve. Top with whipped cream.

*If color is not good, add few drops of red food coloring.

My friend, Hazel Esten, gave this recipe to me. She knows I'm not a good cook. It's easy to make, and very festive on special occasions as well as for the family.

Rose Broderick

WITHOUT RIVAL MERINGUE PIE

4 egg whites
5¼ ounces ground almonds

5¼ ounces sugar

FILLING:

4 egg yolks
1 stick butter
1 teaspoon vanilla

½ cup sugar
½ cup heavy cream

Whip egg whites until stiff. Fold in sugar and almonds which have been previously mixed. Spread on well-greased and floured cookie sheets making two squares approximately ½" thick. Bake in 300° oven until golden brown. Remove immediately from cookie sheets as the squares become very brittle when cool.

Filling: Mix egg yolks, sugar and cream and heat carefully until thickened. Remove from heat and while cooling mix in butter. Add a teaspoon of vanilla. Chill in refrigerator. Spread ½ filling on one square. Cover with 2nd square and spread remaining half.

Kerstin Chapman

Cookies, Bars & Squares

Ladies prepare for a sporting game of croquet in East Sandwich.

Old family store on Liberty Street.

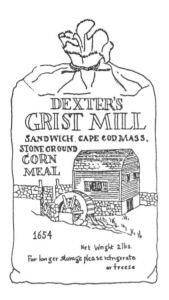

FANNIE FARMER (1857-1915)

Fannie Farmer, born in Boston, became deeply interested in cooking at a young age. She worked at home and for friends and in 1889 graduated from the Boston Cooking School, which trained teachers of cooking. She became Director of the school, and in 1896 edited "The Boston Cooking School Cook Book", which became a classic in its field and was enlarged and reprinted many times. Fannie Farmer's greatest contribution was the development of accurate measurements in recipes.

She has a special connection to Sandwich in that she worked for several years for William A. Foster (1850-1928) of Newton Center and Spring Hill (Skiff House), a well-to-do merchant and importer. William A. Foster was an uncle of Ida Putnam, founder of Green Briar Jam Kitchen.

THE YEAR WITHOUT A SUMMER

The year 1816 was unique in that snow fell in New England in each month of the year, there were frosts in each month, and a wide failure of food crops. The diarist Benjamin Percival records that it was necessary to wear heavy clothes and mittens when working outside even in the summer, and also stated as a matter of even greater amazement that there were no horseflies on the farm that year. The Nye family has a record that the Reverend Levi Nye, a Methodist minister, who lived just north of the present Dillingham House, was the only man in Sandwich who managed to raise any corn. He may have had an unusual south-facing slope with extra protection from winds.

The reason for the extraordinary weather was not appreciated for another sixty years. It was due to the explosive eruption of a volcano called Tamboro in Indonesia, which threw a vast amount of ash into the stratosphere forming a blanket which girdled the earth and only slowly settled out. A similar event occurred in 1883 when the volcano Krakatoa erupted. By that time improved communications allowed the formation of an international committee which studied the world-wide effects of the eruption.

BRANDY SNAPS

¾ cup butter
½ cup sugar
¼ cup dark brown sugar
¼ cup molasses
¼ cup honey
3/8 teaspoon ginger

¾ teaspoon grated orange rind
¾ teaspoon cinnamon
1½ cups flour
1 teaspoon baking soda
1 tablespoon brandy

Melt butter in saucepan. Add sugar, brown sugar, molasses, honey, ginger, orange rind and cinnamon. Stir over low heat until thoroughly blended and sugars are liquefied. Remove from heat. Add flour, baking soda and mix thoroughly with whisk. Add brandy. Stir in. Cool mixture approximately ½ hour. Drop by teaspoonful on unbuttered cookie sheet. Keep cookies several inches apart. Bake in 300° to 325° oven for 10-12 minutes. Yield: 3-4 dozen.

Gerda Geehr

CARROT COOKIES

1 cup butter
¾ cup granulated sugar
1 egg, lightly beaten
1 cup mashed carrots
2 cups flour

pinch salt
2 teaspoons baking powder
½ teaspoon almond extract
½ teaspoon vanilla extract

FROSTING:

confectioners' sugar
water

almond extract

Cream butter and sugar. Add lightly beaten egg, then blend in carrots. Add flour, salt, baking powder and extracts. Mix until smooth. Drop by spoonfuls on greased cookie sheet. Bake for 15 minutes in pre-heated 350° oven. Allow to cool. Frost by blending confectioners' sugar and warm water and almond extract to taste. Spread thinly on cookies.

CHRISTMAS HOLLY LEAF COOKIES

¼ cup butter or margarine
1 10-ounce bag of regular
marshmallows (about 40) or 3
cups miniature marshmallows

green food coloring
5-6 cups corn flakes
red cinnamon candies

In double boiler melt butter, and add marshmallows. Stir and cook until really gooey! Add 1 teaspoon or more green food coloring. Add corn flakes. Take off stove and mix until corn flakes are well blended with green mixture. Drop by teaspoon onto wax paper and form to resemble leaves. Put 2 cinnamon candies on each leaf. Yield: 9 dozen.

Note: *I use these to decorate the cookie trays and desserts during the holiday season.*

Emily Snyder

CHOCOLATE MINT LAYER COOKIES

COOKIE LAYER:

2 1-ounce squares unsweetened
  chocolate
½ cup butter
1 cup sugar

¾ cup flour
2 eggs, slightly beaten
1 teaspoon vanilla

MINT CREAM FILLING:

1½ cups confectioners' sugar
2 tablespoons butter, softened
2 tablespoons heavy cream or
  evaporated milk

¾ teaspoon peppermint
  flavoring
1 drop green food coloring

GLAZE:

3 ounces German sweet
  chocolate
2 tablespoons butter

1 tablespoon vanilla
1 inch-square piece of paraffin

COOKIE LAYER: Melt butter and chocolate over low heat. Mix flour and sugar and add to chocolate mixture. Add eggs and vanilla. Pour into greased pan (9"x9"x2" or 8"x8") and bake at 350° for 20 minutes. Cool.

MINT CREAM FILLING: Combine confectioners' sugar, butter, cream, peppermint flavoring and green food coloring. Beat until smooth. Spread over cookie layer and chill until firm.

GLAZE: Melt chocolate, butter, vanilla and paraffin. Spread over cookies and let set. Cut into 1 inch squares. Yield: 6 dozen. Heavenly eating!!!

Kimberley-Jo Clark

EBBA'S COOKIES

1 pound butter, softened
½ pound sugar
1½ pounds flour

2 eggs, separated
extra granulated sugar
thinly sliced almonds

Cream butter with sugar. Add egg yolks and flour. (Save a little flour to use when rolling out cookies.) Mix thoroughly. On floured board, roll out dough about ⅜" thick. Cut with fancy cookie cutters. Brush over with slightly beaten egg white. Sprinkle with granulated sugar and thinly sliced almonds. Place ¼" apart on ungreased baking sheet. Bake approximately 10 minutes at 400°. They should only be slightly browned (very pale). This recipe makes well over 100 cookies if small cookie cutters are used.

Naomi White

MRS. SWANSON'S CUT-OUT COOKIES

1½ cups shortening
2 eggs
2 cups sugar
½ cup molasses
4 cups flour

2 teaspoons baking soda
2 teaspoons ginger
2 teaspoons ground cloves
1 teaspoon salt

Mix shortening, eggs, sugar and molasses together. Sift flour, baking soda, ginger, cloves and salt together and add to egg mixture. Mix thoroughly. Chill. Roll thin and cut in desired shapes. Bake at 350° for 12 minutes on ungreased cookie sheet.

Nancy Titcomb

SUGAR COOKIE TREE FOR CHRISTMAS

COOKIE DOUGH:

½ cup shortening
1 cup sugar
1 egg or 2 yolks
1 tablespoon cream or milk
1½ cups flour

½ teaspoon vanilla or lemon
flavoring
½ teaspoon salt
1 teaspoon baking powder

FROSTING:

2 egg whites
1½ cups sugar
¼ teaspoon cream of tartar

Plaster of Paris for base

⅓ cup cold water
1 teaspoon vanilla or lemon
flavoring
confectioners' silver balls

Step 1: Mix half a cup of Plaster of Paris with small amount of water to form a paste. Place it in the form of a patty on a metal tray. In a few minutes plaster will begin to set. Sharpen the tip of a 10-inch straight stick or slender dowel and stand it in plaster, butt end down. Set aside to dry.

Step 2: Cut a series of 6 paper stars graduating in size from 7 inches across to 1½ inches. These are patterns for sugar cookies.

Step 3: Beat shortening in large bowl until fluffy; beat in egg, milk and vanilla. Sift together dry ingredients and add to egg/shortening mixture. Should be quite stiff. Chill thoroughly. Roll out portion at a time on floured board. Place star patterns on dough, cut; cut center hole in each star. Bake in 350° oven for about 8 minutes. Cool on wire rack.

Step 4: Cut doughnut-shaped "dividers" from firm slices of bread. Two or three dividers will be needed per star. Dry dividers in warm oven. To build tree, slip 2 or 3 bread dividers onto dowel. These form the hidden trunk of tree. Slip on largest star, then two more dividers, followed by next largest star, rotating points of star so they fall between points of largest star, two more dividers, then star #3, etc. When you reach the top, place a divider on top star, and you are ready for the "snow."

Step 5: Combine frosting ingredients in top of double boiler; place over boiling water. Beat until frosting forms peaks — about 7 minutes. Remove from heat, add flavoring and beat a few more minutes. Frost branches from center to tip, drawing out frosting to form icicles. Place tiny red candles on half the branches (smallest size red birthday candles cut in half). Do not light. Throw on confectioners' silver balls.

These trees are elegant enough for the grandest party, but really belong to the land of fairies, and should be made with and for children.

Shirley Cross

DOUGIE'S COWBOY COOKIES

⅔ cup butter or shortening
½ cup brown sugar
½ cup sugar
1 egg
½ to ⅔ cup rolled oats

1½ cups flour
½ teaspoon baking soda
½ teaspoon salt
½ to ⅔ cup chocolate chips

Cream together butter, sugars and egg. Sift flour, baking powder and salt; add to creamed mixture. Mix well. Add chocolate chips and same amount rolled oats. Drop by spoonfuls onto greased baking sheet; bake for 10 to 15 minutes in 350° oven. Yield: 3 dozen.

Linda McLawhorn-Tracy

FORGOTTEN MERINGUES

2 egg whites
½ cup sugar

½ teaspoon cream of tartar

OPTIONAL:

1 cup rice krispies
¼ cup chopped walnuts

1 6-ounce package mint-flavored
chocolate bits

Beat egg whites to frothy; add cream of tartar and continue beating until whites hold a soft peak. Add sugar gradually, still beating, until stiff but not dry. Optional ingredients may now be added. Drop by teaspoon on lightly greased cookie sheet. Place in middle of preheated 275° oven. Turn off heat as soon as cookies go in; leave for 6 hours (until oven is **stone cold**) or overnight.

Note: This recipe will not work in a gas oven with pilot light. If cooking with gas stove, bake at 250° for 20 minutes or until meringues are dry. Yield: About 3 dozen.

FRUIT DROPS

1 cup soft shortening
2 cups packed brown sugar
2 eggs
½ cup sour milk
3½ cups flour

1 teaspoon baking soda
1 teaspoon salt
1½ cups chopped pecans
2 cups candied cherries — halved
2 cups chopped dates

Mix shortening, sugar and eggs well. Add sour milk. Sift flour, baking soda and salt and add. Add pecans, cherries and dates. Chill at least 1 hour. Drop on cookie sheet by rounded teaspoons. Bake 8-10 minutes at 400°. Yield: about 8 dozen.

Naomi White

BILL FOSTER'S GRANDMOTHER'S GINGERSNAPS

1 cup molasses
1 cup shortening
3¼ cups flour

½ teaspoon soda
1 tablespoon ginger
½ teaspoon salt

Heat molasses to boiling; pour over shortening. Stir other ingredients into it, mix thoroughly, and chill. Roll out one-quarter of the batter at a time. Cut into rounds and bake on a lightly greased cookie sheet for 8-10 minutes at 350°.

COOKIE JAR GINGERSNAPS

2 cups sifted flour	½ teaspoon salt
1 tablespoon ginger	¾ cup shortening
1 teaspoon cinnamon	1 cup sugar
2 teaspoons baking soda	1 egg, slightly beaten
¼ cup sugar in a tray or flat dish	¼ cup dark molasses

Sift flour, ginger, cinnamon, baking soda and salt together. Cream shortening and sugar. Add egg and molasses to shortening mixture and mix well. Add sifted dry ingredients to shortening/egg mixture and mix well. Batter will be somewhat stiff. Roll dough into one inch balls; roll each ball in sugar on tray until coated. Place sugared dough balls one inch apart on lightly greased or non-stick cookie sheet. Bake at 350° for about 10 minutes or until tops are crackly and light brown. Remove with spatula when slightly cool; finish cooling on absorbent paper towels. Yield: 40-50 cookes.

Pat Bryant

Variation: Mary Hall's Gingersnaps added 1 teaspoon of ground cloves to similar recipe.

GRANDMA'S OLD FASHIONED SAND COOKIES

1 cup shortening	1 teaspoon baking powder
1 cup brown sugar	1 teaspoon soda
1 cup white sugar	1 teaspoon cream of tartar
2 eggs, beaten	a little salt
1 teaspoon vanilla	2½ cups flour

Mix all ingredients together in order given. Make balls about the size of golf balls. Roll lightly in white sugar. Put on cookie sheet spaced far apart. Bake at 350° for about 10 minutes.

HARD GINGERBREAD

2½ cups flour	3 tablespoons butter
1 teaspoon ginger	1 teaspoon soda
½ teaspoon salt	3 tablespoons boiling water
1 cup light molasses	

Sift first three ingredients together in a bowl. Cut butter in with a pastry blender. Dissolve soda in hot water and add to molasses. Mix with dry ingredients. Dough will be stiff. Press into greased pan with floured fork. Cook at 350° for about 20 minutes. Cut into squares. Store in cookie jar.

Gramma Armstrong

FOOD AVAILABLE ABOUT 1700

The Sandwich Archives has a journal dated 1699-1704 by a trader named James Mills who sailed back and forth between Sandwich and Boston. Here are cargoes from Sandwich shipped to Boston:

Butter, beeswax, pine-tar, oysters, wheat, pork, barley and corn. Items bought in Boston for Sandwich customers included vegetable oil, licorice, treacle syrup, loaf sugar, nutmeg, cloves, malt, cheese and rum; also kitchen supplies as kettles, lamps, a sieve, earthen pots, platters, a chafing dish, pewter and a warming pan.

JOE FROGGERS

1 cup shortening
2 cups sugar
1 tablespoon salt
¾ cup water
¼ cup dark rum
2 teaspoons baking soda

2 cups dark molasses
7 cups flour
1 tablespoon ginger
1 teaspoon cloves
1 teaspoon nutmeg
½ teaspoon allspice

Cream shortening and sugar until light. Dissolve salt in water and mix with rum. Add baking soda to molasses. Sift flour and spices. Add liquid ingredients alternately with flour mixture to creamed mixture. Stir well between additions. (If your mixer has a dough hook, this works well.) Dough is, and should be sticky. Chill overnight in refrigerator. When ready to bake, roll dough to ½" thickness. Cut with large cutter. Bake in 375° oven for 10 or 12 minutes. I don't grease cookie sheet, and because cookies are large, put only 6 to a sheet to accommodate spreading as they cook. Yield: about 4 dozen.

Recipe over 100 years old — and made of sea water then. (Should be perfect survival food for ambitious field trips!)

KOULOUNA COOKIES

½ pound butter or margarine
2 tablespoons shortening
2½ cups confectioners' sugar
sesame seeds for sprinkling

3 eggs
1 teaspoon vanilla
5-6 cups flour sifted together with
3 teaspoons baking powder

Cream butter or margarine, shortening, and sugar. Beat until fluffy. Add eggs, vanilla, and flour sifted together with baking powder. Add more flour until you can shape the dough. Shape into pretzel form, brush with beaten egg, and sprinkle with sesame seeds. Bake on cookie sheet at 325° until light brown.

Florence Hall

MOLASSES DROP COOKIES

½ cup shortening
½ cup sugar
½ cup molasses
1 egg, beaten
1 teaspoon baking soda
½ cup sour milk
½ cup walnuts, chopped

2½ cups flour
½ teaspoon salt
½ teaspoon ginger
½ teaspoon cinnamon
½ teaspoon allspice or nutmeg
½ cup chopped seedless raisins
1 teaspoon flour

Cream shortening and sugar. Blend in molasses until smooth. Add beaten egg. Dissolve baking soda in sour milk. Sift flour, salt and spices together; add to creamed mixture alternately with milk combination. Dust raisins with spoonful of flour and fold in. Drop teaspoonfuls on well-greased baking sheet. Bake at 350° for 12-15 minutes. Yield: 6-7 dozen.

Recipe was given to me by an elderly friend.

Barbara Keating

MINCEMEAT COOKIES

1 cup soft shortening
2 cups brown sugar
2 eggs
½ cup cold coffee
3½ cups flour

1 teaspoon soda
1 teaspoon salt
1 teaspoon nutmeg
1 teaspoon cinnamon
2 cups well-drained mincemeat

Combine shortening, brown sugar and eggs; add cold coffee. Sift together flour, soda, salt, nutmeg and cinnamon and add to sugar/eggs mixture. Stir in mincemeat; chill for 1 hour. Drop by teaspoonful on greased cookie sheet and bake for 8-10 minutes at 400°.

MINCEMEAT FILLED COOKIES

1 cup shortening
1 cup sugar
1 cup brown sugar
2 eggs
¼ cup buttermilk
1 jar mincemeat

3½ cups sifted flour
1 teaspoon baking powder
1 teaspoon baking soda
1 teaspoon salt
1 teaspoon vanilla

Cream shortening, sugars and eggs together. Add buttermilk and vanilla. Sift dry ingredients and add to above. Mix well. Chill. Cut in rounds (for Christmas can also be cut in star and bell shapes). Place a small spoonful of mincemeat on one round, cover with another round and press edges together. Prick tops with fork. Bake about 10-15 minutes at 400° until cookies are golden brown. Other fillings — dates, apricots, etc. can be used. Yield: about 5 dozen.

FAT-FREE MOLASSES COOKIES

½ cup molasses
1 teaspoon baking soda
½ cup sugar
1 egg, beaten

2 cups flour
¼ teaspoon salt
1 full teaspoon ginger

Boil molasses and add baking soda. Add sugar and beaten egg to molasses mixture. Mix in about 2 cups of flour, the salt and ginger. Drop by tablespoonful onto greased cookie sheet. Cook at 350° about 10 minutes, or until done. Yield: 1 dozen large cookies.

Note: *This recipe came with a note that it is a "hundred-year old Vineyard reeceet" and was given the donor by a 93-year-old friend whose father was a whaling captain in the 1860's. The note went on to say it was an 1800's cheap and easy recipe.*

PECAN CRISP COOKIES

½ cup shortening
½ cup butter
1 box light brown sugar
2 eggs, well-beaten
2½ cups flour

¼ teaspoon salt
½ teaspoon baking soda
1 teaspoon vanilla
1 cup pecans — finely chopped

Cream shortening and butter thoroughly; gradually add sugar and cream well. Add well-beaten eggs. Reduce speed of mixer and add the flour that has been sifted with salt and soda. Add vanilla. Stir in chopped pecans. Drop teaspoonfuls onto greased cookie sheet, two inches apart. Bake at 350° for about 10 minutes. Yield: 5 to 6 dozen.

Mrs. Allen Benner   61

NYE HOMESTEAD
BUTTER-PRINT CUP PLATE COOKIES

½ cup molasses
¼ cup cream
½ cup sugar
½ cup shortening
3 cups flour

½ teaspoon soda
¼ teaspoon salt
¼ teaspoon cloves, ground
½ teaspoon nutmeg

Heat molasses with cream. Cream together sugar and shortening. Sift all dry ingredients, combine with sugar/shortening mixture and liquid. Refrigerate mixture until firm. Form dough into balls about 1″ in diameter. Dust cup plate with Wondra flour EACH TIME a cookie is pressed. Press cup plate onto dough *firmly*. Transfer cookie to cookie sheet. Bake at 325° for 10 minutes. Yield: about 5 dozen.

Dr. Edward Tinney

OAT FLAKE COOKIES

⅔ cup butter
1 cup sugar (can be ½ white
  and ½ brown)
2 eggs, slightly beaten
¼ cup hot water
1 teaspoon baking soda
½ teaspoon salt

2 scant cups flour
1 teaspoon cinnamon
2 scant cups oats
1 cup raisins
1 teaspoon vanilla
½ cup nuts (optional)

Cream butter and sugar until light and fluffy. Add eggs and beat until smooth. Add soda which has been dissolved in hot water and mix thoroughly. Add flour, salt and cinnamon, and then add remaining ingredients and stir until mixed. Drop by spoonfuls on cookie sheet and bake in 350° oven for 10-12 minutes or until slightly browned.

I am sending this note from my father, George L. Kiley, to explain in some measure our long commitment to Burgess and his delightful tales.

"Like Old Mother West Wind and the meadow folk, back in 1915-16, Mother would take a chair in the hallway in ear shot of three bedrooms and read aloud the adventures of Peter Rabbit, Reddy Fox, and Jimmie Skunk just as if they were all gathered around her in the forest glade. It was the same in later years at Grandma's bedside or around her wheel chair.

There seems to have never been a time since 1915 when our family was not exposed to the gentle mysteries of nature by the genius of Thornton Burgess. It is a wonder that Grandma was ever able to do any baking, but she did and the products were especially in demand."

*Submitted by the children, grandchildren and great-grandchildren
of James Patrick Kiley (1876-1961) and Lois Emily Fairchild Kiley (1877-1961)*

Mrs. J. P. Kiley

NO-BAKE PEANUT BUTTER COOKIES

½ cup white sugar
½ cup light corn syrup
¾ cup peanut butter

½ teaspoon vanilla
2 cups rice krispies

Mix sugar, corn syrup and peanut butter together. Bring to a boil. Stir and watch carefully. Add vanilla and rice krispies. Mix well. Drop by teaspoon on wax paper.

Helen Flood

PEANUT BUTTER COOKIES

½ cup butter
½ cup peanut butter
½ cup granulated sugar
½ cup brown sugar
1 egg, well beaten

1¼ cups flour
¼ teaspoon salt
¾ teaspoon baking soda
½ teaspoon baking powder

Cream butter and peanut butter together; add sugars gradually and cream thoroughly. Add well-beaten egg and mix well. Sift flour once before measuring, and then sift flour, soda, salt and baking powder together and add to creamed mixture. Chill dough well; then form into balls the size of walnuts. Place on lightly greased baking sheet. Flatten with fork dipped in flour making criss-cross patterns and bake in 350° oven until lightly browned, or about 10-12 minutes.

Mrs. J. P. Kiley

"REFRIGERATOR" COOKIES

4 cups flour
2 teaspoons baking powder
½ teaspoon salt
1½ cups shortening (part butter,
    part margarine)
1 cup white sugar

1½ cups brown sugar, firmly
    packed
2 eggs, unbeaten
1 tablespoon vanilla
2 cups walnuts, finely chopped
1 package chocolate mini-bits

Sift flour. Add baking powder and salt. Sift again. Cream shortening. Add sugars gradually, beating thoroughly. Add eggs and vanilla. Beat until mixture is light. Add flour and dry mixture gradually and stir until thoroughly mixed. Stir in nuts and chocolate mini-bits. Form in four log shaped rolls about 1½ " in diameter. Wrap each in wax paper and chill in refrigerator. Slice rolls in about one-quarter inch slices and bake in a 400° oven about 5 minutes — or until lightly browned. Remove from sheet promptly. Raw dough can be wrapped in aluminum foil and put in freezer. The rolls can be kept in the freezer for several months and you can have fresh baked cookies in a very short time. This recipe is really a double size because the mini-bits come in a double package, but the frozen rolls keep well.

Alice Wakefield

RUSSIAN TEA CAKES (DIZ'S BUMPS)

½ pound unsalted butter
¼ teaspoon salt
1 teaspoon vanilla

½ cup sifted confectioners' sugar
2¼ cup sifted flour
1 cup finely chopped nuts

Cream butter with sugar. Add vanilla. Blend in flour and salt. Add nuts. Chill dough. Form into small balls. Bake 14-15 minutes at 400°. While warm, roll in confectioners' sugar and again when cool. Makes about 4 dozen.

The sign in the old Blacksmith Shop read: "Call on a man in the hours of business, only on business, transact your business, then go about your business in order to give him time to do his business."

WHOOPIE PIES

FOR PIES:

½ cup shortening
1 cup sugar
1 egg
1 cup milk
1 teaspoon vanilla

2 cups flour
½ teaspoon salt
½ cup cocoa
½ teaspoon baking powder
1½ teaspoons baking soda

FOR FILLING:

2 egg whites
½ cup white shortening
2 cups confectioners' sugar

1 teaspoon vanilla
¼ teaspoon salt

Pies: Cream shortening and sugar. Add egg, milk and vanilla. Sift dry ingredients together and add to shortening mixture. Drop by teaspoonfuls on greased baking sheet and bake 425° for approximately 7 minutes.

Filling: Mix all filling ingredients together and beat until thick. Place filling on half the cookies and top with other half.

This is an old-fashioned recipe that I have had for at least 30 years. It is dependable and, to this day, my children still love it.   Rose Broderick

HERMITS

1 cup white sugar
1 cup brown sugar
1 cup shortening
2 eggs
½ teaspoon baking soda
1 tablespoon hot water

½ teaspoon salt
2 teaspoons cinnamon
1 teaspoon nutmeg
2½ cups flour
2½ cups chopped nuts
1½ cups raisins

Dissolve baking soda in tablespoon of hot water. Cream shortening and sugars. Add unbeaten eggs and dissolved soda. Mix. Add spices to flour and sift into shortening mixture. Add nuts and raisins. Drop onto greased cookie sheet. Bake in preheated oven at 375° until light brown.   Gigi Green

ITALIAN BISCOTTI BARS

¼ pound butter
2 cups sugar
6 eggs
4 cups flour

2 teaspoons baking powder
1½ teaspoons anise extract
1 cup chopped nuts
½ cup confectioners' sugar

Melt butter, add sugar and eggs; beat well. Add dry ingredients gradually, then blend in anise and add nuts. Spread on greased cookie sheet and bake in preheated oven at 375° for 12-20 minutes. While baking, mix confectioners' sugar with enough water to make spreadable. While cookies are still hot, spread with icing. Cut into 36 pieces when cool.   Gerrie Titcomb

MERINGUE BARS

½ cup soft margarine or butter
1 cup cane sugar
2 egg yolks
2 tablespoons water
2 cups flour
2 egg whites

¼ teaspoon salt
1 teaspoon baking powder
¼ teaspoon baking soda
1 teaspoon vanilla
1 6-ounce package chocolate bits
1 cup light brown sugar

Beat yolks slightly with water. Cream shortening and sugar; add yolks and vanilla. Sift salt, baking powder and baking soda into flour; add flour mixture to shortening mixture. Spread on well-greased 14"x10" cookie sheet with edges. Press onto pan with floured hands. Sprinkle chocolate bits on top and press into batter. Beat two egg whites with 1 cup light brown sugar until peaks form. (Add nuts if desired.) Spread on top of bits mixture and bake at 350° for approximately 20-25 minutes. Check with toothpick after 20 minutes — may need only a few more minutes. DO NOT OVERBAKE.

This was always the children's favorite bar recipe for school parties, scouts, etc.

Audrey Johnson

CHOCOLATE BROWNIES

½ cup shortening
¾ cup sifted flour
¾ teaspoon salt
1 cup sugar
1 cup nuts

2 ounces unsweetened chocolate
½ teaspoon baking powder
2 eggs
1 teaspoon vanilla
2 tablespoons corn syrup

In double-boiler melt shortening and chocolate and cool slightly. Sift flour with baking powder and salt. Beat eggs until light, add sugar, then chocolate mixture and blend. Add corn syrup, then flour, vanilla and nuts. Bake in 8"x8" greased pan at 350° for 30-35 minutes.

Robert Swain

MOM'S BROWNIES

½ cup butter or margarine
1 cup sugar
2 squares unsweetened chocolate, melted
2 eggs

¾ cup flour
¼ teaspoon baking powder
¼ teaspoon salt
1 teaspoon vanilla
¾ cup chopped walnuts

Cream butter and sugar. Add chocolate and mix thoroughly. Beat in eggs. Add remaining ingredients, except nuts. When completely mixed, add nuts. Bake in greased 8"x8" pan in 350° oven for 20 minutes. Yield: 16 squares.

Sarah W. Kacprowicz

APPLE SQUARES

1 stick margarine
1 cup sugar
1 egg, well beaten
2 medium apples, chopped fine
½ cup nuts (chopped), if desired

1 cup flour
½ teaspoon baking powder
½ teaspoon baking soda
¼ teaspoon salt
1 teaspoon cinnamon

Cream together margarine and sugar. Add the well-beaten egg. Mix in all remaining ingredients. Stir well. Bake in 8"x8" pan at 350° for 40 minutes. Cut when cool.

Martha Gosse

CARAMEL SQUARES

½ cup butter or margarine,
  melted
2 cups light brown sugar,
  firmly packed
1½ cups flour

2 eggs, separated
1 teaspoon vanilla
1 teaspoon baking powder
1 cup shredded coconut
½ cup chopped nuts

Mix together butter, 1 cup light brown sugar, flour, 2 yolks, vanilla and baking powder. Press on bottom of 12"x8"x2" pan. Beat 2 egg whites stiff; then beat in 1 cup light brown sugar. Add coconut and chopped nuts, spread evenly over mixture in pan; bake in 350° oven for 25-30 minutes. Cut into 2" squares. Yield: 2 dozen.

Elizabeth T. Richards

CHOCOLATE SQUARES

½ cup butter, softened
1 cup + 4 tablespoons all-purpose
  flour
2 tablespoons light brown sugar
2 eggs
1 cup light brown sugar
3 tablespoons cocoa
½ teaspoon vanilla

½ teaspoon salt
¼ cup walnuts, chopped
¼ cup butter, softened
2 cups confectioners' sugar
3 tablespoons cream
1 teaspoon vanilla
1 tablespoon butter
1 square unsweetened chocolate

STEP 1: Blend ½ cup butter, 1 cup plus 2 tablespoons flour. Mix well; pat lightly into buttered 9"x9" pan. Bake 15 minutes at 350°. STEP 2: While above is baking, beat 2 eggs, add 1 cup light brown sugar, 2 tablespoons flour, 3 tablespoons cocoa, ½ teaspoon salt and walnuts. Mix together and spread over first mixture. Bake 20 minutes at 350°. Cool before next step. STEP 3: Mix ¼ cup soft butter, 2 cups confectioners' sugar, 3 tablespoons cream, 1 teaspoon vanilla. Mix well and spread over cooled bars. STEP 4: Melt 1 tablespoon butter and 1 square unsweetened chocolate. Dribble over top of frosting. Yield: 16 squares.   *Alice Mullen*

HONEY BEAR SQUARES

½ cup sugar
½ cup honey
½ cup peanut butter

3 cups Cheerios
½ cup salted peanuts

Boil sugar and honey; remove from heat and stir in peanut butter until mixture is smooth. Put Cheerios and salted peanuts in bowl; pour peanut butter mixture over and stir to coat. Press in 9"x9"x2" greased pan. Cool and cut.

Nancy Titcomb

CRANBERRY SQUARES

2 cups all-purpose flour
1 cup sugar
1½ teaspoons baking powder
1 teaspoon salt
½ teaspoon baking soda
*streusel topping

¾ cup orange juice
2 tablespoons shortening
1 egg, well-beaten
1½ cups fresh or frozen
  cranberries, coarsely chopped
½ cup chopped nuts

Preheat oven to 350°. In bowl mix together flour, sugar, baking powder, salt and baking soda. Stir in orange juice, shortening and egg. Mix until well blended. Carefully fold in cranberries and nuts. Turn into greased 9"x13"x2" pan. Sprinkle with streusel topping. Bake 30 to 35 minutes. Serve warm.

*Streusel topping: mix together until crumbly ¼ cup flour, 2 tablespoons butter or margarine, ⅓ cup sugar and ¾ teaspoon cinnamon.

NOTE: To prepare Cranberry Squares using cranberry sauce, substitute one 8-ounce can whole berry cranberry sauce for fresh cranberries, reduce sugar to ½ cup and orange juice to ½ cup.

LEMON FRESH NUT SQUARES

CRUST:

1¾ cups flour
1 cup butter or margarine, cut
  in small pieces

½ cup confectioners' sugar
½ cup finely chopped walnuts

TOPPING:

4 eggs
⅓ cup fresh lemon juice
½ teaspoon baking powder

1½ cups sugar
¼ cup flour

Combine flour and sugar, add butter and blend to coarse, crumbly stage. Add nuts. Press into ungreased 13"x9"x2" pan and bake 20 minutes at 350°. For topping, beat all ingredients together until fluffy. Pour over crust and bake 15 or 20 minutes at 350° until lightly browned. Cool before cutting. Yield: 30 bars.

Bea Blondell

OLD FASHIONED HINTS

When cake or pastry is to be made, take care not to make trouble for others by scattering materials, and soiling the table or floor, or by the needless use of many dishes. Put on a large and clean apron, roll your sleeves above the elbows, tie something over your head lest hair may fall; take care that your hands are clean, and have a basin of water and a clean towel at hand. Place everything you will need on the table. Butter the pans, grate the nutmeg, and squeeze the lemons. Break the eggs, each one in a cup by itself, lest adding a bad one to the others should spoil the whole. Make your cake in an earthen, not a tin pan.

DID YOU KNOW THAT

★ Salted water boils faster. ★ A tablespoon of butter or oil added to the cooking water for pasta will keep the water from boiling over. ★ All vegetables that grow above the ground should be put on to cook in rapidly boiling water. ★ All vegetables that grow below the ground should be put on to cook in cold water. ★ The addition of parsley in a recipe containing garlic will offset the aftertaste and odor. ★ Ginger will accomplish the same thing in Oriental recipes. ★ Whipped butter is more attractive, easier to spread, and one tends to use less. Although whipped butter is more expensive at the market, you can whip your own with your electric mixer and enjoy the difference without the expense. ★ Relishes were the colonial substitute for salads. To "eat with relish," as the saying goes, is to enjoy indeed, and Americans are the greatest users of relish in the world.

Puddings & Desserts

Cranberry harvest on Cape Cod, showing string lines used to assure complete hand-picking of berries.

A family in West Barnstable enjoying dessert on the porch. 69

CRANBERRIES ON CAPE COD

Cape Cod did not have the broad acres needed for the efficient production of food grains, but certain crops, like onions, turnips and strawberries, did grow well here and commanded a ready market. Cranberries were a special case which their growers regarded as an art and science distinct from all other agricultural production. Bogs had been built from about 1850, requiring an expensive process of preparing a wide flat surface, a controlled water supply, drainage ditches, water run-off and exact soil preparation. It was found that Finnish immigrants had a natural understanding of this construction and the annual cycle of growth. By 1921 there were 3500 acres of bogs in this county, and the first power-assisted devices for gathering the crop were then tried. It was early recognized that unlike other fruit and vegetables a cooperative marketing organization was a necessity to process, pack and release cranberries to the national consumer. Mr. Isaiah Tobey Jones of Sandwich (1838-1898) was an early leader in establishing this approach. Through the efforts of the Cape Cod Cranberry Growers Association the State established an experimental station at East Wareham as part of the Agricultural College, later the University of Massachusetts. The first director was Dr. H.J. Franklin, then Dr. Chester Cross of Sandwich. Cranberry production has continued to increase and is one of the Cape's only remaining exports.

FOOD DURING THE AMERICAN REVOLUTION

Due to blockade of ports shutting off most imports and coastal trade, food and commodities at markets became scarce out of season, and prices rose steeply. This was worsened by inflation of paper currency which had no special backing. Accordingly each town tried to fix ceiling prices for food, commodities and labor rates, and published these lists. Some rates for 1777 in shillings and pence in the Cape Cod area:

Indian corn	4 - 0	per bushel
Peas	8 - 0	per bushel
Potatoes	1 - 6	per bushel
Fresh beef	0 - 3	per pound
Salt beef	0 - 4	per pound
Chicken	0 - 5	per pound
Milk	0 - 2½	per quart
Cheese, local	0 - 7	per pound
Flour	24 - 0	per hundred pounds
Sugar	60 - 0	per hundred pounds
Molasses	4 - 0	per gallon
Chocolate	1 - 8	per pound
Butter	0 - 10	per pound
Coffee	1 - 4	per pound
Salt	13 - 0	per bushel from sea water
Rum	7 - 8	per gallon West Indies
Rum	4 - 8	per gallon New England

There were 12 pence to the shilling, and 6 shillings to a Spanish Milled Dollar. The Spanish Dollar was also worth 8 pieces of eight, whence our expression "two bits" for a quarter.

In spite of these posted prices, inflation continued with prices in 1779 being ten to twenty times the above rates. If one had silver shillings or Spanish Milled Dollars, much different rates prevailed. It is remarkable that stocks of coffee, tea, chocolate, sugar and molasses still remained for sale, probably from hoarded stocks.

BAKED APPLES WITH MINCEMEAT

6 apples	juice of one lemon
⅓ cup mincemeat	6 tablespoons light brown sugar
grated rind of one lemon	2 tablespoons honey
cream or soft custard	

Wash apples and core without cutting through stem end. Hollow out apples leaving ½″ thick wall. Chop pulp fine and combine with mincemeat and lemon rind. Mix well and fill apples. Arrange in medium baking dish, add lemon juice and enough water to make ½ cup. Sprinkle apples with sugar and drizzle with honey. Bake in preheated 350° oven, basting occasionally, 50-60 minutes. Serve slightly warm with cream or custard topping. Serves: 6.

Judy Harrington

BLANCMANGE — SEA MOSS PUDDING

Collect white bleached pieces of Irish moss from the wrack at the high line at the beach. Wash out sand in cold water at home. Cook a cup full (do not pack tightly) in double boiler with 1 quart of milk about one-half an hour. Strain out seaweed — don't worry about small bits in the milk. Add 1 teaspoon lemon flavoring to milk solution. Pour into custard cups and chill. Unmold into saucers. Serve with cream and sugar. Great project for beach scavengers. Irish moss (Chondrus Crispus) is not always present on the beach but usually enough can be found; sometimes quantities.

Shirley Cross

BLUEBERRY FLUFF

1 envelope plain gelatin	¼ teaspoon salt
¼ cup water	1 teaspoon grated lemon rind
½ cup sugar	1 teaspoon vanilla
2 eggs, separated	1 cup blueberries
1 cup low-fat milk	2 tablespoons sugar

Sprinkle gelatin in water to soften. Set aside. Combine ½ cup sugar, egg yolks, milk and salt in saucepan and cook while stirring over low heat for three minutes. Add softened gelatin, lemon rind and vanilla. Cool. Then chill until thickening begins, fold in blueberries. Beat egg whites until soft peaks form, gradually beat 2 tablespoons sugar into them. Fold mixture into blueberry custard and chill until serving time. Serve in sherbet dishes. Serves: 6.

BLUEBERRY GRUNT* (DUMPLINGS)

2½ cups fresh blueberries	2 tablespoons sugar
⅓ cup sugar	2 teaspoons baking powder
dash salt	¼ teaspoon salt
1 cup water	1 tablespoon butter
1 tablespoon lemon juice	½ cup milk
1 cup flour	

Bring first 4 ingredients to boiling. Cover; simmer 5 minutes. Add lemon juice. Sift together dry ingredients. Cut in butter until like coarse meal. Add milk all at once, stirring only until flour is dampened. Drop batter from tip of tablespoon into bubbling sauce, making six dumplings. Don't let them overlap. Cover tightly. Cook over low heat 10 minutes without peeking. Serve hot. Serves: 6.

Grunt is Cape Cod name for steamed berry pudding.

Shirley Canning

EAST SANDWICH CHEESECAKE

FOR SHELL:

2 cups flour
½ cup sugar
2 teaspoons grated lemon rind

2 sticks butter
2 egg yolks
½ teaspoon vanilla

FOR FILLING:

2½ pounds cream cheese
1¾ cups sugar
1 teaspoon grated lemon rind
¼ teaspoon vanilla
3 tablespoons flour

¼ teaspoon salt
4 whole eggs
2 egg yolks
¼ cup heavy cream

FOR TOPPING:

¾ cup sugar
3 tablespoons light cornstarch
2 tablespoons corn syrup

3 to 4 drops red food coloring
4 cups raspberries

Shell: In bowl combine flour, sugar, and lemon rind. Blend in butter until mixture resembles meal. Add egg yolks and vanilla. Combine mixture until forms dough. Press ⅓ of dough onto bottom of 10″ springform pan (leaving off ring). Bake in preheated oven 400° for 8 minutes. Let cool on rack. Return ring to pan and pat the remaining dough onto the sides of pan, at least 2 inches high.

Filling: Beat cream cheese until smooth and beat in sugar (electric mixer), lemon rind, and vanilla. Beat in flour, salt, whole eggs and yolks, one at a time, and cream. Pour into shell and bake on baking sheet (preheated 425° oven) for 12 minutes. Reduce heat to 300° and continue baking for 1 hour more (it will not be set). Let cool on rack.

Topping: In saucepan combine ¾ cup water, sugar, and cornstarch. Cook mixture over moderately high heat, stirring until thick and clear. Remove from heat, stir in corn syrup and food coloring. Let cool until lukewarm. Arrange raspberries on cheesecake and pour the topping over them. Chill cheesecake 3 hours or overnight.

Paul J. White
Down East, Woodcarver

BLUEBERRY APPLE CRISP

3 cups blueberries
3 cups very tart sliced apples
brown sugar (to taste)
1 cup flour
¾ cup white sugar
1 teaspoon baking powder

¾ teaspoon salt
1 egg
⅓ cup butter, melted
½ teaspoon cinnamon
2 tablespoons milk

Grease baking dish and put in apples and blueberries. Add brown sugar to taste. Mix together flour, white sugar, milk, baking powder, salt, unbeaten egg and melted butter with a fork. Drop this mixture over top of fruit. Sprinkle with cinnamon. Bake in 350° oven for 30 minutes or until top is golden brown. Serve warm with cream. Serves: 6-8.

Augusta Jillson

CRANBERRY CRISP

1 cup sugar
½ teaspoon cinnamon
¼ cup water
¼ cup orange juice

2 cups fresh cranberries
⅓ cup butter, melted
3 cups soft bread crumbs
grated rind of 1 orange

GOLDEN SAUCE:

1 egg yolk
½ cup heavy cream, stiffly
whipped

2 tablespoons sugar
1 teaspoon orange flavoring

Combine sugar, cinnamon, water, and orange juice and bring to boil. Add cranberries. Mix grated orange rind in melted butter and pour over crumbs. In buttered baking dish, put alternate layers of crumbs and cranberry mixture, with top layer of crumbs. Cover, bake at 375° for 20 minutes. Uncover and bake an additional 15 minutes, or until top is browned.

Serve with GOLDEN SAUCE (makes 1 cup): Beat egg yolk until thick. Gradually add the sugar. Fold in whipped cream and mix in orange flavoring. Serves: 8

Barbara Tomlinson

CHOCOLATE MINT DESSERT CUPS

1 cup white cream mints
¾ cup milk
few drops green food coloring
1 cup heavy cream, whipped

1 7-ounce package chocolate mint
candy wafers or 1 6-ounce
semi-sweet chocolate chips
2 tablespoons shortening

Combine mints and milk. Cook over low heat, stirring frequently — about 15 minutes or until mints are melted. Cool to room temperature. Stir in food coloring. Fold in whipped cream. Pour into refrigerator tray and freeze until firm. Melt candy wafers or semi-sweet pieces with shortening over hot, not boiling, water, stirring until smooth. Cool to room temperature. Place 8 paper baking cups in muffin pans. With teaspoon, swirl chocolate mixture around inside cups, covering entire surface with a thin layer of chocolate. Chill. When chocolate cups harden, remove paper. Fill with rounded scoops of frozen mint mixture. Top each dessert with a chocolate mint wafer. Serves: 8.

Emily Snyder

HONEY PECAN ICE CREAM

2 cups heavy cream, whipped
4 stiffly beaten egg whites
4 egg yolks

¾ cup honey
3 teaspoons vanilla
1 cup chopped pecans

Beat egg yolks, honey and vanilla together until light and smooth. Fold in whipped cream. Fold in stiffly beaten egg whites. Fold in nuts. Freeze.

Lucille Mullaly

MAPLE MOUSSE

½ cup maple syrup
2 eggs, separated

½ pint whipping cream, whipped

Heat syrup. Pour slowly on beaten egg yolks. Fold in whipped cream, then beaten egg whites. Put in freezer. (Makes enough to fill a 6"x10" dish).

Harriet Clark

BEEHIVE PEACHES

Make up a double pie crust recipe or use 2 packages of a ready mix crust. Roll into an oblong and cut into strips 1" wide. Wash and dry eight large peaches. **They must be perfect.** Wrap strips of the pie crust around, starting from the bottom until the peach is entirely covered. Pat and patch as you go along, being careful that there are no gaps or holes. Place them in a pan. Bake 30-40 minutes at 400°. Serve hot with a hard sauce or ice cream. Each person breaks his crust and peach in half. Remove the stone. (The peach skin has completely disappeared). Serves: 8.

Carol Jillson

PEACH FREEZE

4 peaches, peeled and diced
1¼ cups soured cream
½ cup sugar

1 teaspoon lemon juice
¼ teaspoon almond extract

GARNISH:

1 teaspooon Grand Marnier or
   Cointreau liqueur

fresh fruit

Combine all ingredients in covered blender. Blend until smooth. Pour into 9" metal pan. Freeze one hour or until solid but not firm. Spoon into mixer bowl. Beat at medium speed until smooth. Pour into mold or individual cups. Freeze until set. Before serving, top with fresh fruit (strawberries, raspberries, sliced peaches, etc.) and 1 teaspoon Grand Marnier or Cointreau liqueur. Serves: 6.

Dorothy Clark

AMERICAN PUDDING — BLUEBERRY

3 cups blueberries
1 cup brown sugar
6 tablespoons butter
1 cup sugar
⅔ cup softened butter
dash vanilla
2 eggs
2 cups heavy cream

1½ cups flour
2 teaspoons baking powder
½ teaspoon salt
2 teaspoons grated orange rind
¾ cup orange juice
6 tablespoons Grand Marnier
   (optional)

Preheat oven to 350°. Simmer blueberries in brown sugar and 6 tablespoons butter. Cream sugar, ⅔ cup butter, and vanilla. Add eggs and beat. Sift flour, baking powder, and salt into creamed sugar and butter mixture. Add orange rind and juice. Place blueberry mixture in bottom of 3-quart baking dish. Pour batter over berries. Bake 45 minutes. Whip cream and add Grand Marnier and serve as topping. Serves: 10-12.

This is an old family recipe.

Mary C. Gleason

BIRD'S NEST PUDDING

8 tart apples, peeled and sliced
¾ cup sugar

½ teaspoon cinnamon
biscuit dough (below)

BISCUIT:

2 cups flour
½ teaspoon soda
1 teaspoon cream of tartar

½ teaspoon salt
¼ cup shortening
1 cup milk

SOUR SAUCE:

½ cup sugar
1 tablespoon flour
2 or 3 tablespoons vinegar

¾ cup water
2 tablespoons butter

Biscuit: Combine all ingredients and roll into a ball.

Sour Sauce: Cook sugar, flour, water and butter until smooth and thick. Remove from heat; add vinegar. If vinegar is strong, 2 tablespoons will be enough.

Fill deep buttered dish with tart apples to within 2 inches of top. Add sugar mixed with cinnamon. Roll biscuit crust 1″ thick and cover. Bake in moderate oven 350° for 40 minutes. Serve with sour sauce.

This old New England recipe comes in many forms, some with a baked custard mixture poured over the unsliced apples, and baked 1 hour. But this is my favorite.

Wendy Klein

MRS. CAPEN'S BREAD PUDDING

2 cups soft bread crumbs
4 tablespoons jam
¼ teaspoon salt
½ teaspoon soda

2 eggs, beaten
⅓ cup butter
¾ cup sugar (or less)

Mix ingredients together in top of double boiler and steam 2 hours. Top with whipped cream or sugar. Serves: 4-6.

A similar recipe using raisins was submitted by Barbara Keating.

Jackie Staples

CHOCOLATE BREAD PUDDING

2 cups stale bread crumbs
4 cups milk, scalded
2 squares unsweetened chocolate
1 teaspoon vanilla

⅔ cup sugar
2 eggs
¼ teaspoon salt

Add bread crumbs to scalded milk; melt chocolate over hot water, add one-half sugar and enough hot milk to make of pouring consistency. Add chocolate mixture to hot milk and bread crumbs. Beat eggs with remaining sugar, salt and vanilla. Mix all together. Bake in 350° oven until silver knife comes out clean. Serve with cream.

One of the recipes Mother learned when she went to Fannie Farmer's Cooking School. This was my father's favorite dessert.

Rosanna Cullity

CRANBERRY BREAD PUDDING

½ cup butter
½ cup white sugar
4 beaten eggs
2 cups fresh cranberries
4 cups bread crumbs

2 teaspoons grated orange rind
⅓ cup chopped walnuts
1 teaspoon salt
½ cup brown sugar
⅓ cup cream

Preheat oven to 350°. Cream butter, sugars, and salt. Stir in eggs. Add cream, stirring constantly. Fold in remaining ingredients. Pour into 8 greased custard cups or 9"x9" greased casserole dish. Set in a pan of warm water. Bake 1 hour. Serve hot or cold, plain or with whipped cream. Serves: 8.

Ruth Anderson

CHOCOLATE STEAMED PUDDING

3 tablespoons butter
⅔ cup sugar
1 well beaten egg
1 cup milk
2¼ cups flour

¼ teaspoon salt
4½ teaspoons baking powder
2½ squares unsweetened baking
   chocolate

FLORADORA SAUCE:

2 eggs, separated
½ to 1 cup confectioners' sugar
a few grains salt

¾ cup stiffly whipped heavy
   cream
⅔ teaspoon rum flavoring

Cream butter and sugar and add egg. Mix and sift flour, salt, and baking powder. Add flour mixture alternately with milk to creamed mixture. Melt chocolate and add to batter. Turn into a buttered mold or buttered top of a double boiler. Steam two hours.

Floradora Sauce: Beat egg whites and salt until stiff. Beat in half sugar. Without washing beater, beat yolks thick with remaining sugar. Combine two egg mixtures and flavoring. Fold in stiffly whipped cream. Serve as topping to steamed pudding.

A small scoop of vanilla ice cream and hot fudge sauce can be served as topping for pudding.

Ethel W. Holmes

CRANBERRY PUDDING — STEAMED

1½ cups flour
1 teaspoon soda
½ teaspoon salt
½ cup molasses

⅓ cup boiling water
2 cups raw cranberries, whole
butter sauce

BUTTER SAUCE:

½ cup butter
1 cup sugar

½ cup cream (can use
   evaporated milk, undiluted)

Sift dry ingredients. Add molasses and hot water. Stir in cranberries. (If frozen, you do not need to thaw.) Pour into buttered 1½ quart mold. Cover tightly with lid or double thickness of foil and secure with string or rubber band. Place on rack in large container. Add boiling water to half-way up mold. Cover and steam for 2 hours. Unmold and serve with Butter Sauce.

Butter Sauce: Cook slowly, stirring, until sugar dissolves. Can add any flavored extract to taste after sugar is dissolved. Rum is excellent with the cran-molasses pudding.

GRAPENUT PUDDING

2 eggs
½ cup sugar (or light molasses,
   maple syrup or honey)
½ teaspoon vanilla

speck of salt
⅓ cup grapenuts (generous)
2 cups milk
cinnamon

Beat eggs and add other ingredients. Pour into casserole. Sprinkle top with sugar and cinnamon. Set in pan of water. Bake at 350° for 30 minutes.

Mrs. Kershaw

INDIAN PUDDING

5 cups scalded milk
⅓ cup Indian meal
½ cup molasses

1 teaspoon salt
1 teaspoon ginger

Pour milk slowly over meal. Cook in double boiler 20 minutes. Add molasses, salt and ginger. Pour into a buttered pudding dish. Set in pan of hot water. Bake 2 hours in slow oven (300°). Serve with cream or ice cream.

Mary Thomas

LEMON PUDDING

1 cup sugar
3 tablespoons flour
½ teaspoon salt

2 eggs (separated)
1 cup milk
1 lemon, juice and grated rind

Mix sugar, flour and salt. Beat egg yolks in large bowl. Add ⅓ milk, dry ingredients, remaining milk and lemon. Carefully fold in stiffly beaten (not dry) egg white. Put in buttered dish, set in water. Bake at 325° for about 45 minutes. Pudding will be custard on bottom, sponge on top. Serve hot or cold.

Tink Miller

GRANDMOTHER'S POMPADOUR PUDDING

1 quart milk
¾ cup sugar
2 tablespoons cornstarch

dash salt
3 eggs — separated
2 teaspoons vanilla

TOPPING:

2 squares unsweetened chocolate
¾ cup sugar

4 tablespoons milk
3 egg whites

Pudding: Scald milk. Add sugar, cornstarch and salt. Cook 15 minutes. Add egg yolks and cook 5 minutes longer. Add vanilla and fill baking casserole.

Topping: Melt chocolate. Add sugar and milk. Beat egg whites until stiff and dry. Add to chocolate mixture. Place topping on pudding. Bake in preheated 325° oven for 45 minutes. Set pudding container in water when baking. Serves: 6-8.

"This pudding was by my Grandmother and Mother and I believe it is French in origin and comes from Canada."

Barbara Maxwell

RHUBARB TAPIOCA PUDDING

2 cups rhubarb, cut into 1" pieces   ¾ cup sugar or ½ cup honey
1 cup hot water   ¼ cup tapioca

Combine ingredients in top of double boiler and cook for about 25 minutes or until rhubarb is tender. Cool and serve with plain or whipped cream.

SNOW PUDDING

1½ packages plain gelatin   ½ cup lemon juice
¼ cup cold water   generous teaspoon of grated
¾ cup boiling water   lemon rind
1 cup sugar   3 egg whites

CUSTARD SAUCE:

1 tablespoon cornstarch   1½ cups scalded milk
⅓ cup sugar   1 teaspoon vanilla
1/8 teaspoon salt   2 egg yolks
½ cup cold milk

Soak gelatin in cold water, dissolve in boiling water, add sugar, lemon juice and grated rind. Set in freezer until thick enough to hold mark of a spoon. Beat egg whites in bowl until stiff. Beat gelatin mixture until frothy, add beaten egg whites and beat until stiff enough to hold its shape. Chill overnight. Serve with a soft custard sauce.

Custard Sauce: Mix cornstarch, sugar and salt. Combine with cold milk and gradually add hot milk. Cook in double boiler stirring until thickened. Cover and cook 15 minutes. Mix 2 egg yolks (only 2) with 2 tablespoons cold milk and stir into custard mixture. Cook 5 minutes more. Remove from heat and add 1 teaspoon vanilla extract.

Note: I do not unmold mine, but set my glass bowl in a large bowl and fill the space between with ice. Garnish with strawberries and their leaves.

Mrs. Gale

AUNT FANNIE'S RASPBERRY SHERBET

1 pint raspberries (or strawberries)   juice of one lemon
1 cup sugar   whites of 2 eggs, slightly beaten
½ cup water   fresh berries for garnish

Press the berries, sugar, water and lemon juice through a strainer and put into tray. Freeze until firm. Remove to a bowl and beat until pink. Add two egg whites slightly beaten. Beat until mixture is fluffy. Place in tray and freeze overnight. Garnish with fresh berries.

Aunt Fannie Davis was our dear landlady when we came in 1941 to live at 10 Spring Hill Road. She had inherited this Nye Homestead from Aimée Sears whose mother was a Nye.

S.G.C.

STRAWBERRY SHORTCAKE

1 cup flour	¼ cup shortening
½ teaspoon salt	⅓ cup milk
2 teaspoons baking powder	1 quart strawberries
3 tablespoons sugar	whipped cream

Cut strawberries lengthwise, sugar well, and set aside. Sift flour with salt, baking powder, and sugar. Cut in shortening until mixture resembles coarse crumbs. Add milk. Mix just until dough follows fork around the bowl. Roll ⅛″ thick on floured surface. Cut in rounds with scalloped cookie cutter. Bake on ungreased cookie sheet in hot oven (350°-400°). Serve warm with generous topping of strawberries and whipped cream. These cakes can be piled 3 or 4 high with strawberries in between. They are known as "Towers of Babel". Whipped cream is loaded on the tops which are then decorated with a big strawberry, green hull up. Trick is to get them to the table without toppling. Two cakes usually satisfy senior citizens. Extra cakes can be frozen.

CRANBERRY ORANGE TORTE

2 cups all-purpose flour	1 cup sugar
2 teaspoons baking powder	1 teaspoon vanilla
¼ teaspoon salt	½ teaspoon grated orange
½ cup margarine (or butter)	1 cup milk

FILLING:

1 cup sugar	1½ cups heavy or whipping
2⅔ cups cranberries	cream
1 cup water	2 tablespoons confectioners' sugar
	1 teaspoon vanilla

Preheat oven to 350°. Grease and flour two 9″ round pans. In medium bowl combine flour, baking powder and salt. In mixing bowl cream butter (or margarine) with sugar and add eggs one at a time beating after each. Beat in orange peel and vanilla. Add dry ingredients alternately with milk beginning and ending with dry. Spoon in pans evenly. Bake 25 minutes. Cool in pan 15 minutes and remove. (Can be made ahead and kept frozen up to one week.)

Filling: In sauce pan combine cranberries, water and granulated sugar. Simmer for 20 minutes. Cool. (Can be made ahead and refrigerated for two days.) In large bowl whip cream with confectioners' sugar and vanilla until stiff.

Slice each cake horizontally into two layers. Place one layer on serving dish and spread on half the filling; add a second layer and spread with cream. Repeat layers with cranberry filling and cream. Refrigerate for four hours. Garnish if desired.

Betty Lundgren

In July of 1847 the last wolf in Sandwich was killed and hung up between the columns of the Town Hall. The bells rang in celebration as the farmers rejoiced in relief as they had been losing many sheep to the wolves.

FESTIVE CRANBERRY TORTE

FOR CRUST:

1½ cups graham cracker crumbs　　¼ cup sugar
½ cup chopped pecans　　6 tablespoons butter, melted

FOR FILLING:

1½ cups ground fresh cranberries　　1 teaspoon vanilla
　　(2 cups whole)　　1/8 teaspoon salt
1 cup sugar　　1 cup whipping cream
2 egg whites　　1 recipe cranberry glaze
1 tablespoon frozen orange juice　　fresh orange slices, quartered
　　concentrate, thawed

FOR GLAZE:

½ cup sugar　　¾ cup fresh cranberries
1 tablespoon cornstarch　　⅔ cup water

Crust: In mixing bowl combine cracker crumbs, pecans, sugar and melted butter. Press onto bottom and up sides of an 8" springform pan. Chill.

Filling: In large mixer bowl combine cranberries and sugar. Let stand 5 minutes. Add unbeaten egg whites, orange juice concentrate, vanilla and salt. Beat on low speed of electric mixer until frothy. Then beat at high speed 6 to 8 minutes or until stiff peaks form. (Tips stand straight.) In small mixer bowl whip cream to soft peaks (Tips curl over.) Fold into cranberry mixture. Turn into crust. Freeze firm. Spoon cranberry glaze in center. Place orange slices around outside.

Glaze: In saucepan stir together sugar and cornstarch. Stir in cranberries and water. Cook and stir until bubbly. Cook, stirring occasionally, just until cranberry skins pop. Cool to room temperature. (Do not chill.) Makes one cup. You can make cranberry glaze ahead of time. Serves: 8-10.　　*Barbara Tomlinson*

Of the many buildings at Heritage Plantation of Sandwich, the Daniel Wing House, dating back to 1686 is of major historic interest in Sandwich. The home, in its original location, was built as a half-house. Shortly thereafter, an addition expanded it to a two-family home and through many years and various additions it has maintained its integrity as a two-family Colonial.

——————————————————————

The Wing Fort House, which was placed on the National Register of Historic Places in 1977, has been restored and preserved by the Wing Family of America, Inc. It appears in the records of Sandwich in July 1640 when Andrew Hallett sold his dwelling, land and "ye cowhouse" to Daniel Wing of "ye same towne".

Confections

Cutting ice on Shawme Pond for the ice house on Grove Street.

A Wing family house on Sandy Neck Road and cows from a nearby farm. 81

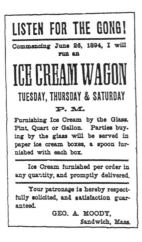

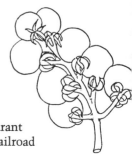

ICE CREAM

There was a restaurant in the new Sandwich railroad terminal in 1848, and according to its broadside, ice cream was always available here.

The Sandwich newspaper *Seaside Press* in the 1870's advertised Gus Pope's ice cream at food and general stores along Jarves Street. Gus owned an ice house on Grove Street next to the old cemetery. Above is a broadside by George A. Moody of Sandwich in the summer of 1894, which tells householders to "Listen for the Gong" when his Ice Cream Wagon will pass along the streets. The first ice cream in Sandwich was probably much earlier as the book "The American Economical Housekeeper" of 1852 provides several recipes and recommends the use of A.H. Reip's Patent Ice Cream Freezer made in Baltimore and sold by Ballard & Stearns at 16 Bromfield St., Boston. The freezer was to be placed in a tub of ice and salt, and the ice cream ingredients in the freezer chilled and then beaten to smoothness by an internal paddle. After 20 minutes, the paddle was removed and ice piled around the freezer top and covered with a rug for about an hour. Recipes are provided for lemon, vanilla (take a large vanilla bean and boil it . . .) and strawberry ice cream, two sherbets and a frozen custard.

THE ICE KING AND HIS FAMILY

Frederick Tudor of Nahant and Boston (1783-1864) was an enterprising merchant who conceived the idea of shipping ice to the tropics, packed in sawdust. He not only shipped to the West Indies but got cargoes to Bombay and Calcutta, with about 50% loss in the 5-month voyage. Tudor became known as "The Ice King".

He wrote in 1821 "Sandwich is one of the most pleasant villages in Massachusetts. To persons fond of fishing, sporting or riding it offers greater resources than any other spot in this country". Among Tudor's companions in Sandwich sports were Daniel Webster and Deming Jarves.

Tudor's son, Frederick, Jr., was an inventor who loved the Buzzards Bay area. In 1869 he built a large house in Monument Beach called Tudor Haven. It was sold to Grover Cleveland in 1890, renamed Grey Gables, and became the first summer White House.

The family of Frederick Tudor Jr. continued their connections with Sandwich and Bourne. His daughter Marie married James Garland and bought the Monument Club on Head-of-the-Bay Road, now known as Grazing Fields Farm, owned by Marie's daughter, Hope G. Ingersoll. Frederick Tudor III came to Sandwich and occupied the Wing Howland house at 8 Morse Road which he named Wamdosa Farm; he is famous as the man granted the right to use Mass. One as his license plate by the State Legislature. His sister Rosamund Tudor married W. Starling Burgess, a yacht designer, poet and aviator, and is the mother of famous artist Tasha Tudor.

BUCKEYES

½ pound soft margarine or butter
1 pound (2 cups) smooth peanut
   butter
1½ pounds (5¾ cups)
   confectioners' sugar

1 teaspoon vanilla
12 ounces chocolate bits
one quarter of a ¼ pound cake
   of paraffin wax

Mix thoroughly butter, peanut butter, confectioners' sugar and vanilla. Roll into balls ½ to 1 inch in diameter. Put in refrigerator. Melt chocolate and paraffin in double boiler. (Dipping chocolate can be used if available.) Pick up chilled balls on toothpicks and dip into chocolate to ALMOST cover (leave their "eyes" open). Remove excess chocolate with knife. Place on waxed paper; refrigerate until firm. Yield: 120-140.

Ellen Holway

CANDIED GRAPEFRUIT PEEL

3 grapefruit
water
salt

sugar
confectioners' sugar

Wipe grapefruit and remove peel in 6 sections, lengthwise of fruit. Soak overnight in one quart of cold water and 1 tablespoon of salt. Drain, cover with cold water, and boil 20 minutes. Repeat three times and cook in last water until tender (could be 2 hours). Drain, cut in strips ⅛" wide. Weigh peel and put an equal amount of sugar in pan (heavy aluminum stockpot is best) and add ½ as much water as sugar. Bring to boil, add peel, cover and cook until clear. Remove cover and let syrup boil until very little remains. Remove peel to rack and let dry until just tacky. Roll in confectioners' sugar and resume drying until desired consistency is reached. Store in tin or glass jar. The halves from breakfast grapefruit can be used for this delicious holiday confection.

CARAMELS

1 cup butter
1 14-ounce can condensed milk
1 cup corn syrup

1 16-ounce box light brown sugar
   (2¼ cups packed)
1 teaspoon vanilla

Line a 9"x9" pan with buttered aluminum foil. Melt butter in a 3-quart saucepan. Add remaining ingredients except vanilla. Using a candy thermometer, bring to 248° (firm-ball stage), stirring frequently. Remove from heat, add vanilla and quickly pour into pan. Cool to room temperature. Cut into 1 inch squares using a buttered knife. Wrap in plastic or dip in milk or dark chocolate. Yield: 2 pounds.

Jeanne Stone

An order was passed in 1695 that every unmarried man in the Township should kill six black birds yearly, or three crows, while he remained single. In Sandwich men over 70 were excused.

credit: A Bit Of Sandwich History, 1939

NUTTY CARAMELS

2 cups sugar
1 cup brown sugar
1 cup light corn syrup
1 cup milk

1 cup heavy cream
1 cup butter
1 cup chopped nuts
1½ tablespoons vanilla

Cook sugar, brown sugar, light corn syrup, milk, cream and butter VERY slowly (several hours), stirring occasionally to clear the sides of the pan. When temperature reaches 248° (a firm ball) remove from stove and add nuts and vanilla. Pour into lightly greased 9"x13" pan. Let cool thoroughly before cutting. Yield: 2½ pounds.

Mary Winings

CHINESE FRIED WALNUTS

6 cups water
4 cups walnuts, shelled
½ cup sugar

1 cup salad oil
salt

In a 4-quart saucepan over high heat, heat water to boiling. Boil nuts one minute, then rinse under running hot water. Wash pan and dry well. In large bowl, stir walnuts and sugar until sugar is dissolved. In 4-quart saucepan heat oil to 350°; add half the nuts to the oil using a slotted spoon, and fry 5 minutes or until golden. Stir often. With slotted spoon, place nuts in coarse sieve over bowl to drain. Sprinkle very lightly with salt; toss gently to keep nuts from sticking together. Cool on paper towel. Fry remaining nuts in same manner. Store in tightly covered container. Yield: 4 cups.

Myra Winings Ummel

CHOCOLATE FUDGE

2 cups granulated sugar
⅓ cup baking cocoa
1 cup homogenized milk
1 teaspoon vanilla

1 heaping teaspoon butter or
   margarine
chopped nuts, raisins, or other
   choice

Mix dry ingredients thoroughly, and blend in milk, stirring until smooth. Heat over moderate heat, stirring frequently. A long, slow boil is preferable. Boil (15 to 20 minutes) to soft ball in water stage (238°). Other indications are (a) mixture stops rising in pan and bubbles slowly, sullenly, and insolently; (b) residue around rim of pan near top crystallizes as it cooks. Add butter or margarine, vanilla, and nuts, raisins, or other choice. Beat thoroughly until mixture begins to stiffen. Pour into greased pan, cool, slice and eat.

George E. Williams

MICROWAVE FUDGE

3 cups chocolate chips
1 can sweetened condensed milk

½ stick butter
chopped nuts (optional)

Put all ingredients in mixing bowl. Microwave on medium 3-8 minutes, until butter melts. If desired, add chopped nuts. Mix well. Pour into lightly greased 9"x9" pan. Refrigerate, cut into squares and enjoy!

Gerrie Titcomb

THREE-MINUTE FUDGE

2 cups sugar
½ cup milk
piece of butter, size of a walnut
 (1 tablespoon)

dash of salt
½ cup peanut butter
½ cup marshmallow fluff
1 teaspoon vanilla

Cook sugar, milk, butter and salt just three minutes. Then whip in peanut butter, fluff, and vanilla. Pour onto platter. Peanuts may be added if desired.

Nancy Koder

MARSHMALLOWS

1 envelope unflavored
 gelatine
⅓ cup cold water
½ cup sugar

⅔ cup light corn syrup
½ teaspoon vanilla
fine granulated sugar and
 cornstarch

Soften gelatine in cold water in small saucepan. Stir until dissolved over boiling water. Add sugar and stir until dissolved. Pour corn syrup in large bowl and add gelatine, vanilla and sugar mixture. Beat with electric mixer until thick and of marshmallow consistency. Pour into 11½"x10"x2" pan covered with a thick layer of equal parts fine granulated sugar and cornstarch — smooth top and cool for about an hour or more (not in refrigerator). Loosen edges with knife and invert on to board covered with a layer of sugar and cornstarch. Cut with sharp knife dipped in water and roll in sugar and cornstarch mixture. Makes about a pound.

Dorothy Holway

MOLASSES CANDY

½ can molasses
1 tablespoon butter

1 pinch saleratus (baking soda)

Combine ingredients and cook in a skillet until mixture forms a HARD ball when dropped into cold water. Then pour into buttered pan and cool before cutting.

Eleanor Heckler

MOLASSES TAFFY

1 cup molasses
2 teaspoons vinegar
¾ cup sugar

1 tablespoon soda
2 tablespoons butter
1/8 teaspoon salt

Combine first three ingredients and bring to hard boil (265° to 270°). Remove from heat and add soda, butter and salt, and blend. Pour into buttered pan to cool. When cool, pull until firm and light-colored. Snip off chunks with scissors.

As a young boy, Thornton Burgess sold his mother's molasses candy to the workers at the Boston and Sandwich Glass Factory.

PEANUT BRITTLE

2 cups sugar
½ cup water
1 cup white corn syrup
1 teaspoon soda

1/8 teaspoon salt
2 cups raw Spanish peanuts
  (1 pound)
1 tablespoon butter

Cook sugar, water and corn syrup in a large frying pan until it forms a soft ball. Add salt, peanuts and butter. Cook to hard crack and brown in color. Remove from heat; add 1 teaspoon soda and stir briskly. Pour quickly into buttered pans — 1 large cookie sheet and 1 round cake pan.

Tink Miller

OLD FASHIONED POPCORN BALLS

1 cup dark corn syrup
1 cup brown sugar
¼ cup water

1 teaspoon vinegar
2 teaspoons butter
2 quarts unsalted popcorn

Combine syrup, sugar, water and vinegar and cook over medium heat stirring constantly to hard ball stage (260°). Remove from heat and add butter, stirring well. Pour over popcorn and mix thoroughly. Butter hands and make balls, using as little pressure as possible. Yield: 15 2½ inch balls.

Dorothy Holway

VINEGAR CANDY

1½ teaspoons butter
2 cups sugar

½ cup vinegar
½ cup water

Mix all ingredients together. Boil in saucepan until mixture forms a hard ball in cold water. Pour into buttered tins and cool before cutting.

Eleanor Heckler

WALNUT TOFFEE

1 cup sugar
½ teaspoon salt
¼ cup water
½ cup butter or margarine

1½ cups chopped nuts
1 package (12 ounces) semi-sweet
  chocolate bits

In a saucepan combine sugar, salt, butter and water; stir and heat to boiling point. Cook *without stirring* or until it "cracks" when tested. Remove from heat. Stir in ½ cup nuts and turn onto greased cookie tin. Cool. Melt half chocolate bits over hot water; spread over toffee and sprinkle with ½ cup nuts. Cool until chocolate is firm. Turn candy upside down on cookie sheet. Melt remaining chocolate bits, spread on candy, and sprinkle with remaining ½ cup nuts. Cool until chocolate is firm. BREAK candy into pieces and serve.

Mary Winings

Eggs, Cheese, Rice & Sauces

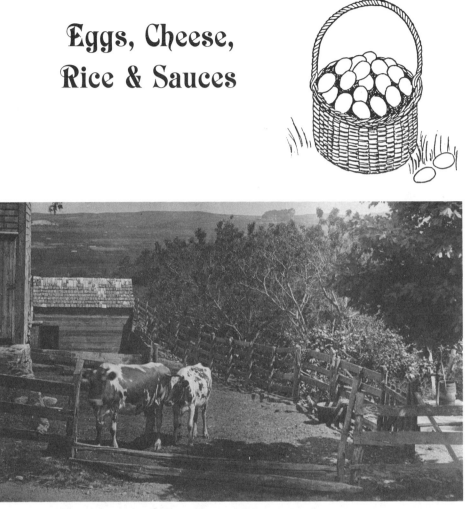

Hilliard's farm off Old County Road, East Sandwich.

The egg-producers at Hilliard's farm.

THE EGG

I sing the praise of the versatile egg,
    Clean and pure in its germ proof shell;
Easy to come by and cheap to use,
    It has more uses than I can tell.

Boiled or fried, or poached or scrambled,
    Main dish or extra, on the side,
Sponge cake light, and pleasingly high,
    Its many uses can't be denied.

Mile high meringue on a fine lemon pie,
    Custards or icing on cake,
Omelets light as fleecy white cloud,
    It's wonderful what eggs can make.

Brown ones or white ones, what matters the shade
    The treasure is what the shells hold.
The white can be whipped to a snowy white peak,
    The yolks are a beautiful gold.

Queen of the barnyard, my hat's off to you,
    Never stop laying, I beg!
Meals would be duller, and life would be drear,
    Without the magnificent egg!

CREAMED EGGS À L'ONION

1 cup onion, chopped	2 cups milk
4 tablespoons butter	6 hard cooked eggs, halved
4 tablespoons flour	6 slices buttered toast
salt and pepper	

Cook onion in butter. Add flour and seasonings. Add milk and cook until thickened. Place eggs on toast. Pour the onion sauce over. Season with salt and pepper (or lemon pepper). Serves: 4-6.

SCOTCH EGGS

4 eggs hard boiled	1 pound sausage meat*
1 egg beaten	fine breadcrumbs or cracker meal

Peel eggs. Dip in beaten egg, and cover thickly with sausage meat. (It should be about the size of a large duck egg when covered.) Dip, or brush again with beaten egg, then in breadcrumbs or cracker meal. Fry in deep fat about ten minutes. Drain well on paper towelling. Serve hot or cold. Serves: 4 — One egg per person.

*Ground beef/pork or plain hamburger meat would serve equally well.

This is a well known recipe in the U.K. but hard to find in other than Scottish cook books. Two, with a green vegetable or salad, would be a good emergency meal.
                                            Francis Elphinstone Dalrymple

SANDWICH FILLING
for a large group. Sometimes called
"POOR MAN'S CAVIAR"

6 eggs — hard cooked	1 cup olives
2 cups pecans	mayonnaise to moisten well

Chop and combine ingredients. This recipe is always appreciated by both men and women. Yield: 2 cups .
                                            Florence Eaton

ORIGINAL MASHPEE INDIAN "JAG"

4 cups cooked rice	1 pound salt pork
1 package baby lima beans,	salt and pepper
cooked and drained	

Cut salt pork into strips, then into small pieces the size of the end of your thumb. Fry salt pork until golden; drain on paper towels. Keep fat from salt pork warm in frying pan. Mix rice and lima beans, add salt pork fat and salt and pepper to taste. Keep warm on hot tray (covered). When ready to serve, mix in all pieces of crisp, drained salt pork into rice and lima beans. Serve immediately so salt pork retains its crispness. Serves: 6.

This is the real jag, not to be confused with the linguiça and rice dish often called jag.
                                            Fay W. Robbins

PERSIAN RICE CASSEROLE

2 cups long grain rice washed
4 cups water
1 teaspoon salt
3 tablespoons anisette

4 ounces butter
1 cup seedless raisins
1 cup cream sherry

Bring to boil 4 cups water; add rice, reduce heat to lowest, cover and cook until all liquid is absorbed; do not stir. Add butter and raisins and mix by lifting with fork — do not stir. Add sherry and turn all into casserole; drizzle with 3 tablespoons anisette; cover and keep warm in low oven 30 minutes or until serving. Serves: 8.

Elsa R. Gerling

RICE SOUFFLÉ

1 tablespoon butter, melted
1 tablespoon flour
1 cup milk
2 eggs, separated

2 cups cooked rice*
¼ pound grated cheddar cheese
onion salt, to taste
pepper

Mix flour with butter; slowly add milk, stirring 'til smooth. Beat in egg yolks. Fold in rice, cheese and seasonings. Lastly, gently add stiff-beaten egg whites. Pour into buttered dish; bake about 40 minutes in preheated 350° oven, until puffed up and browned. This soufflé doesn't fall. Serves: 4.

Helen Clark

*2 cups cooked farina may be substituted for cooked rice.

RED BUNNY

2 tablespoons butter
2 tablespoons flour
½ cup milk
1 can tomato soup into which 1/8
  teaspoon soda has been stirred

2 cups grated cheese
2 eggs, slightly beaten
salt and pepper to taste
¼ teaspoon dry mustard

Melt butter and add flour and milk to make white sauce, stirring constantly until thickened. Place pan over hot water, (if using double boiler) and add the rest of ingredients to white sauce. Blend and cook over hot water until piping hot. Serve on crackers, such as saltines, with chopped pickles for a relish. Serves: 4.

Mrs. Leon Burgess

WELSH RAREBIT

1 tablespoon butter
½ pound cheddar cheese, cut fine
½ cup cream or "good milk"

2 egg yolks
salt and pepper

Melt butter in chafing dish, then cheese. When creamy, add the cream or milk, then egg yolks. Season with salt and pepper. Serve on toast. Serves: 4.

Christy Lowrance

On April 10, 1867 a severe snow storm surprised the people of Cape Cod. The passenger train from Sandwich to Boston became stalled in the deep snow near Rock station. The passengers obtained milk from the near-by farms for the babies and wood to burn on the train for heat.

PATTI'S CHEESE QUICHE

6 link sausages
½ pound provolone cheese
1 small container ricotta cheese
6 eggs

1 small package mozzarella
cheese
2 tablespoons chopped parsley

Cook sausage and drain. Grate provolone and mozzarella cheeses. Arrange sausage slices on bottom of 9" pie plate. Layer cheeses on top of sausage. Beat eggs and add parsley, and pour slowly over cheese. Bake at 350° for one hour. Can be served hot or cold. Serves: 6.

Pat Weaver

SWISS PIE

6 slices bacon
1 cup chopped onion
¾ cup sour cream
2 eggs

dash of pepper
12 ounces Swiss cheese, cut up
1 9-inch unbaked pastry shell

Cook bacon until crisp. Drain, but reserve drippings. Crumble bacon and set aside. Cook onion in drippings until tender. Blend sour cream, eggs, pepper and onion. Add cheese and bacon. Pour into pastry shell, and bake at 375° for 30-40 minutes. Serves: 6.

This recipe is great for substitutions: Yogurt instead of sour cream has fewer calories. Ham or sausage can be used instead of bacon. Cheddar or mozzarella can be used instead of Swiss cheese, etc.

Nancy Logan

EGGS FLORENTINE

1 package frozen spinach
6 eggs
12 tablespoons parmesan cheese

6 tablespoons sour cream
salt and pepper

Cook, drain, and season spinach. Place in 6 buttered custard cups. Sprinkle each with 1 tablespoon cheese. Place an egg on top, and cover each with a tablespoon of sour cream. Then sprinkle with rest of cheese. Place in moderate oven (350°) for six to eight minutes. Serves: 4 to 6.

Jacqueline Jacobsen

EGG-POTATO-CHEESE SCALLOP

2 medium potatoes
1 medium onion
½ pound cheddar cheese

4 eggs
½ teaspoon each salt, pepper
4 tablespoons parmesan cheese

Cook potatoes until tender. Peel and slice thinly. Slice onion and cheese, thinly. Start oven at 400° and grease baking dish. Put layer of potatoes on bottom of dish, and cover with onion and cheese. Break eggs over cheese, and sprinkle with salt and pepper and parmesan cheese. Bake 20 minutes. Serves: 4.

CARROT CHEESE PIE

bread slices, buttered	2 eggs
4 ounces grated cheese	1 cup milk
4 ounces grated carrots	salt and pepper

Butter bread slices and fit in shallow pan, or deep dish pie plate, butter-side down. Cover with cheese, and then with grated carrots. Beat eggs and add milk, salt and pepper. Pour over casserole. Bake at 350° for 30 minutes. Serves: 6.

CHILI PUFF OR "LA STRADA"

24 slices bread, crusts off	2 cups milk
Monterey Jack cheese	Worcestershire sauce
butter	1 can green chilies
4 eggs	

Make 12 sandwiches (crusts cut off) of Monterey Jack cheese. Butter outsides of sandwiches and place in large utility dish. In blender: combine 4 eggs with 2 cups of milk, dash of Worcestershire sauce, and 1 can green chilies. Pour mixture over cheese sandwiches and refrigerate overnight. If the product seems dry the next day, add more eggs and milk. Bake for one hour at 325°. Serves: 12.

May be modified for smaller numbers. Excellent served with tossed salad.

Carol Colburn

BRUNCH CASSEROLE

4 cups cubed day old firm white bread	1 teaspoon salt
	¼ teaspoon onion powder
2 cups (8 ounces) shredded cheddar cheese	dash of ground pepper
	8-10 slices cooked bacon, crumbled
10 eggs, lightly beaten	½ cup sliced mushrooms
4 cups (1 quart) milk	½ cup chopped peeled tomato
1 teaspoon dry mustard	

Generously butter 9"x13" baking dish. Arrange bread cubes in dish and sprinkle with cheese. Beat together next 5 ingredients with pepper to taste and pour evenly over cheese and bread. Sprinkle with bacon and mushrooms and tomato. Cover and chill up to 24 hours. Preheat oven to 325°. Bake casserole uncovered until set — about one hour. Tent with foil if top begins to overbrown. Serves: 12.

Susan Flaws

CHEESE SPECIAL FOR LUNCH

¾ pound cheddar cheese, grated	1 chopped green pepper
½ pound bacon, cooked, but not crisp	mayonnaise to moisten
	English muffins

Mix four ingredients together, and place on toasted English muffins (or buns), halved. Place under broiler to melt cheese and brown lightly. Serves: 6.

Lib Andrews

EGGS PORTUGAL

8 slices bread, cubed, no crust
1 pound, browned, drained
  sausage
4 whole eggs
¾ teaspoon dry mustard

2½ cups milk
¾ pound shredded cheddar
  cheese
fresh or canned mushrooms
¼ cup dry Vermouth

Place bread cubes in bottom of casserole; sprinkle cheese over bread; add browned, drained sausage. Mix eggs, milk and mustard and pour over all. Refrigerate, covered, overnight. Before serving, add mushrooms and Vermouth, and bake at 300° for 1½ hours, or 350° for 1 hour. Serves: 8.

This makes a tasty brunch dish, which can be prepared the night before.

Laurie Clark Crigler

FROZEN CHEESE SAUCE CUBES

8 ounces sharp cheese, grated
¾ cup water
⅓ cup butter or margarine
½ cup flour
2 tablespoons water

1½ teaspoons salt
1 teaspoon dry mustard
2 teaspoons Worcestershire sauce
½ cup instant dry milk

Add cheese to ¾ cup water. Heat 'til cheese is melted. Melt butter in separate pan. Remove from heat and add flour. Stir until smooth and add salt, mustard and Worcestershire sauce. Add to melted cheese. Stir until smooth and add milk and 2 tablespoons water. Stir to smooth and pour into 8½"x4½" bread pan. Freeze until consistency of ice cream and cut into 32 cubes. Put on chilled tray and freeze until solid. Store in plastic bags. Yield: 32 cubes.

To use: Cook lima beans or any vegetable — add 8 cubes and cook until smooth.

To make sauce separately, stir 6 to 8 cubes into ¾ cup milk, and cook until thick and smooth.

Lib Andrews

BARBECUE SAUCE*

½ cup light or dark corn syrup
½ cup catsup
½ cup finely chopped onions

¼ cup cider vinegar
¼ cup prepared mustard
¼ cup Worcestershire sauce

In saucepan combine all ingredients. Stirring frequently, bring to boil. Reduce heat and cook for 15 minutes until thick. Brush on meats, turning frequently during the last 20 minutes of cooking. Makes two cups. If too thick, thin with vinegar.

*Oriental Barbecue Sauce: Omit Worcestershire sauce and add ¼ cup soy sauce and 1 teaspoon ground ginger. Delicious with pork. Can be served hot in pitcher to pour over meats.

Diana Payne

PEANUT SAUCE

1 cup peanut butter
4 tablespoons soy sauce
juice of half a lemon

2 cloves of garlic, crushed
cayenne pepper to taste

Mix all together in saucepan, adding enough warm water to pour. Heat just before serving. Delicious on steamed vegetables. Serves: 6.

BLANCHE'S MT. WASHINGTON CHOCOLATE SAUCE

8 tablespoons sugar
6 tablespoons butter

4 tablespoons cream
2 tablespoons cocoa

Make NO substitutions for the above ingredients. Mix all together over medium low heat, stirring constantly. When thoroughly blended, let stand a few minutes over low heat. Serve while warm. Store leftover sauce in refrigerator. Rewarm gently over very low heat. This is the best chocolate sauce ever! Double the recipe, for it will keep for weeks in the refrigerator (if well hidden).

Gladys M. Burgess

SUNNY'S CHOCOLATE SAUCE

4 squares baking chocolate
½ cup butter
4 tablespoons cocoa

1½ cups sugar
1 cup evaporated milk
1 teaspoon vanilla

In top of double boiler, add all ingredients. Heat and stir until well mixed and smooth. Store in refrigerator. Heat before serving.

Judy Harrington

Fish & Shellfish

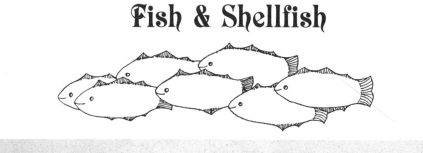

Fisherman's house at Mill Creek, Sandwich near the Boardwalk.

Sam Jillson digging clams at Scorton Creek, East Sandwich.

TREASURE FROM THE SEA

This is not about fish but about cargo from ships wrecked or seized. Cape Codders expected ships ashore with every storm and had a quick eye for possible benefits.

Here are three diverse incidents involving food.

On December 26, 1872, the Bark Francis loaded with tin and sugar came ashore at North Truro. The Francis had an iron hull and came straight in on the sand so that the crew were not in great danger and were all soon rescued. Tugs and lighters were brought to the scene and work began on saving the cargo. Some of the sugar, which was in great bags of heavy matting, broke free spilling on the deck during salvage operations. A work gang of 25 men were put aboard to hoist out the cargo and stow it on the lighters. These men brought their lunch and worked all day on the vessel, and were allowed to fill their pockets and lunch boxes with loose sugar each evening. The lunch boxes grew amazingly from little paper bags to big sacks and boxes holding 50 pounds of sugar per man. The contractor learned of this and stopped it, but the men are said to have laid in a year's supply for their families.

Benjamin Percival of South Sandwich reported in 1814 that cargo from British vessels seized by American privateers was being brought into Chatham and Hyannis and loaded onto carts for shipment to Boston. The British Navy at this time still controlled Massachusetts Bay and threatened to land anywhere. The carters were paid one quarter cent per pound Barnstable to Sandwich and one cent per pound Sandwich to Boston. The first cargo sent was 300 tons of sugar.

Clarence Pope of Sagamore, in his fine historical articles "Looking Backward" for the *Sandwich Independent* reported that in April 1870 a schooner came ashore on Sagamore Beach and had to be offloaded. The hold cargo was bulk corn, with barrels of kerosene on the deck. In the wreck many of the barrels leaked and the corn became soaked with oil. The owner nevertheless brought the corn ashore and heaped it in 600 bushel lots on the beach and asked for bids. William Swift of Sagamore (father of the famous Gustavus F. Swift of Swift & Company) owned ten western mules and believed that his mules would eat anything a goat would. He bought up 1200 bushels of kerosene corn at eight cents a bushel, and reported that his mules appeared to thrive on this diet.

SIMPLE CAPE COD FOODS

Some of those helping with "Flavors of Cape Cod" remember when the usual fare in a Cape Cod family of modest means was nutritious but had few frills. Those who did not have a cow or chickens could buy milk and eggs from a neighbor. According to former Selectman J. Louis Roberti in the 1920's there were twenty dairies selling milk in Sandwich (part of two hundred Cape-wide) not counting those with one or two cows who supplied neighbors unofficially. Everyone had a vegetable garden, and fresh seafood was plentiful. The weekly fare included:

Quahaug Chowder; Sea Clam Pie; Corned or Smoked Herring.

Vegetable: Baked Beans & Brown Bread; Parsnip Stew; Potato Bargain; Corn Fritters; Corn Chowder; Corn Bread.

Desserts: Indian Pudding; Sea Moss Pudding (Blanc Mange); Hard Gingerbread; Blueberry Muffins; Hasty Pudding (fried when cold); Apple, Pumpkin & Mince Pies; Rose Hip Jelly.

BOUILLABAISSE

1½ quarts water
1 level tablespoon salt
1 pound fresh unpeeled shrimp
1 pound scallops
1 pound haddock fillet
1 pound cod fillet
1 pound cooked lobster meat
2 dozen oysters
½ pound fresh mushrooms, sliced
2 large onions, diced
salt and pepper to taste

2 cloves garlic, finely minced
2 tablespoons butter
1½ teaspoons curry powder
2 tablespoons flour
1 can tomato soup
1 cup water
½ cup dry sherry
3 bay leaves
12 whole cloves
8 peppercorns

Bring 1½ quarts water, tablespoon salt, and four cloves to a boil. Add unpeeled shrimp and bring water back to boiling point. Immediately remove shrimp with slotted spoon. Reserve water. Cool shrimp enough to handle, peel, de-vein, and slit lengthwise. Set aside.

Sauce: Melt butter in large frying pan. Add onions, garlic, curry powder. Sauté lightly; add flour. Sauté until light golden brown. Add tomato soup, 1 cup water, ¼ cup sherry, four cloves, bay leaves. Simmer for 30 minutes. Set aside. Add sherry to shrimp water, bring to boil, reduce heat. Add scallops and fish and simmer until fish flakes. Add oysters. When edges curl, remove all fish carefully to a heated platter. Strain broth and reserve. Heat sauce, add mushrooms, lobster cut in bite-sized pieces, and shrimp. Cook gently for five minutes. Pour over fish in platter and serve. Strained broth from cooked fish may be served in cup to accompany bouillabaisse or saved for soup at another time. Serves: 10.

The Ballad of Bouillabaisse

This Bouillabaisse a noble dish is
A sort of soup, or broth, or stew,
Or hotchpotch of all sorts of fishes
That Greenwich never could outdo;
Green herbs, red peppers, mussels, saffron,
Soles, onions, garlic, roach, and dace:
All these you eat at Terre's Tavern
In that one dish of Bouillabaisse.

— *Thackeray*

BLUEFISH TERIYAKI

2 to 3 pounds fresh bluefish
    fillets

⅔ cup soy sauce
⅔ cup fresh orange juice

This is a very simple way to eliminate the strong oily taste in bluefish to which some people object. Combine soy sauce and orange juice in a glass container large enough to hold fish. Marinate fish in sauce for 2 to 3 hours in refrigerator. Remove fish from marinade and broil, skin side down, until done. Excellent with boiled new potatoes and cherry tomatoes sautéd with garlic and herbs.

Michael Grigg

CAPE COD TURKEY (SALT COD FISH)

4 potatoes	1½ cups milk
½ pound salt pork	¼ cup flour
1 pound salt cod	½ cup water

Soak cod fish in warm water for several hours, changing water three times. When ready to serve, simmer fish about ten minutes until fish will flake. Drain. Cut salt pork into fine cubes and try out* slowly in an iron spider. Remove pork scraps. Add flour to fat in spider and stir until it bubbles, then add water and stir. Add milk and continue stirring until smooth. Season with salt and pepper. In the meantime, boil or bake the potatoes. Serve as accompaniment. To serve, put fish on hot platter and cover with pork scraps and serve with milk gravy. Boiled onions and beets are usually served with Cape Cod Turkey.

*"Try out" is an old whaling term referring to the rendering of the oil from the blubber of the whale. This was done in a try pot.
                                                                    Abigail Cullity

CODFISH CAKES

1 pound salt codfish, freshened	1 egg
and shredded	2 tablespoons butter
5 or 6 potatoes, cubed	salt and pepper

To freshen fish, soak in warm water for several hours, changing water three times. When ready to prepare recipe, simmer in fresh water until fish will flake easily. Cook potatoes and mash together with codfish. Add other ingredients. Mix well. Shape into patties and fry in ¼" oil in fry pan.

We always had codfish cakes with baked beans on Saturday night, and I think everyone else on Cape Cod had the same 50 years ago.
                                                                    J. L. R.

KEDGEREE

2 cups cooked, flaked fish (cod,	2 cups cooked rice
salmon, haddock or halibut)	¼ teaspoon cayenne
3 tablespoons butter	salt to taste
1 teaspoon finely minced onion	2 sliced hard cooked eggs
½ cup heavy cream	parsley, paprika garnish
¼ teaspoon turmeric	

Over medium heat melt butter and add onions. Cook until onions become translucent, about 3 minutes. DO NOT BROWN. Stir in turmeric, cayenne, and salt to taste. Add cream. Mix. Gently fold in rice and fish. Bring to boiling point. Eggs may be folded in at this point or used as garnish. Serve piping hot. Works well in chafing dish.

Kedgeree — sometimes referred to as "Indian Hodgepodge" was brought to these shores by our sailing men. It is basically a fish and rice dish, with local variations, some version of which can be found in seaports all over the world. The name comes from the Hindi — Krichi, and references to it have been found in manuscripts dating back to the 1300s.
                                                                    Laura Maleady

COD BAKED IN WINE WITH BÉCHAMEL SAUCE

½ pounds fresh cod fillets
¼ cup butter

½ cup dry white wine

Preheat oven to 400°. Butter baking dish generously. Place fish in dish in single layer, and fold tail under so that fish is of even thickness. Drizzle with melted butter and wine. Bake until fish flakes easily. Place fish on serving platter and keep warm. Reserve liquid from fish to add to sauce.

SAUCE BÉCHAMEL:

2 tablespoons butter
3 tablespoons flour
1 cup chicken broth
fish stock from baked fish

¼ cup fresh lemon juice
salt to taste
thinly sliced lemon and parsley
for garnish

Melt butter over medium heat. Add flour and blend well. Remove from heat. Add chicken broth and fish stock. Stir to blend. Return to heat and stir constantly until sauce thickens. Whisk in lemon juice. Taste for seasoning. Pour over fish. Garnish with lemon slices and parsley. Serve sliced hard-cooked eggs on side or place on top of fish.

Laura Maleady

DEEP SEA CLAM PIE

¼ pound salt pork
1 tablespoon butter
4 tablespoons flour

4-5 large sea clams
1 cup clam water
pepper (no salt)

Try out salt pork in iron fry pan. Add butter, blend in flour, add clam broth. Cook until broth is thickened. Grind meaty portion of clams, leaving out stomachs. Throw ground clams in pot with broth. Season with pepper. Cook slowly for 10 minutes. Line deep pie dish with rich pastry. Put in clam mixture, cover with top crust, and surround with twist of crust. Bake in pre-heated oven, 450°, for 15 minutes. Reduce heat to 350° and bake 15 minutes longer. Serves: 6.

"I won a Boston newspaper contest with this and received $5.00 for best recipe sent in that month in 1912. Also asked to contribute this recipe for "The Yankee Cook Book" to sell at the New York World's Fair in 1939. Originally it came from my grandmother, Mrs. Parker L. Paine of North Truro."

Emma Knowles Cross

CLAMS AGROUND — SAM WHITE'S

1 pint ground clams
1 small grated onion
1 cup sliced potatoes
2 cups liquid — milk and
    clam broth

2 tablespoons butter
2 tablespoons flour
buttered breadcrumbs
salt and pepper to taste

Simmer clams in own juice a few minutes until tender. Drain and reserve liquid.

White sauce: Melt butter, add flour, blend. Add clam liquor and enough milk to make 2 cups. Cook, stirring constantly, until thickened. Add potatoes, onion, and clams. Put in casserole and cover with breadcrumbs. Pre-heat oven to 350° and bake for 30 minutes.

CAPE COD CLAM FRITTERS

1 pint clams or quahaugs	1½ to 2 cups flour
2 eggs	2 teaspoons baking powder
salt and pepper to taste	

Enough clam water or milk to make fritter batter. Clean clams, drain and chop. Beat eggs; add flour and baking powder and enough liquid to make fritter batter; should be just stiff enough to hold shape. Add chopped clams and season with salt and pepper. Drop by spoonfuls into ¼ " fat in fry pan or deep fry. Serve with tartar sauce.

CRAB CAKES

2 cups fresh crabmeat	2 eggs, well beaten
¼ cup milk	1 teaspoon Worcestershire sauce
1 tablespoon finely chopped	1 teaspoon Dijon mustard
parsley	4 tablespoons butter
salt to taste	lemon wedges
½ cup fresh breadcrumbs	

Pick over crab to remove shell and cartilage. Blend crab with milk, parsley, salt, breadcrumbs, Worcestershire sauce, and mustard. Shape into 4 to 6 cakes. (Can be smaller for appetizers.) Fry in butter on both sides until golden brown. Serve with lemon wedges.

Makes an excellent luncheon menu — serve with green salad or fresh asparagus in season and hot rolls.

Janet Grigg

CRAB IMPERIAL

1 pound crabmeat, picked over	1 tablespoon chopped pimento
1 tablespoon chopped green	1 tablespoon butter
pepper	

CREAM SAUCE:

4 tablespoons butter	¼ teaspoon dry mustard
5 tablespoons flour	1 tablespoon Worcestershire
1 cup milk	sauce
½ teaspoon salt	white pepper to taste
1 egg yolk	½ cup mayonnaise

Make cream sauce; whisk in egg yolk and seasoning. Carefully fold in crabmeat. Heat through. Serve in chafing dish for hors d'oeuvre with toast points or spoon into shells, spread with mayonnaise, bake in 375° oven, 30 to 35 minutes for main dish.

Sarah Fisher

HERRING

In 1737 it is said that herrings were so scarce no one was allowed to use them "to fish their corn". In 1787 records show that the saw mill over the Herring River at North Sandwich was closed at stated times to allow the herring to run.

CRAB CASSEROLE

¼ cup butter
1 tablespoon flour
1 cup light cream
1 teaspoon prepared mustard
1 teaspoon lemon juice

1/8 teaspoon ground mace
1 can crabmeat
2 hard-boiled eggs, chopped
salt and pepper to taste
breadcrumbs

Melt butter, stir in flour, add cream. Cook, stirring constantly, until sauce is smooth and thickens. Add all other ingredients except breadcrumbs. Stir and place in buttered casserole. Top with breadcrumbs. Bake in 350° oven 20 minutes or until bubbly. Serves: 4-6.

Mae Foster

CRABMEAT QUICHE

½ pound Swiss cheese cut in
   strips
1 cup crabmeat
½ cup small shrimp
2 cups light cream
4 eggs, beaten
1 tablespoon flour

½ teaspoon salt
dash pepper
dash of cayenne
¼ teaspoon nutmeg
2 tablespoons melted butter
2 tablespoons sherry wine
9" unbaked pie shell

Line pie shell with cheese. Cover with layer of crabmeat and shrimp. Combine cream, eggs, flour, salt, pepper, cayenne, nutmeg. Stir in melted butter and sherry. Beat well and pour over seafood. Refrigerate or freeze. When ready to serve, bake at 375° for 40 minutes until brown. Let stand 20 minutes before serving.

Evelyn Mora

FINNAN HADDIE (SMOKED HADDOCK)

2 pounds finnan haddie
2 cups lukewarm milk or water
1½ cups Béchamel sauce

4-6 potatoes, parboiled and
   quartered

Soak finnan haddie which has had skin and bones (if any) removed in lukewarm milk or water for 30 to 40 minutes. Drain well. Put fish in 9"x13" baking dish. Surround the fish with the quartered potatoes. Cover with Béchamel sauce. Bake in a 350° oven until potatoes are done — 45 to 60 minutes. Serves: 4-6.

Joan Kilman

BAKED FLOUNDER

2 flounder fillets
milk to cover
breadcrumbs
¼ cup melted butter

slivered almonds, toasted
parmesan cheese, grated
salt

Soak fillets in milk, with salt to taste, for 45 minutes before baking. Drain and dry. Place in buttered baking dish. Cover with breadcrumbs. Pour melted butter over top. Bake in hot oven, 450°, 5 to 7 minutes. Remove from oven. Sprinkle almonds and cheese over top. Return to oven to toast cheese and almonds. Serve immediately.

101

HADDOCK WITH SOUR CREAM

3 pounds haddock fillets
1 pint sour cream
½ package prepared stuffing mix

1 teaspoon marjoram
1 teaspoon paprika
salt and pepper

Place haddock on aluminum foil in pan and cover with soured cream. Sprinkle with salt and pepper, then spread stuffing mix over all. Sprinkle with marjoram and paprika over stuffing. Bake at 350° for 30 minutes or longer, depending upon thickness of fish.

Evelyn Mora

BAKED STUFFED HADDOCK
WITH COTTAGE CHEESE DRESSING

2 pounds fillet of haddock (or cod)
6 slices white bread
1-1½ pounds cottage cheese
1 egg
salt and pepper to taste

1 medium onion, minced
1 small can evaporated milk
(⅓ cups)
Accent

Place haddock, skin side down, in a well greased shallow baking pan. In large bowl tear bread as for turkey stuffing. Add cottage cheese, egg, onion, milk, Accent, salt and pepper. Mix well and spread over fish so that there are no air spaces at sides of pan. Dot with butter and bake in hot (475°) oven for 30 minutes. Check at 25 minutes.

Robert Gerling

BAKED HADDOCK WITH OYSTER STUFFING

2 thick haddock fillets
½ teaspoon salt
juice of 1 lemon
1 tablespoon melted butter

½ pint oysters
½ teaspoon pepper
1 cup cracker crumbs

Place one fillet on greased baking dish. Sprinkle with salt and pepper. Wash and clean oysters. Dip oysters in cracker crumbs and spread on fillet. Lay second fillet on top and hold in place with toothpicks. Sprinkle with lemon juice and remaining crumbs. Bake 1 hour at 350°. Remove toothpicks and serve.

Pat Morgan

BAKED HALIBUT

1½ pounds fillet of halibut
1 small shredded green pepper
5 strips thinly sliced salt pork

5 thick slices tomato
2 tablespoons butter
1 tablespoon flour

Place fillet in buttered baking dish. Fold tail under so fish is even thickness. Melt butter and blend in flour. Spread evenly over fish. Top fish with tomato slices, pepper, and salt pork. Pre-heat oven to 375°; bake for 25 minutes. Serves: 4.

Mrs. J. Raymond Smith

THATCHED FISH, BAKED

2 pounds fish - haddock, cod,
  flounder

2 tablespoons butter

SAUCE:

3 tablespoons butter
2 teaspoons dry mustard
2 cups milk

3 tablespoons flour
salt and pepper to taste

TOPPING:

4 potatoes
1½ cups grated sharp cheese

2 tablespoons butter

Use 2 tablespoons butter to grease oval or round baking dish. Arrange fish in baking dish. In saucepan melt tablespoons butter, add flour. Cook and stir with whisk, constantly, one minute. Stir in mustard and gradually whisk in milk. Whisk until thick and boiling. Simmer 2 minutes. Add salt and pepper. Ladle sauce over fish. Peel potatoes. Cut in thin slices. Cut across several slices at a time to make matchstick pieces. Put in saucepan with cold water to cover. Bring to boil. Cook 2 minutes or until almost tender. Drain in collander, shake. Melt 2 tablespoons butter, add potatoes. Toss to coat. Spread potatoes on top of fish. Sprinkle cheese over all. Pre-heat oven to 400°. Bake 30 minutes or until potatoes are crisp and golden. Serves: 4.

Bea Blondell

CAPE COD CORNED HERRING

5 or 10 gallon crock
fresh herring, whole, uncleaned

coarse salt — table salt will do

Layer salt and herring in crock, using as much herring as you wish to corn. Cover layers with small board or plate. Place a weight, a rock or jar filled with water, on plate/board to keep the herring below brine. Let herring remain in brine for three days and two nights (or between 55-60 hours). Any longer herring will be too salty. Length of time herring is left in brine is quite important. In earlier times a stick would be run through the gills of a dozen or so herring and they would be hung in sun to dry. After they were thoroughly dry they would be re-hung in the attic for future use. Today you can keep a few in the refrigerator or hang them up covered with cheese cloth to keep flies away. Herring are smoked after being salted, and attain a delicious flavor.

BAKED CORNED HERRING

Line a 9"x13" baking tin with brown paper. Lay three or four corned herring across pan on brown paper. Bake in pre-heated 350° oven for 30 minutes or until skin lifts off fish easily. Herring, baked whole, should then have skin and head removed before serving. It takes a bit of patience to remove the meat and avoid the many bones, but the delectable morsels are well worth the effort. If you are lucky and have herring roe, you've got it made!

"Herring are Running" was the cry which foretold the coming of Spring. The herring start to appear in many fresh water streams in the latter part of March and continue to run through May, swimming upstream to ponds to spawn. Colonial laws allowed each taxpayer to have a barrel of herring each year, and nearly every household had its supply of dried herring for winter use. Herring roe, dipped in cornmeal and fried in bacon or salt pork fat was also highly esteemed by Cape Codders.

Rosanna Cullity

NOUVEAU FISHE

For years the so-called "trash fish" has been either thrown back or sold for fish meal and fertilizer. As fishing stocks have become depleted the useful, tasteful pout, whiting, dogfish, cusk, hake, monkfish, pollock and squid have begun to come into their own. "Trash Fish" Banquets and recipe contests have added to their popularity and quite recently they have been termed "nouveau fishe" (pronounced feesh). Our thanks to the proprietors of Napi's Restaurant of Provincetown for the following recipe, served at a recent meeting of the International Association of Cooking Professionals.

HELEN'S OCEAN POUT TARATOUR

*1 pound ocean pout fillets, pounded**	*3 eggs*
1/8 cup milk	*¼ cup flour*
¼ cup sesame seeds	*¼ cup vegetable oil*
1/8 cup coarsely ground pepper	*2 cloves garlic*
1 cup fresh lemon juice	*1/8 teaspoon salt*
1/8 teaspoon pepper	*½ cup tahini sauce*

Mix eggs and water into an egg wash. Dip fillets in egg wash and coat with flour, sesame seeds and pepper. Heat vegetable oil in a saut9 pan. Lay fillets in the pan, gently fry until brown. Pat dry and squeeze fresh lemon over fish before adding a ribbon of Taratour Sauce.

Taratour Sauce: In a blender, chop garlic with lemon juice. Add salt, another ⅛ teaspoon pepper, and tahini sauce. If sauce becomes too thick, add enough water to give it texture of very heavy cream.

*Pout is a tough fish and must be pounded to tenderize, as veal cutlets and abalone are pounded. If you don't have a mallet, the bottom of a cast iron skillet does an even better job, although somewhat hard on your kitchen counter — as well as the house.

Helen Van Dereck

BROILED CUSK

(Cusk is an ocean catfish, a nice firm fish. If unavailable, cod or haddock can be substituted.)

fresh cusk	*lemon*
salt pork	*parsley*
melted butter	

Cut cusk into fat chunks. Place on greased broiling pan. Top each chunk with thin strip of salt pork. Broil until pork is brown and curly and fish is white. Remove to platter. Spoon melted butter over fish. Serve with parsley and lemon wedges.

This recipe comes from an old Salem Sea Captain who lived across the street from the House of Seven Gables. He fished in the morning and served the fresh cusk in the evening, but only to recommended patrons.

FISH PUDDING, AZORES STYLE

1¼ to 1½ pounds hake fillets
1 large onion, chopped
1 cup fresh breadcrumbs
salt

4 tablespoons butter
2 tomatoes, peeled and chopped
3 eggs

Chop hake into very small pieces. Melt butter in large saucepan, add onion, and cook until soft, but not browned. Add tomatoes, salt, and fish. Cook over moderate heat, 7 to 8 minutes. Add breadcrumbs and beaten eggs. Mix well and place in buttered 1 quart baking dish. Put dish into pan and set on rack in oven pre-heated to 350°. Pour hot water into pan to depth of approximately 1 inch. Bake for one hour. Chill overnight in refrigerator. When ready to serve, turn out pudding onto platter, and garnish with parsley, celery leaves, lettuce, etc.

FISHERMAN'S STEW, PORTUGUESE STYLE

2 pounds cusk, monkfish, or
   striped bass fillets
1 tablespoon butter
1 garlic clove
3 cups water
1 teaspoon thyme
1 teaspoon salt

4 cups pumpkin or winter
   squash, cut into small cubes
1 cup onions, chopped
2 pounds canned tomatoes
1 tablespoon basil
¼ teaspoon red pepper, crushed
2 ears corn

Skin fillets and cut into small cubes. Melt butter in large saucepan. Add onion, crushed garlic clove, and cook until tender. Add tomatoes, undrained but chopped, water, basil, thyme, red pepper, salt, pumpkin/squash, and corn (cut crossways in 1" pieces). Cover pan, bring to boil, simmer 10 to 15 minutes until vegetables are cooked. Add fish and cook until fish flakes easily, 5 to 10 minutes.

SALMON STEAKS WITH LEMON MUSHROOM SAUCE

4 salmon steaks 1½" thick

butter for frying

LEMON MUSHROOM SAUCE:

¼ cup butter
1/8 teaspoon white pepper
½ teaspoon salt
2 tablespoons flour

1½ cups milk
2 egg yolks
3 tablespoons lemon juice
1 small can sliced mushrooms

Sauce: Melt butter over medium heat. Add flour and seasonings, stir, add milk, and cook, stirring constantly until sauce is smooth. Whisk in egg yolks and lemon juice. Mix in mushrooms. Keep warm.

In skillet, melt butter over medium heat. Fry salmon until fish flakes easily. Place on platter, pour sauce over, and garnish with parsley and paprika. Serves: 4.

Sarah Fisher

LOBSTER CUTLETS

2 cups cooked lobster meat	1 cup breadcrumbs
¼ teaspoon mustard	1 egg
1 cup very thick white sauce	1 tablespoon water
1 teaspoon salt	¼ cup melted butter
1 teaspoon lemon juice	Hollandaise sauce

Cut lobster into small cubes. Blend lobster, mustard, white sauce, salt, and lemon juice. Cool. Shape into cutlets, dip in crumbs and beaten egg diluted with water. Dip in crumbs again. Place in buttered baking dish, drizzle with melted butter, and bake 15 to 20 minutes in 375° oven.

Hollandaise sauce: In double boiler put 2 beaten egg yolks and ½ cup melted butter. Blend well, add lemon juice and seasoning. Serve at once. Serves: 4.

Mrs. J. Raymond Smith

LOBSTER DING

2 cups cooked, diced, cold lobster meat	4 tablespoons cooking oil
1 cup whole blanched almonds	1 slice chopped fresh ginger
4 scallions, chopped fine	1 cup chicken stock
1 tablespoon dry sherry	1 tablespoon light soy sauce
¼ teaspoon sugar	1 tablespoon cornstarch dissolved in 1 tablespoon cold water

Mix chicken stock with sherry, soy sauce, sugar, and cornstarch mixture. Heat 2 tablespoons oil in wok to 400°. Add almonds, ginger, and scallions. Stir fry until almonds are lightly toasted. Remove from wok. Heat remaining two tablespoons oil in wok to 375°. Add lobster and stir fry quickly just to heat through. Add sauce mixture and stir until slightly thick. Return almond mixture to wok and stir to combine. Serve over hot steaming rice.

Janet Grigg

MERRYMOUNT LOBSTER

3 cups cut-up lobster, crab, shrimp or sea legs	2 cups light cream
1 tablespoon lemon juice	1 cup soft breadcrumbs
2 eggs, slightly beaten	2 tablespoons butter
dash of cayenne pepper	1 cup buttered cracker crumbs
black pepper, freshly ground, about ¼ teaspoon	1 heaping teaspoon prepared mustard
	salt to taste

Lobster may be frozen, canned, or fresh. Sprinkle lemon juice and beaten eggs over lobster. Bring cream, butter, and breadcrumbs just to boil, stir well together, and pour over lobster. Stir mustard, cayenne pepper, black pepper, and salt carefully into lobster mixture. Pour into buttered casserole dish and top with 1 cup buttered cracker crumbs (saltines). Bake, uncovered, in pre-heated oven at 350° until crumbs are brown and lobster bubbly: no more. Can be prepared ahead of time. Excellent for large buffets. Serves: 8.

Jeanne Stone
Laura Maleady

MUSSELS IN CREAM

2 quarts mussels	2 cups white wine
½ cup finely chopped onions	2 tablespoons flour
1 stick butter	2 cups hot milk
2 egg yolks	1 cup heavy cream
pinch mild curry powder	pinch fennel
1 bay leaf	1 sprig parsley
salt and pepper to taste	1 sprig English thyme or 1/8
drops of lemon juice to taste	teaspoon dried whole thyme

To prepare mussels: Scrub each mussel with brush; scrape off beard with sharp knife. Put mussels down in enough cold water to cover, to which has been added ¼ cup flour. Soak 2 hours. Mussels will eat flour and disgorge their sand. Drain when ready to cook.

Place onion, parsley, wine, bay leaf, thyme, salt, pepper and 4 tablespoons butter in large kettle and boil for three minutes. Add mussels, cover, and cook over high heat. Stir mussels and shake pan so mussels cook evenly. Cook just until mussels open — 5 to 10 minutes. DO NOT OVERCOOK!

Remove mussels from broth, place in bowl, and set aside. Strain cooking liquor through fine sieve or muslin cloth. Boil to reduce liquor by half to concentrate flavor. Melt butter and stir in flour to make roux. Strain both again and add to butter/flour mixture. Add curry, salt, pepper, and several drops of lemon juice to taste. Add enough milk to bring to creamy soup consistency. Add mussels and bring to simmer. In bowl, blend egg yolks and cream and gradually add to soup. When ready to serve, re-heat and adjust seasoning.

To serve: Serve soup as is, or garnished with paprika and chopped parsley, or remove mussels and serve separately with green vegetable, such as Frenched green beans, with soup on the side.

Jane Vaughan

ANGELS ON HORSEBACK

oysters	lemon juice
small piece of toast for	cayenne pepper
each oyster	thinly sliced bacon

Season oysters with a little lemon juice and sprinkle lightly with cayenne pepper. Cut bacon strips in half, crosswise. Wrap piece of bacon around each oyster and secure with toothpick. Place on rack or in grilling basket. Broil or grill, turning once, until bacon is crisp all around. Place each on small piece of toast. Sprinkle with a little more lemon juice and cayenne pepper. Serve with whipped potato and green vegetable or salad.

Jane Vaughan

SCALLOPED OYSTERS

1 pint oysters	1½ cups ground saltines
½ cup butter	1 egg, beaten
1 pint milk or cream	

Mix all ingredients together. Place in buttered casserole. Bake at 350° for 25-30 minutes.

Fran Tidmarsh

BAKED/BROILED SCALLOPS

1 pound scallops
¼ cup dry white wine
1 clove garlic
breadcrumbs

6 mushrooms, sliced
¼ medium onion, minced
½ stick butter
parsley

Place scallops in casserole. Add garlic, wine, butter, mushrooms, and onion. Sprinkle lightly with breadcrumbs and parsley. Bake at 350° for 15 to 20 minutes. Place under broiler until top browns lightly. Serves: 2.   *Barbara Lantery*

COQUILLES SAINT JACQUES

2 pounds scallops
3 tablespoons peanut oil
fresh soft breadcrumbs
garlic butter

2 tablespoons butter
flour, salt, white pepper
paprika

Wash, dry, season, and flour scallops. Shake off all flour. In large skillet, heat oil and butter; when foam subsides, sauté scallops in two batches. Shake pan and stir until firm. DO NOT OVERCOOK. With split spoon transfer to heated platter or individual shells.

GARLIC BUTTER

1 stick butter
2 tablespoons parsley

1 tablespoon finely minced
garlic

Heat butter. DO NOT BROWN. Stir in garlic and parsley. Pour over scallops. Sprinkle a few breadcrumbs and paprika over top. Place in pre-heated oven, 450°-500°, until slightly brown. Sprinkle with fresh lemon juice. Garnish with fresh lemon wedges. Serves: 4.

SHRIMP CASSEROLE

6 tablespoons butter
1 large can mushrooms, stems
  and pieces
1 cup chopped green pepper
2 cups chopped celery
¾ cup ketchup

1 pint half and half cream
2 teaspoons Worcestershire sauce
½ teaspoon tabasco
1 package (20 ounces) frozen
  shrimp
2 cups cooked long-grain rice

Sauté mushrooms, pepper and celery in butter. Mix together ketchup, cream, Worcestershire sauce, tabasco, shrimp and rice. Place all ingredients together in 3-quart casserole and bake at 350° for 30 minutes or until bubbly. Note: this recipe can be doubled. Serves: 8.   *Rainy Reagen*

SEA FOOD PIE

2 cups chicken broth or stock
1 dozen oysters
½ pound scallops
½ pound fresh cod
¼ cup dry sherry
salt and pepper
pastry for double crust 10" pie

5 tablespoons butter
1 small onion, finely minced
1 tender stalk celery, finely
minced
4 tablespoons flour
1 cup cooked cut lobster in
bite-sized pieces

Bring chicken broth/stock to boil. Add scallops, oysters and fish. Cook until oysters curl at the edge and fish flakes. Separate fish, with fork, into bite-sized pieces as it cooks. This takes 4-5 minutes. DO NOT OVERCOOK. Transfer to bowl. Reserve stock. Melt butter in 1-quart saucepan over medium heat. Add onions and celery. Cook until soft. DO NOT BROWN. Stir in flour and add chicken broth/stock. Cook until thickened. Carefully fold in lobster, scallops, fish, oysters, sherry. Season to taste. Set aside to cool. Line deep-dish pie plate with prepared pastry. Pour in seafood mixture. Roll out top crust. Cut three small fish shapes for vents. Reserve cutouts. Place top crust on pie. Seal and crimp edges. Dampen underside of fish cutouts with water and place between vents on top of pie. Preheat oven to 375°. Bake in center of oven until golden brown, about 30 to 35 minutes. Serves: 4-6.

Jane Vaughan

SHRIMP CURRY

4 tablespoons butter
1 large onion chopped — about
1 cup
4 tablespoons flour
1 red apple, skin left on,
cored, and chopped
1½ pounds cooked, shelled,
deveined, medium sized shrimp

½ cup plain yogurt
2-3 teaspoons curry powder
2 teaspoons salt
1 cup water
2 cucumbers, peeled and seeded,
cut in pieces same size as
shrimp
1 cup tomato juice

Sauté apple and onion in butter until soft — about 5 minutes. Stir in curry powder. Cook, stirring constantly, one minute. Mix in flour, stir for one minute, add salt, tomato juice, and water. Bring to boil and simmer for 5 minutes covered. Add shrimp and cucumber. Heat, stir often, until curry is very hot and cucumber tender. Stir in yogurt. Serve in chafing dish with toast points as an hors d'oeuvre or with rice as a main dish with Indian sideboy — salted peanuts, kumquats, chutney, sliced banana, coconut, chopped radishes, chopped green pepper, etc.

Sarah Fisher

MUSTARD SHRIMP

1 pound shrimp, cooked
4 tablespoons Dijon mustard
¼ cup red wine vinegar
¼ cup tarragon vinegar
½ cup vegetable oil

¼ cup chopped shallots
¼ cup chopped parsley
2 teaspoons red pepper flakes
garlic to taste

Whisk together mustard, both vinegars, and vegetable oil. Add shallots, parsley, pepper and garlic. Add shrimp. Let marinate 2 hours. Serve with garlic bread.

Brian Cullity

109

SHRIMP NEWBURG

1 pound cooked, deveined shrimp
1 cup milk
2 tablespoons flour
½ teaspoon dry mustard
2 tablespoons sherry
salt and pepper to taste

2 tablespoons butter
3 tablespoons tomato ketchup
1 scant tablespoon
  Worcestershire sauce
cayenne pepper

Whirl milk, flour, and dry mustard in blender. Pour into top of double boiler and cook over boiling water, stirring constantly, until smooth and thickened. Stir into thickened sauce butter, ketchup, Worcestershire sauce. Season with salt, pepper, and cayenne to taste. Stir in shrimp and heat thoroughly. At this point, dish may be held in refrigerator all day and re-heated at serving time. Just before serving, stir in sherry. Serve over rice. A great shrimp recipe! Serves: 4.

Marion Francis

SHRIMP SCAMPI

1½ pounds clean, shelled shrimp
  — 15 to 18 count
½ stick melted butter
1 tablespoon oil
1 teaspoon salt

black pepper
2 cloves finely minced garlic
2 tablespoons chopped parsley
fresh breadcrumbs
lemon slices for garnish

Remove shell from shrimp, leaving tail; devein and butterfly. Place in bowl. Mix melted butter, oil, salt, pepper, garlic, and parsley. Pour over shrimp. Marinate for one hour. Place shrimp on shallow baking pan, one layer. Spoon marinade over shrimp; sprinkle with breadcrumbs. Put in hot, 500°, oven. Cook just until shrimp turns pink — about 5 minutes. Remove to warm serving platter. Serve as hors d'oeuvre or main course.

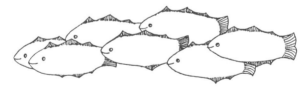

FOOD BY RAIL

A record exists of the freight brought in daily to the North Sandwich station from 1863 to 1870. The food in bulk includes:

> Hogsheads of molasses, also barrels and kegs
> Firkins or tubs of butter and lard
> Barrels of crackers, dried beef, dried fish, rice, beans, corn,
>   oats, dried pork, tripe, apples
> Bags of flour, corn meal, sugar, salt, potatoes
> Chests of tea
> Bundles of salt fish
> Barrels of oil (vegetable), vinegar and "syrup"
> Boxes or baskets of spices, pepper, raisins, yeast

Meats & Poultry

A COLONIAL KITCHEN

This scene is from a cookbook entitled "The American Economical Housekeeper and Family Receipt Book" by Mrs. E.A. Howland. It was published in Worcester in 1845 and again in 1852, selling thousands of copies. The cookbook recipes here assume a big iron stove, but the illustration is of a century earlier with pots hung from a swing arm in the fireplace, and a portable metal reflector in front of the fireplace for roasting meat on a spit or for cooking pastry. In households of either period, a great deal of work was needed to prepare food for each meal and to store things for the long winter — "putting food by" it was called, through smoking, preserving, drying, salting, storing in dry sand or other processes. Most food had to be home grown or bartered with neighbors, rather than bought with money. They acquired by the barrel, not in daily or weekly batches.

In this view the woman at the left is preparing to skewer a large bird, probably a goose. A leg of pork or beef hangs nearby. The woman at the right is rolling out pastry, and behind her on the wall is a lamb and a pair of chickens. The basket from the fields shows potatoes, turnip, cabbage, squash, etc. The housewife would be assisted by an older daughter, an unmarried sister, or someone from the older generation.

Many of the "receipts" given in the book are for long-term preservation of food, such as keeping apples year round, keeping cheese from insects, preserving potatoes and how to deal with rats, flies, ants and mildew.

GUSTAVUS FRANKLIN SWIFT (1839-1903)

Gustavus was the fifth son in a family of twelve born to William Swift and Sally (Crowell) in Sagamore. He early learned butchering as his father and elder brothers bought cattle or hogs in Brighton and brought them to Sagamore for slaughter, and sold the meat in this area. His older brothers, Noble and William Jr., both owned buildings on Jarves Street in Sandwich. Possibly it was this family competition that drove Gustavus in his early 20's to move to Barnstable and start a meat business there. He was intensely ambitious and analytical as to what was involved in business success. This drove him to Brighton at 30 where he joined partners and formed a much larger business in the Boston area and other cities. Chicago was the next big leap, where he went in 1875 at 36. He particularly developed the shipment of live animals to eastern markets, and then typically helped to develop refrigerated cars to ship dressed meat East. He incorporated Swift and Company in 1885 and displayed great skill not only in the business but in matters of financing for rapid growth and in the selection of business associates. When he died in 1903 his firm had over 22,000 employees and did $200,000,000 in business.

His elder brother, Noble Parker Swift (1830-1911) remained in Sagamore and continued in butchering, farming and real estate all his life, acquiring a considerable fortune in his own right.

SANDWICH TAXES IN 1666

Plymouth Colony in 1666 advised the various towns as to the value of goods produced on the farms which could be used to pay taxes. This included grains, pork, beef, butter, peas and pine tar. Town taxes could be paid in a mix of commodities:

> *one third — wheat or pork or both*
> *one third — butter or barley or both*
> *one third — beef, corn, peas, rye, or tar*

These goods were to be laid down, freight paid, with the Plymouth Colony agent in either Plymouth or Boston by the first week in November.

EYE OF ROUND ROAST

3 to 5½ pounds eye of the round
    roast

2 cloves garlic
garlic salt

Cut 4 pockets in bottom of roast and stuff each pocket with ½ clove garlic and pre-heat oven to 500°. Place roast in shallow pan and roast 4 minutes per pound. Turn oven off and leave door closed. Keep roast in oven for 2 hours without opening door. Remove and sprinkle with garlic salt. Slice thin diagonally. It will cook perfect medium rare roast, every time!

FILET OF TENDERLOIN ROAST

Order several days ahead, if possible. Have butcher trim and tie for roasting. Early on day of use, rub filet with garlic clove and lard with bacon strips. Filet may be lightly coated with flour, if desired. Just before roasting, lift bacon strips and season with salt and pepper.

Return bacon strips, secure with toothpicks, and place meat on rack in roasting pan. Roast in 500°, pre-heated oven, approximately 10 minutes per pound or to an internal temperature of 125° (for rare). Roast will continue to cook after it is removed from oven. Let rest for 10 minutes before carving. Serve with Béarnaise sauce and sautéd mushrooms.

Peter Maleady

GRANDMA'S POT PIE

FILLING:

1 pound top round steak
1 medium onion, chopped
2 diced potatoes

6 cups water
3-4 beef bouillon cubes

PASTRY DOUGH:

2 cups flour
1 teaspoon salt

½ cup shortening
water

Cut beef into thin slices. Simmer meat, onions, potatoes in 6 cups water and bouillon cubes for about 1 hour or until the beef is tender.

Pastry: Blend together 2 cups flour, salt and shortening. Add small amount of water until the dough is the consistency of pie dough.

When meat is tender, roll out dough and cut into 1 inch strips. Bring meat to a boil and criss-cross dough strips on top of meat mixture. Boil for 5 minutes. Season and serve. Better on the second day.

Nan Geertz

THE FIRST SURVEY

The first survey of the original Sandwich land grant was made by New England's early military hero, Captain Miles Standish assisted by his friend, John Alden. The first houses were built around the town's bay shores and along the banks of the Shawme River. Both areas chosen provided food and water.

ONION-GLAZED SHORT RIBS

meaty short ribs — English cut	salt
if possible	water to cover
bay leaf	pepper

ONION GLAZE:

1 finely chopped onion	¼ cup brown sugar
2 tablespoons paprika	2 teaspoons salt
1 teaspoon dry mustard	½ teaspoon pepper
1 cup water	½ cup vinegar
¼ cup Worcestershire sauce	¼ cup corn oil

Place the short ribs in kettle with bay leaf, salt and pepper to taste. Add water to cover. Simmer until tender (about 1 hour).

Onion Glaze: Place remaining ingredients in saucepan and cook over low heat until onion is tender. Brush short ribs which have been drained with onion glaze. Grill on outdoor grill or in oven for about ¼ hour. Keep meat covered with glaze as it browns.

STEAK AU POIVRE

1 tablespoon cognac or whiskey	1 tablespoon drained green
½ teaspoon Dijon mustard	peppercorns crushed in mortar
¼ cup heavy cream	and pestle

Cut piece of fat from steak, render in skillet. Add whiskey or cognac to small amount of fat. Add peppercorns and cream. Bring to simmer, stirring. Stir in mustard and pour over steak that has been cooked on charcoal grille. Serves: 3.

This sauce makes a good steak very elegant!

Barbara Maxwell

OLD FASHIONED BEEF STEW

½ cup flour	1 cup water
1 tablespoon salt	½ teaspoon marjoram or oregano
½ teaspoon pepper	1½ pounds potatoes
2 pounds stew beef	1 pound carrots
¼ cup salad oil	1 pound pearl onions
14 ounces beef broth	1 can green beans
16 ounces chopped tomatoes	½ cup dry red wine
(drain and reserve liquid)	

In plastic bag combine flour, salt and pepper; add meat and shake until well coated. In Dutch oven, over medium high heat, brown meat in salad oil, ½ at a time. Stir in broth and scrape pan to remove browned bits. Add meat, water, wine, tomato liquid, marjoram and remaining flour. Bring to boil and stir. Reduce heat and simmer 1½ hours, stirring occasionally. Add carrots, onions, potatoes, and tomatoes. Cook until vegetables are done, stirring occasionally. Add green beans and cook until heated through. Serves: 6.

BEEF AND BEER STEW

2½ pounds lean boneless beef
   cut into 1" cubes
¼ cup salad oil (optional)
6 medium sized onions, sliced
1 large garlic clove, finely
   chopped (or garlic powder)

1 bay leaf
¼ teaspoon thyme
5 tablespoons flour
1 teaspoon salt
½ teaspoon pepper
12 ounces beer

Either brown in skillet or put all ingredients in large casserole dish. Cover and bake at 325° for three hours or more until meat is tender. Serve over hot buttered noodles. Serves: 4 to 6.

Rainy Reagen

POLISH HUNTER'S STEW

¼ cup flour
1 teaspoon paprika or caraway
   seed
2 tablespoons butter
2 pounds sauerkraut, rinsed and
   drained
1 beef bouillon cube
1 cup water

2 medium onions, sliced
1 small can tomato paste
12 ounces kielbasa, cut into 1"
   pieces
1 four-ounce can mushrooms,
   undrained
½ cup white wine
1 can boiled potatoes

Combine flour and paprika. Dredge cut-up meat in flour mixture. Brown meat in melted butter in heated heavy pot. Add sauerkraut, onion, mushrooms including liquid, wine, tomato paste, bouillon cube and water. Cover and cook over low heat for 1½ to 2 hours. Serve with pumpernickel bread. Garnish with parsley. Use other meats if desired. Serves: 4.

Mark Kacprowicz

GOURMET BEEF RAGOUT

2 pounds chuck, cut in 1" cubes
¼ cup flour
1½ teaspoons salt
shortening for browning meat
1 clove garlic, minced
3 cups boiling water
2 cans (8 ounces each) tomato
   sauce
3 tablespoons butter or margarine

4 sprigs fresh parsley
2 bay leaves
½ teaspoon each, dried
   marjoram, thyme, rosemary
2 tablespoons sugar
8 small white onions
4 carrots in bite-size pieces
4 large potatoes, pared and cubed
1 can drained cooked peas

Shake meat in bag containing salt, pepper, flour. Brown meat on all sides in heavy kettle or Dutch oven. Drain on absorbent paper. Pour any remaining shortening from pan; return meat to pan; add garlic, water, tomato sauce. Simmer, covered 1½ hours or until meat is almost tender. Tie parsley and herbs in small cloth bag. Place in kettle with meat. Melt butter and sugar in medium-sized frying pan; add onions and carrots; heat, stirring often until well glazed. Add these and potatoes to meat. Simmer, covered, about 30 minutes or longer until all are tender. Remove spice bag; stir in peas. Serve piping hot. Adapts well to crockery cooker. Serves: 6.

Carol Jillson

BEST EVER COTTAGE PIE

2 pounds very lean ground beef
2 large onions, chopped
1 bay leaf
1 tablespoon chopped parsley
2 pounds cooked, washed
   potatoes

½ teaspoon marjoram
2 teaspoons Worcestershire sauce
2 tablespoons ± flour
2 cups ± good beef stock or
   consomée

Place meat in large skillet, break up with spoon; add onion and bay leaf; brown. Add enough flour to bind mixture and cook 2 minutes. Add enough stock to make thick sauce, stirring constantly. Add parsley, marjoram and Worcestershire sauce. Simmer meat mixture 30 minutes adding stock to keep it from sticking to pan. Remove bay leaf. Place meat in deep casserole and top with potatoes. Sprinkle with paprika to give color. Bake at 400° until potatoes are lightly browned. Serves: 6-8.

Monique Leonard

COLORADO CASSEROLE

½ pound bacon (cut in small
   pieces)
1 pound chopped meat
1 large onion, chopped
½ cup catsup
2 tablespoons vinegar

1 one-pound can kidney beans,
   undrained
1 one-pound can lima beans
   (cannellini)
1 28-ounce can pork & beans
¼ cup brown sugar

Fry bacon, remove from pan and pour off grease. Brown meat and onion, add bacon. Mix beans with meat then add catsup, vinegar, brown sugar. Bake 1 hour at 350°.

Phyllis Colucci

LINDSTROM'S BEEF STEAKS

2 pounds hamburg
3 cooked beets, sliced
4 cooked potatoes, sliced
1 tablespoon white onion,
   mashed

2 tablespoons capers
3 eggs
salt and white pepper to taste
butter to fry
2 onions, sliced

Grind hamburg with beets, potatoes, white onion, and capers. Beat eggs and spices and add to hamburg mixture. Mix well. Make patties — larger than hamburgers. Fry them in butter slightly on both sides. Place steaks on oven proof serving dish in 325° oven. Slice 2 onions and fry lightly in butter in frying pan. Divide browned onions over beef steaks and continue cooking until done to taste. Serve when ready with potatoes, rice, or noodles. Serves: 4-6.

A family favorite from my sister Ilona in Finland.

Salme Mikkonen

MOCK ITALIAN MEATBALLS

½ cup finely ground pecans
  or walnuts
3 eggs beaten
¾ cup prepared stuffing mix
  (herb seasoned)

1 medium finely chopped onion
½ teaspoon sage
1½ teaspoons parsley, chopped
1 clove garlic, chopped
salt to taste

TOMATO SAUCE:

2 cups stewed tomatoes
1 small can tomato paste
1 small can water
1 tablespoon sugar
½ teaspoon salt

3 tablespoons oil
1 diced onion
½ teaspoon basil
½ teaspoon oregano
½ cup chopped celery

Meatball Mixture: Combine and let stand awhile. Form into small balls. Roll in cracker crumbs and brown in hot oil. Use with any prepared spaghetti or homemade sauce.

Tomato Sauce: Combine ingredients and bring to boil. Add meatballs. Simmer 1 hour. Serves: 6.

Christina Murley

NEW ENGLAND GOULASH

2 pounds hamburger
1-2 cloves garlic, minced
1 tablespoon brown sugar
2 teaspoons salt
¼ teaspoon seasoned salt
1/8 teaspoon paprika
1 bay leaf
12 ounces tomato paste
2 cups elbows or other macaroni
16 ounces tomato sauce

1 onion, chopped
2 tablespoons oil
1 tablespoon Worcestershire
  sauce
¼ teaspoon celery salt
¼ teaspoon pepper
¼ teaspoon basil
1 28-ounce can tomatoes
1 pound longhorn or mild
  cheddar cheese

Brown meat, onion and garlic in oil in large frypan or Dutch oven. Add seasonings to meat mixture and mix well. Add tomatoes, paste, sauce and bay leaf to meat mixture and cook while macaroni cooks. Cook macaroni according to directions. Drain. Cut cheese into ½" cubes. Add macaroni to meat mixture and fold in cheese. Place in 2-quart casserole. Bake at 350° for 20-30 minutes. Serves: 6-8.

Pam Anderson

PASTA POT

2 pounds ground meat
2 chopped onions
½ cup chopped green pepper
14-15 ounces spaghetti sauce
1 pound stewed tomatoes
3-ounce can sliced mushrooms
8 ounces shell macaroni

crushed clove of garlic or
  1 teaspoon garlic powder
1½ pints sour cream
½ pound provolone, round slices
½ pound mozzarella cheese,
  sliced

Brown meat, onion and green pepper; then add garlic, spaghetti sauce, tomatoes and mushrooms. Cook macaroni shells. In deep 4-quart casserole put half the shells, half the meat mixture, half the sour cream, and ALL the provolone. Put another layer of shells, meat, sour cream. Top with mozzarella. Cover and bake at 350° for 30 or 40 minutes. Uncover for another 10 minutes to melt top. Serves: 10 to 12.

Polly Leis

PASTEL DE CHOCLO (CORN PIE)
(A Chilean Specialty)

1 pound lean ground beef
1½ pounds chicken breasts,
  cooked, skinned, boned
1 clove garlic, minced
2 medium onions, chopped
2 crushed dried chilies or ½-¾
  teaspoon crushed red pepper
½ cup raisins

4½-ounce can chopped olives
⅓ teaspoon cumin powder
½ teaspoon paprika
salt and pepper
26 ounces frozen corn, thawed
sugar and salt
½ cup - 1 cup milk (the less the
  better)

Soak crushed chilies in very hot water to cover, at least ½ hour. Soak raisins in hot water to cover ½ hour. Brown beef in skillet. Add garlic, onions, chilies, raisins, cumin, paprika, salt and pepper and skim fat if necessary. Simmer until excess liquid has evaporated, about 15 minutes. Reserve. Put corn with milk through blender a little at a time and place in large saucepan. When all corn is pureed, cook, stirring constantly over medium heat until thickened. Add sugar and salt to taste. Assemble in individual 1 pint oven-proof serving bowls or in a 2-quart casserole as follows: 1 layer beef, 1 layer chicken, 1 layer olives, 1 layer corn mixture. Sprinkle top of corn mixture with a little sugar. Bake at 325° for 1 hour or until golden brown and firm looking. Makes 4 individual pasteles or 1 pastel serving 4.

Monique Leonard

RALPH'S BARBECUE BEANS

1 pound ground beef (chuck or
  round)
1 pound bacon, chopped
1 onion, chopped
½ cup barbecue sauce
2 16-ounce cans red kidney beans
2 16-ounce cans pork and beans

¾ teaspoon pepper
1 teaspoon chili powder
4 teaspoons molasses
4 tablespoons prepared mustard
½ cup ketchup
1 teaspoon salt
2 16-ounce cans butter beans

Brown ground beef, onion and bacon. Drain the excess fat. Combine and add all other ingredients except beans. Stir thoroughly. Add beans and mix well. Bake for one hour at 350°. Serves: 20-24.

Fun for family cookouts and large gatherings. A favorite at Green Briar Nature Center summer picnics.

RIBBON MEATLOAF

3 slices soft bread, diced
1 cup milk
1 pound ground beef
½ pound ground pork or veal
1 egg yolk
¼ cup minced onion
4 slices cooked ham

1¼ teaspoons salt
¼ teaspoon each dry mustard,
pepper, sage, celery salt,
garlic salt
1 tablespoon Worcestershire
sauce

CHEESE FILLING:

1 egg white, slightly beaten
2 slices soft bread, diced
1 tablespoon water

4 ounces shredded cheddar
cheese

Mix together ingredients in Cheese Filling section. Set aside. Stir together bread and milk, mix in remaining ingredients, except cheese filling and ham. Pat half meat mixture in 9"x5"x3" loaf pan. Cover with ham slices and cheese mixture. Top with remaining meat mixture. Bake 350° for 1½ hours. Serves: 6-8.

Susan Fellows

SHEPHERD'S PIE

10 pounds potatoes (peeled)
6 cups milk
4 eggs
4 cups grated Swiss cheese
salt and pepper to taste
3½ tablespoons butter, in pieces

pinch of nutmeg
4 cups leftover meat or poultry,
chopped
.1 small can tomato paste
additional butter to grease
baking dish

Boil potatoes in salted water, then mash or purée them. Add milk, beat in eggs, cheese, salt, pepper and nutmeg. Butter a baking dish, spread ½ mashed potatoes evenly over bottom of baking dish; pour in meat mixture and spread evenly over potatoes. Top with remaining potatoes and spread over meat with fork. Dot surface with remaining butter. Place in pre-heated 400° oven and bake 45 minutes or until golden brown on top. Serve with a green salad.

Walter Dennison
Simple Fare Restaurant

CHICKEN CREOLE

1 chicken
onion salt

water to cover
pepper

CREOLE SAUCE:

¼ can pimentoes
2 green peppers, chopped
½ can whole tomatoes or
4 fresh ones
½ teaspoon salt

dash of poultry seasoning
2 onions
dash of nutmeg
pepper

Simmer chicken in water with spices until tender. Mix flour and water to make thickening or use a prepared chicken gravy mix. Add creole sauce ingredients. Pour over pieces of chicken, removed from bones. Heat until very hot.

Louise R. Briggs

CHICKEN SUPREME

¼ cup elbow macaroni —
  cooked, drained
2 cups Velouté sauce
1 cup sautéed mushrooms

2 tablespoons sherry
2 cups diced chicken (white
  meat)
⅓ cup grated Italian cheese

VELOUTÉ SAUCE:

2 tablespoons butter
3 tablespoons flour
½ cup chicken stock

⅓ cup cream
pepper and salt to taste

In casserole dish, combine macaroni, mushrooms, sherry, chicken; stir in Velouté sauce and sprinkle with cheese. Bake at 350° for about 1 hour.

JEAN'S TAJINE

¼ cup olive oil
1 large onion, sliced or scallions
1 clove garlic, mashed
1 tablespoon parsley, chopped
⅓ cup green olives
1 lemon, cut in wedges

1 tablespoon coriander (optional)
1 teaspoon salt
ground black pepper to taste
1/8 teaspoon saffron
1 cut-up chicken, skin removed

Place oil in large, top of stove casserole or pot. Add all the ingredients except olives. Stir to coat with flavors. Cover and simmer for about 1 hour, stirring occasionally. When done, stir in olives to heat. Serves: 4-6.

Serve on platter of rice. Add salad, pita bread and mint tea for a delightful Moroccan flavor.

Jean Stott

ORANGE CHICKEN

chicken pieces for frying
salt pork
sliced onions
butter

sliced mushrooms (3-ounce can),
  boiled in butter
1 can frozen orange juice
bourbon

Fry chicken pieces coated with flour, salt, pepper to taste, in salt pork until browned. Remove from pan. Add butter, sauté sliced onions until translucent. Add mushrooms. Put chicken pieces back in and pour frozen orange juice concentrate over all. Cook until chicken is tender, add ¼-⅓ cup bourbon. Serve over rice.

Robert Swain

CHICKEN BREASTS SUPREME

2 whole chicken breasts, split
  and boned
8 tablespoons butter
½ cup chicken broth

½ cup dry white wine
2 tablespoons flour
½ teaspoon salt and dash pepper
¼ cup heavy cream

Sprinkle chicken breasts with salt; cook in butter over medium heat about 4 minutes each side or until done. Remove chicken. Blend and stir chicken broth, wine, the remaining 2 tablespoons butter, flour, salt and pepper, until smooth. Cook over low heat until thick and comes to boil. Stir in cream. Heat gently. Pour over chicken. Serve with rice. Serves: 6.

CHINESE CHICKEN WITH CASHEWS

2 large whole chicken breasts
  skinned, boned and halved
¼ cup water
¼ cup dry sherry
¼ cup soy sauce
1 tablespoon + 1 teaspoon
  cornstarch
2 tablespoons dark corn syrup

1 tablespoon vinegar
¼ cup peanut oil
½ cup chopped green pepper
½ cup cashews
2 tablespoons sliced green onion
¼ teaspoon ground ginger
2 cloves garlic, minced

Cut chicken into 1″ pieces. Set aside. Combine water, sherry, soy sauce, cornstarch, syrup, vinegar and set aside. Heat wok to 375° or high heat 1 to 2 minutes. Add chicken, stir fry 2-3 minutes until white and push up sides of wok. Add green pepper and cashews, stir fry thirty seconds and push up sides of work. Add onion, garlic and ginger, stir fry one minute and push up sides. Add cornstarch mixture, bring to boil, stirring constantly. Cook one additional minute, stirring all ingredients into sauce. Serve over hot cooked rice. Serves: 4.

Vicky T. Uminowicz

CHICKEN DIVAN

4 chicken breasts, boiled and
  sliced
2 packages frozen broccoli —
  cooked or 1 each of asparagus
  and broccoli
1 can cream of chicken soup

juice of ½ lemon
pinch cayenne pepper
1 tablespoon curry powder
1 cup grated cheddar cheese
½ cup mayonnaise
butter dabs

Arrange layers of chicken and vegetable in baking dish. Top with heated sauce made of remaining ingredients, except cheese. Sprinkle with cheese and butter dabs. Bake in 350° oven until bubbly. Serves: 4-6.

Helen Jacobsen

THE HONEYSUCKLE HILL CHICKEN DISH

2 whole chicken breasts, boned
  and cut into fingerlike strips
1 package frozen or fresh broccoli
  spears
1 can cream of celery soup

8 ounces sliced Swiss cheese
2 cups dry stuffing mix (crumb
  style)
½ cup melted butter

In 6"x10" baking dish put broccoli (precooked), chicken strips, cheese, in layers; pour undiluted soup mix over all. Add stuffing mix, pour melted butter over crumbs and bake at 375° for 45 minutes.

Barbara Rosenthal

CHICKEN RIVIERA

6 boneless chicken breasts
2 cans cream of mushroom soup
1 cup fresh mushrooms
1 large green pepper
salt and pepper to taste

1 medium onion
1 teaspoon seasoning salt
¼ teaspoon celery salt
¼ cup butter
paprika, if desired

Brown skinned chicken breasts in melted butter. Place chicken in baking dish. Wash and cut up mushrooms and place on top of chicken. Add seasoning, salt and pepper to taste. Spoon soup on top. Cut up green pepper and onion, add to top of everything. If desired, sprinkle with paprika. Bake at 350° for 45 minutes to 1 hour, uncovered. Serves: 4-6.

Jane Nye

CHICKEN AND RICE CASSEROLE

1½ cups cooked chicken, bite-size
1 cup chopped celery
¾ cup mushrooms, cut up fresh
  or canned
1 medium onion, chopped
¾ cup mayonnaise & ¼ cup
  water
1 can cream of chicken soup with
  ½ can water

½ cup broken pecans or walnuts
1 tablespoon lemon juice
butter crackers
potato chips
parmesan cheese
paprika
butter or margarine
1½ cups cooked rice

Sauté onion, celery, and mushrooms in butter until onions are transparent. Mix together with ½ can water, chicken soup, mayonnaise mixed with ¼ cup water, and the rest of the ingredients. Put in buttered casserole.

Topping: Crush crackers and potato chips in equal parts. Toss in melted butter and put on top of casserole. Sprinkle with parmesan cheese and paprika. Put in 350° oven until brown and bubbly. Serves: 6.

Audrey Johnson

CHICKEN PATTIES WITH MARSALA MUSHROOM SAUCE

½ cup chopped onions
¼ pound sliced mushrooms
2 tablespoons chopped garlic
6 skinned, seeded and chopped
  tomatoes (fresh or canned)
¼ cup dry Marsala wine
3 tablespoons unsalted butter

½ pound coarsely chopped lean
  pork
¾ pound chopped chicken
  breasts
1 egg
¼ cup bread crumbs
⅓ cup chopped parsley

SAUCE:

5 tablespoons butter
2 tablespoons onion
¼ pound sliced mushrooms

½ cup Marsala wine
1½ cups chicken stock

Sauté in 3 tablespoons of unsalted butter ½ cup chopped onions and mushrooms. Cook until dry. Add chopped garlic, tomatoes and ¼ cup Marsala wine. Cook until almost dry; cool. Add to chopped pork and chicken. Add egg, bread crumbs and parsley. Mix thoroughly. Form into patties. Cook in oil for about 10 minutes. Keep warm.

Sauce: Sauté onions and mushrooms in 3 tablespoons melted butter. Add wine and chicken stock. Reduce to one-half. Whisk in rest of butter; add some chopped parsley and the cooked patties. Heat through and serve.

Brian Cullity

BAKED STUFFED HAM

Prepare a smoked shoulder in spiced water: cloves, allspice, peppercorns. Simmer until meat is tender and comes away from bone easily. Remove bone carefully so as to retain shape of meat. Remove excess fat and prepare surface for glaze or coating. Fill cavity with corn bread stuffing. Bake until heated through in 350° oven. Reduce 1½ cups of cider by half, and baste ham with cider to form a glaze.

Corn Bread Stuffing:

⅓ cup melted butter
2 tablespoons chopped parsley
4 cups cornbread crumbs
1 teaspoon salt
1/8 teaspoon pepper

1 cup chopped celery
2 tablespoons chopped onion
¼ teaspoon dried, whole thyme
  leaves crushed

Sauté celery, parsley, and onions in butter. Do not brown. Add rest of ingredients and mix lightly.

Gloria Fox

Sandwich Boardwalk

CRANBERRY MEAT LOAF

2 cups ground cooked ham
½ cup dry bread crumbs
3 tablespoons chopped parsley
1 teaspoon salt
1/8 teaspoon pepper

1 pound ground raw veal
2 eggs
1 teaspoon chopped onion
2 cups 10-minute cranberry
   sauce*

Combine cooked ham, veal, bread crumbs, eggs, parsley, onion and seasonings. Add half cup cranberry juice (from the sauce) and blend well. Form mixture into loaf; bake in moderate oven at 375°F. for about one hour. Pour remaining cranberry sauce over meatloaf during last 15 minutes of baking. Serves: 6.

*Ten Minute Cranberry Sauce

2 cups sugar
4 cups fresh cranberries

2 cups water

Boil sugar and water together for 5 minutes. Add cranberries and boil without stirring until all the skins pop (5 minutes usually sufficient). Remove from heat and allow the sauce to remain in saucepan until cool. Makes 1 quart sauce.

HAM LOAF WITH HONEY MUSTARD SAUCE

1 pound ham
1 pound pork
1 cup soft bread crumbs
1 cup milk

½ can tomato soup
2 eggs
salt and pepper

SAUCE:

½ cup honey
¾ cup ginger ale
1 tablespoon cornstarch

¼ cup prepared mustard
1 tablespoon horseradish

Grind together ham and pork. Mix in crumbs, milk, soup, eggs; salt and pepper to taste. Bake in loaf pan set in hot water for 1½ hours at 350°.

Sauce: Combine honey, ginger ale, cornstarch, mustard and horseradish. Cook over low heat, stirring until sauce is thick and clear. Serve with the ham loaf. Serves: 8.

HAM ROLLS WITH EGGS

8 thin slices cooked ham
¾ cup tropical relish

scrambled eggs, made your own
favorite style

Tropical Relish:

4 cups cranberries
1 cup shredded pineapple
(canned) (crushed)

1 lemon
2 cups sugar

Relish: Put cranberries through food chopper. Quarter lemon, remove seeds and put through chopper. Add pineapple and blend all with sugar. Chill in refrigerator before using. Makes 1 quart. This keeps well in refrigerator for weeks.

Main Dish: Place tablespoon of relish on each slice of ham and roll up. Arrange, folded side down in pan and spoon a little syrup from relish over top of each. Broil slowly to glaze ham and heat filling. In the meantime scramble eggs according to your favorite recipe. Pile eggs in center of heated dish and surround with ham rolls.

LAMB PILAF

2 cups chicken broth (or 3
    bouillon cubes dissolved in
    2 cups boiling water)
3 tablespoons butter
2 teaspoons lemon juice
1 teaspoon salt
1 bay leaf
1 cup raw rice

2 tablespoons butter
1 medium onion, diced fine
1 small green pepper, diced
1 to 1½ cups cooked lamb, cut
    into small cubes
1¼ teaspoons thyme
salt
pepper

Combine chicken broth, butter (3 tablespoons), lemon juice, salt, and bay leaf in saucepan and bring to boil. Add rice, cover tightly, lower heat and cook 20 minutes or until rice is tender and all liquid absorbed. While rice is cooking, melt 2 more tablespoons butter in skillet, add onions and pepper, sauté until tender. Add lamb and seasonings, cook 5 minutes more. Add rice to lamb mixture. Turn into buttered 1½ quart casserole. Cover and bake 15 minutes at 350°. Serves: 6-8.

This is an excellent way to use up that cold lamb leftover from roast lamb dinner.

Helen Hayward

CROWN ROAST OF PORK

Have crown prepared at market from strip of pork containing 10-12 chops. For easy carving, have backbone removed. Season with salt and finely ground black pepper. Place in roasting pan, bone ends up. Wrap bone ends in foil to prevent excess browning. Roast uncovered in slow oven, 325°, 35 to 40 minutes per pound. An hour before meat is done, fill with favorite stuffing. Continue roasting until meat is done. To serve, remove foil from bone ends. Place paper frills, steamed prunes, or crab apples over bone ends.

Kevin Mullaly

VEAL SCALLOPINI À MA FAÇON

4 ounces veal per person
seasoned flour to dredge
2 tablespoons clarified butter
handful of sliced mushrooms
1 tablespoon minced shallots
black pepper

splash of brandy
3 tablespoons white wine
¼ cup rich chicken stock
chopped parsley
lemon juice

Lightly pound best quality veal scallopini with flat side of cleaver. Dredge in seasoned flour and sauté briskly in clarified butter until done. Remove from pan. Add large handful of sliced mushrooms, shallots and sauté in pan. Do not allow mushrooms to give up water. Flame the pan with a splash of brandy and add a little white wine. Reduce until almost dry. Add chicken stock, very lightly thicken with cornstarch slurry. Add freshly chopped parsley, a good squeeze of lemon juice and pepper to taste. Replace meat in pan and gently reheat. Serve with homemade fettucini tossed with cream, parmesan cheese and butter. Serve with fresh steamed asparagus.

David Williams
Vittorio's Restaurant, Milford, Mass.

WASH DAY LONG AGO

This is an authentic washday "receipt" in its original spelling as it was written for a bride four generations ago:

" 1. bild a fire in back yard to heet kettle of rain water.

2. set tubs so smoke won't blow in eyes if wind is pert.

3. shave one hole cake lie soap in biling water.

4. sort things, make three piles, 1 pile white, 1 pile cullort, 1 pile work britches and rags.

5. stir flour in cold water to smooth, then thin down with biling water.

6. rub dirty spots on board, scrub hard, then bile — just rench and starch.

7. take white things out of kettle with broom stick, then rench, blew and starch.

8. spread tee towels on grass.

9. hang ole rags on fence.

10. pore rench water on flower bed.

11. scrub porch with hot soapy water.

12. turn tubs upside down.

13. go put on cleen dress — smooth hair with side combs — brew cup of tee — set and rest and rock a spell and count blessings."

Author Unknown.

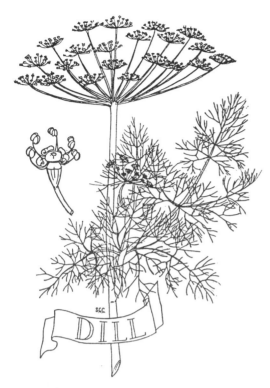

Pickles
& Preserves

DILL

Green Briar Jam Kitchen.

Frank H. Burgess, uncle of Thornton Burgess, was
a cranberry grower and town treasurer.

FROM SANDWICH GARDENS

The weekly newspaper in Sandwich in the 1870's was *The Seaside Press.* It
supplied personal news,events in churches, plus lectures, plays and musical shows
at Town Hall, and other happenings such as runaway horses, robberies, races in
sleighs and accidents in the homes, factories or on the trains. Among the reports
are those of record production from the garden:

T.F. Atkins grew a cucumber of 2½ pounds and a beet of 24 pounds.

W.E. Boyden grew a potato of 1 pound 6 ounces.

Samuel Chipman grew a strawberry 5½ inches in circumference.

Benjamin Haines grew a cauliflower of 11 pounds at his home in
Spring Hill which was Green Briar.

George F. Hoxie found an ear of corn with 20 rows and over 800
kernels.

The keeper of the Almshouse Farm grew a turnip of 11 pounds 6
ounces.

Ezra T. Pope caught a snapping turtle of 34 pounds in Shawme Pond.

When the spring was warm, there were races for early production. On June 26
James A. Bicknell harvested new potatoes bigger than hen eggs, and on the same
day Benjamin Irwin ate new peas. On July 3 Mr. R.C. Clark Esq. had a new potato
of 7½ ounces. Ansel Tobey found a single bean vine with 235 pods and counted
1300 beans. Russell Blackwell displayed a strawberry plant with 194 berries on it.

Samuel H. Nye of Old County Road was a scientific gardener who displayed
his products at Barnstable County Fair, and on Sept. 29, 1877 surpassed all competition with nine top prizes.

Gustavus Howland, the popular lumber dealer and house mover who built the
boardwalk in 1875, had a prize garden which was described as 16½ square rods,
which would be 4492 square feet or about 45x100. On this one plot in 1875 he
grew 12 bushels of peaches, 3 bushels of apples, 12 bushels of corn, 1½ bushels of
cukes, 3 pecks of beans, 6 bushels of potatoes, 2 bushels of beets and 375 squashes
or pumpkins.

APRICOT DATE CHUTNEY

1 pound dried apricots
1¼ cups dates, coarsely chopped
½ cup preserved ginger, chopped
4 teaspoons salt
1 teaspoon chili powder
1¼ cups water

1½ cups golden raisins
zest of 1 orange, cut in fine strips
1½ cups dark brown sugar,
  packed
1 teaspoon mustard seed
1½ cups white vinegar

Combine all ingredients. Bring to boil, then simmer (covered) for 2 hours. Allow to cool to room temperature before storing in jars. Yield: 4 cups.   *Carol Jillson*

CRANBERRY CHUTNEY

4 cans whole cranberry sauce
1 cup chopped pitted dates
1 cup currants
1 cup slivered almonds
1 cup cider vinegar

2 tablespoons chopped candied
  ginger
1 teaspoon ground allspice
1 cup packed dark brown sugar

In large stainless steel or enamel pan, combine all ingredients. Bring slowly to boil, stirring constantly. Simmer uncovered for 30 minutes, stirring constantly. Can be stored in large plastic container for use as desired. Yield: 4 pints.

PEACH CHUTNEY

1 cup chopped onions
½ cup raisins
1 clove garlic
2 tablespoons mustard seed
1 tablespoon salt
⅔ cup candied ginger

4 pounds peaches, slightly
  underripe
2 tablespoons chili powder
1 quart vinegar
1½ pounds brown sugar

Put onions, raisins, garlic through grinder. Cut peeled peaches into small pieces. Mix fruit with vinegar and brown sugar and spices. Boil together for one hour or more until brown and thick. Seal at once in sterile jars. Yield: 3 pints.

Note: Peaches are an excellent substitute for hard-to-find mangoes, which are commonly used in commercial chutneys.

The Green Briar Nature Center has an illustrious past in the history of Sandwich as the site of what may be the oldest continuously used sun-cooking center in New England. The 1780 house has undergone many changes over the years including the addition of the long narrow ell which forms the kitchen. This addition, and the 20-foot long sun cooker on the south wall, were both due to the success and far sightedness of founder Ida Putnam, who in 1903, started making jams and jellies on the stove in the old kitchen of her home at Green Briar.

PEACH PLUM JAM

5 cups plums (3 pounds)   4 cups peaches (3 pounds)
8 cups sugar   1 lemon

Seed and slice lemon thin and cook in small amount of water until tender. Put fruit in kettle. Add sugar and lemon. Boil until thick. Skim and stir 5 minutes. Put in sterilized jars and seal.

SPICED PEAR JAM

3 pounds ripe pears (Anjou)   1 orange, seeded
1 lemon, seeded   1 cup chopped pineapple
1 teaspoon cinnamon   ½ teaspoon cloves
chopped ginger to taste   4 cups sugar

In large pan, cook orange, lemon and pineapple until tender. Add cut-up pears, sugar, spices and ginger. Cook about 30 minutes. Put in sterilized jars and seal.

Martha Blake

FRESH MINT JELLY

MINT INFUSION:

1½ cups mint leaves and stems   2¼ cups water
(firmly packed)

JELLY:

1¾ cups mint infusion   juice of 1 lemon, strained
3½ cups sugar   ½ bottle liquid fruit pectin or
green food coloring   equivalent

Place mint leaves and stems in large saucepan and crush with a masher or tumbler. Add 2¼ cups water and quickly bring to a boil. Remove from heat, cover and let stand 10 minutes. Strain. Measure 1¾ cups into kettle; add strained lemon juice and few drops green coloring. Add 3½ cups sugar. Mix well and over high heat, bring to a boil stirring constantly. At once stir in ½ bottle liquid fruit pectin.* Bring to full rolling boil and boil hard 1 minute, stirring constantly. Remove from heat, skim off foam and pour quickly into glasses. Cover at once with ⅛" hot paraffin.

*Footnote: Do not use apples to supply pectin as their use will dilute the fresh mint flavor.

Having ascertained that diners of my acquaintance do not use the fresh mint of their garden in making their jelly, I submit this recipe for their consideration urging its adaptation at their earliest convenience to the great benefit of their household cuisine.   Goodwife S. Cross, Spring Hill

GERANIUM JELLY

2-4 rose geranium leaves
1½ cups sugar

2 cups apple juice

Add rose geranium leaves to apple juice. Bring to boil and boil for 4-6 minutes, depending on desired strength of flavor. Remove leaves. Bring juice back to boiling and add sugar. Boil rapidly until jelly stage is reached. Pour at once into hot, sterilized jars and seal.

PEPPER JELLY

6 sweet red peppers
1½ cups vinegar
1 bottle liquid fruit pectin

6 green peppers
6½ cups sugar
10 drops green food color

Wash peppers. Cut peppers and remove seed and membrane. Put through food chopper twice (fine). Measure 2 cups chopped pepper (press solidly). Add vinegar and sugar and heat quickly to boiling, stirring constantly. Remove from heat and add pectin. Cool 5 minutes, stirring and skimming. Pour into hot jelly glasses and seal. Yield: 12 6-ounce jars.

Betty Duquet

ROSE HIP JELLY

JUICE:

rose hips

water

JELLY:

2½ cups juice
1 box pectin

1 cup apple juice
4½ cups sugar

Pick stem ends from rose hips and wash in cold water. Add 2 cups water to each cup hips and boil 15 minutes. Mash hips and simmer 10 minutes more. Set aside for 24 hours in glass or enamel container. Strain juice through cloth, squeeze lightly. To 2½ cups juice add 1 cup apple juice and 1 box pectin. Bring mixture to rolling boil. Add 4½ cups sugar, stirring occasionally. Boil 6-7 minutes or until jelled. Remove from heat, skim and pour into hot jars and seal.

Jackie Staples

ROSÉ WINE JELLY

3 cups sugar
1½ cups rosé wine
1 tablespoon finely shredded
orange peel

½ cup orange juice
½ bottle (3 ounces) liquid fruit
pectin
paraffin

Combine sugar, wine, orange peel and orange juice in 5-quart Dutch oven. Bring to full rolling boil. Boil hard for 1 minute, stirring constantly. Immediately stir in pectin and mix well. Skim off foam if necessary. For gift item, pour into heatproof wine glasses. Cover with hot paraffin and cool. Yield: 5-6 glasses.

CRANBERRY-APPLE MARMALADE

1 large orange, seeded and sliced
   thin
3 cups cranberries

1 cup water
4 apples, peeled and cored
4 cups sugar

Parboil orange in water until very tender. Put cranberries and apples thru grinder. Place in large kettle and add sugar and orange. Cook on low heat until thickened, about 20 minutes. Put in sterilized jars and seal.

Martha Blake

GINGER MARMALADE

about 1 pound fresh ginger root
1¾-ounce package powdered
   pectin

2 tablespoons lemon juice
5 cups sugar

Thinly pare ginger root and cut in ½" slices. In 5-8 quart saucepan cover ginger *thoroughly* with cold water. Bring to boil; boil gently 20 minutes. Drain thoroughly. Generously cover with fresh cold water. Boil until ginger is tender/crisp enough to be pierced with fork, about 50-60 minutes. Drain carefully. Cover with fresh water and allow to stand 15 minutes; drain completely. With either a kitchen appliance or by hand, chop ginger so it is rice grain size. *Do not purée.* Turn into saucepan and add 1 cup fresh cold water, lemon juice and pectin. Over high heat bring mixture to full rolling boil, stirring constantly. Immediately add all the sugar and bring back to boil. Stir constantly and boil hard for 1 minute. Remove from heat, skim off foam. Ladle into hot sterilized jars. Seal tightly. Yield: 7 to 8 6-ounce jars.

PUMPKIN MARMALADE

1 5-pound pumpkin
1 orange
2 teaspoons ground ginger

3 lemons
4 pounds sugar
4 drops yellow food color

Cut pumpkin in half; remove seeds. Cook in microwave oven or regular oven until tender. Quarter lemons and oranges and remove seeds and white pith at center. Chop by hand or in food processor. Remove cooked pulp of pumpkin from shell. Add to citrus in large pan. Add sugar, ginger and food color. Simmer until thick (about 30 minutes) stirring often to prevent scorching. (A small lump of butter or margarine helps prevent foaming of jam). Skim and pour into sterilized jars and seal. Yield: about 8 jelly jars.

Betty Duquet

PICKLED NASTURTIUM SEEDS

2 cups small green ripe
  nasturtium seeds
4 cups water
2 bay leaves (small)
1 teaspoon white peppercorns

⅓ cup salt
3 cups white vinegar
1 large whole mace
¼ cup sugar

Dissolve salt in water and soak seeds for 48 hours. Drain and rinse with cold water. Cover with fresh cold water and let stand for 24 hours. Drain and pack in hot sterilized jars. Bring remaining ingredients to boil, reduce heat and simmer 20 minutes. Strain liquid and pour over seeds. Seal and let ripen for 3 months before using. Can be used in any way you would use capers. Try some nasturtium blossoms and/or chopped leaves in your green salads. Has a nice peppery flavor. Very tasty.

PUMPKIN PICKLE

1 pumpkin (large)
1 gallon cider vinegar
1 box (1¼ ounces) whole cloves

10 pounds sugar
1 box (1¼ ounces) stick
  cinnamon

Prepare a syrup made of sugar and cider, cooked until slightly thickened. Place cloves and cinnamon in spice bag and add to syrup. Cut pumpkin into 1″ cubes, rind removed. Place in colander and pour boiling water through until pumpkin is thoroughly hot. Drain and cook in boiling syrup. Remove each piece as it becomes clear and set aside. When all pumpkin is cooked, allow syrup to cool. Return pumpkin to syrup and let stand in a cool place overnight. Syrup can be re-used. Simply discard spice bag, strain and store in covered jars. *Muriel Raymond*

BEACHPLUM CRANBERRY CONSERVE

2 cups beachplums
2 cups grapes
2 cups sugar

2 cups cranberries
1 or 2 oranges
1 cup chopped walnuts

Pick over and clean fruit. Put beachplums in kettle and add water just until you can see it, not quite covered. Boil until partly soft. Add grapes and boil until all is soft. Strain through sieve. Seed and thinly slice orange. In kettle put sieved fruit, cranberries and orange; cook until all is soft. Add sugar and boil until thick; add nuts. Pour into sterilized jars and seal. *R.C.*

133

CHOW CHOW

½ peck green tomatoes (4 quarts)	⅓ small cauliflower
3 small cucumbers	1 bunch celery
1 pint small onions	2 green peppers
2 tablespoons mustard seed	2 tablespoons cinnamon
1 tablespoon cloves	1 tablespoon allspice
1 tablespoon pepper	2 cups salt
2 quarts vinegar	

Prepare the vegetables and cut them into small pieces. Put them in a large preserving kettle and sprinkle them freely with the salt. Let stand for 24 hours and then drain well. Boil vinegar and spices together 10 minutes. Add vegetables and cook until very soft. This Chow Chow may be kept in a stone jar. Whole spice may be used instead of ground spice.

Delicious . . . an old family recipe.

Louise Martens

GRANDMA NYE'S FOREIGN PRESERVE

2 pounds green tomatoes	1½ pounds sugar
1 lemon, seeded and sliced thin	

Core tomatoes and cut in thin wedges. Put sugar in kettle on stove with very little water. Add tomato and lemon and cook gently until transparent and thick. Put into sterilized jars and seal.

WILD STRAWBERRY PRESERVE

wild strawberries	*an equal amount of sugar*

Wash and hull strawberries and measure the amount to be used. Put berries in broad based, stainless steel kettle. Add an equal amount of sugar. Let stand overnight to dissolve sugar. Next day, bring to boil. Let boil rapidly for 3 minutes. Set aside, uncovered, until the next day. If the berries are thick enough, put into sterile jars and process. If not, bring again to boil for 3 minutes and let stand overnight. They should now be thick enough to process. Cultivated strawberries may be processed in the same manner.

The strawberry was first cultivated during the 15th century for medicinal purposes and was considered the only fruit safe to eat uncooked. The name derives from the fact that they were first brought to the marketplace strung on straws.

British soldiers assigned to service in the American colonies complained bitterly in their letters home of stains on their boots and white leggings from the wild strawberries which covered the ground in great profusion.

Wild strawberries can still be found in areas of the Cape, if you know where to look for them. They make a superb preserve.

BLUEBERRY RELISH

6 cups blueberries
2 cups sugar
10 whole cloves
1 teaspoon whole allspice
grated rind of 1 large orange,
    orange part of skin only

1 cup water
1 cup cider vinegar
½ teaspoon coriander seed
2 sticks cinnamon, 2" to 3" long,
    broken in pieces

Rinse and drain berries. Tie spices in small piece of cheese cloth. Bring sugar and water to boil in large kettle. Boil until sugar is dissolved. Add berries, reduce heat, and simmer until berries begin to burst. Remove berries to bowl and set aside. To syrup, add vinegar, orange rind, spice bag, and bring to boil. Reduce heat and cook gently until syrup is reduced by half as syrup reaches the jelly stage. Add berries and cook gently until thickened. Put in large containers and keep refrigerated to use as needed. Will keep for 4 to 5 months, if it lasts that long. Great with chicken or pork.

Blueberries grow in great profusion on Cape Cod in both the wild and cultivated form. They are one of the first plants to reclaim the soil after a forest fire.

They were a staple of the Indian's diet, a major element of his food supply, and were dried for winter use. They were sometimes referred to by early American cooks as "pie timber," and blueberries do, in fact, make a great pie, as well as many other delicacies.

RAW CRANBERRY RELISH

2 cups raw cranberries
½ cup sugar
2 tablespoons horseradish

1 small onion
½ cup sour cream

Chop cranberries and onion in blender or food processor. Add remaining ingredients. Mix well. Freeze. Remove from freezer 2 hours before serving.

HOT DOG RELISH

4 cups onions, ground
10 green tomatoes (4 cups,
    ground)
6 sweet red peppers
6 cups sugar
2 tablespoons mustard seed
4 cups cider vinegar

1 medium cabbage (4 cups,
    ground)
12 green peppers
½ cup salt
1 tablespoon celery seed
1½ teaspoons turmeric
2 cups water

Prepare vegetables and grind using a coarse blade. Sprinkle with ½ cup salt. Let stand overnight. Rinse and drain. Combine remaining ingredients. Pour over vegetables in large kettle. Mix. Heat to boiling. Simmer 3 minutes. Place in hot jars and seal. Process 10-15 minutes. Excellent! Yield: 9 pints.

June Ashley

135

PEPPER RELISH

12 large red sweet peppers,
   seeded
3 cups light brown sugar

12 large green peppers, seeded
15 small onions
1 quart vinegar

Chop vegetables together. Pour boiling water over — let stand 10 minutes. Pour off water. Add more boiling water — let stand 5 minutes, drain. Place in large pot. Add vinegar and brown sugar. Boil until soft and thick — stirring all the time. Pour into sterilized jars and seal.

Helen J. Flood

M. L. POOLE'S FRENCH CORN RELISH

6 large onions, peeled
6 green tomatoes
3 red peppers, seeded
1¾ teaspoon celery seed
½ ounce turmeric
1 cup brown sugar

6 large cucumbers
1 small cabbage
6 ears corn, husked
½ ounce mustard seed
1 tablespoon ground mustard
about 1½ quarts vinegar

Chop or grind onions, cucumbers, tomatoes, cabbage and red peppers. Place in large kettle. Mix together with ¼ cup salt. Let stand overnight. In morning drain well. Add corn cut from cobs, sugar and spices. Cover with vinegar and boil mixture 15 minutes. Put in jars and seal. Be sure not to add corn until the ingredients are ready to cook.

TOMATO-APPLE RELISH

16 ripe tomatoes (about 10½
   pounds)
16 tart apples (about 6 pounds)
8 onions
3 pounds sugar

2 tablespoons salt
1 teaspoon each of dry mustard,
   ginger, allspice and cinnamon
1 quart vinegar

Chop onions, tomatoes and apples. Add rest of ingredients. Bring to boil; simmer for about 1 hour. Place in sterilized jars and seal.

Anne Allen

SPICED GRAPES

9 pounds grapes
6 pounds sugar
6 cups vinegar

1 tablespoon each: clove,
   cinnamon, allspice, black
   pepper

Boil grapes until soft, and put through sieve. Add sugar and boil until thick. Then add vinegar and spices and cook again for 15-20 minutes. Pour into sterilized jars and seal.

Wild grapes are good to use if one can find them. This sauce is good on meats, etc. — somewhat like a catsup. From an old Nye family recipe (Mrs. Lennie Nye). Can also be made with gooseberry.

Mae Foster

SPICED PEACHES

4 pounds firm, ripe, cling peaches
2 cups cider vinegar
1 tablespoon whole cloves
4 2 to 3" sticks cinnamon

4 cups sugar
1 cup water
1 tablespoon whole allspice

Pour boiling water over peaches. Let stand a few minutes until skin slips easily. Dip in cold water and peel. Stick 2 or 3 cloves into each peach. Tie remaining cloves, allspice, and broken sticks of cinnamon in a piece of cheese cloth. Into a large kettle put sugar, vinegar, water, and spice bag. Bring to boil and cook for 5 minutes. Add peaches and cook gently until peaches are tender. Remove peaches with slotted spoon to 1½ to 2 quart jar. Remove spice bag from syrup and pour syrup over peaches. Should stand for about three weeks before serving. Will keep for several months refrigerated.

CLOVER HONEY

24 red clover blossoms
petals of 6 roses
½ teaspoon alum powder

35 white clover blossoms
10 cups sugar
3 cups water

Combine sugar, water, and alum in saucepan and boil for 5 minutes. Pour the syrup over blossoms and let stand for 15 minutes. Strain through cheesecloth and bottle.

The making of honey without the help of bees dates back many years. This is my grandmother, Nettie Dame's recipe.

Harold Ericksen

MARINATED PEPPERS WITH GARLIC

2 cups water
1 cup white vinegar
2-3 cloves garlic, split
1 teaspoon sugar

1 teaspoon salt
1 teaspoon oregano
green and red peppers, sliced
    lengthwise

Pack peppers in jar. Mix water and vinegar. Add other ingredients. Pour over peppers and tightly cover. Leave in refrigerator for one week before using. Delicious with steaks or salads or as an appetizer.

Diana Payne

MINCEMEAT BY JANE BEARD

3 pounds lean brisket or
   rump beef
1 fresh tongue (about 3 pounds)
1½ pounds beef suet, finely
   chopped
2 pounds raisins
2 pounds sultanas
2 pounds currants
½ pound citron (diced or
   shredded)
½ pound orange peel (diced or
   shredded)
1 bottle (a fifth) sherry

¼ pound lemon peel (diced or
   shredded)
2 cups sugar
1 pint strawberry preserve
1 tablespoon salt
2 teaspoons nutmeg
1 tablespoon cinnamon
1 teaspoon allspice
1 teaspoon mace
1 teaspoon ground cloves
2 bottles cognac — enough to
   make loose mixture

Boil the brisket and the tongue in water until tender. Cool and put through coarse
grinder and then combine with all other ingredients. Mix thoroughly and place in
large crock (covered). Let stand month or so before checking each week to see if
mixture needs more spirits.

To make a pie: Combine 2½ cups mincemeat with 1 cup chopped apples and bake
in a double crust at 450° for 10 minutes and then 350° until brown.

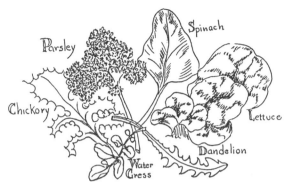

Salads

Mowing on the salt meadows.

Typical Cape Cod salt works.

SALT-MAKING

The Revolution brought about many adjustments in the everyday lives of the colonists. In addition to the interruption of the tea trade, importation of salt was halted. Salt was a necessity of life useful in the preservation of meats and fish. In an attempt to replace the unavailable commodity, salt water was boiled on the beaches in the huge kettles used to reduce whale blubber. Unsurmountable difficulties arose in keeping the kettles boiling in that they required an inordinate amount of fuel and constant tending. A brilliant innovator, John Sears in Dennis built a huge wooden pan for evaporating sea water by solar radiation. This was called Sears Folly because it had to be supplied by hand, the roof let in rain and the pan leaked. Improvements were made and with a windmill to pump water and an easily moveable roof, the arrangement worked and produced salt cheaply. Labor was intermittent and could be done by women, children and the elderly. About 350 gallons of sea water produced one bushel of sea salt.

When the Revolution was over, construction of salt works was undertaken in every town, using cheap lumber available from Maine. Sandwich had eight such works, 3 on Massachusetts Bay and 5 on Buzzards Bay; by 1830 there were 442 salt works Cape-wide. The top level of vats was called the "water room" where initial evaporation produced slimy deposits and vegetation on the edges of the vats; the next lower level was the "pickle room" where "lime" was deposited; the concentrated brine then flowed to the "salt room" where sodium chloride was deposited. This was shoveled out, dried and bagged for shipment. The process took about six weeks. By-products included Glauber's salt for tanning and Epsom salt, a medicinal.

Production on Cape Cod peaked at over a half million bushels per year in the 1830's, but declined thereafter as the price of salt fell due to efficient production from saline springs and solid salt deposits, also as lumber costs rose and Massachusetts dropped its bounty on solar salt production. The sprawling vats were subject to damage from storms and fires, and were dismantled for other construction. The last vestiges were gone by 1900.

The rebuilt Aptucxet Trading Post in Bourne has a two-part saltworks to demonstrate the process to visitors during the summer season.

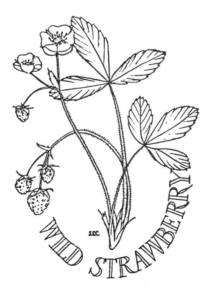

WILD STRAWBERRY

CELERY SEED SALAD DRESSING

½ cup sugar
1 teaspoon salt
⅓ cup vinegar
1 teaspoon celery seed

1 teaspoon mustard (either dry or
  commercial)
½ small onion, grated
1 cup salad oil

Mix all dry ingredients in bowl. Add few drops of vinegar, shake vigorously to blend. Add oil very slowly, beating constantly. When thoroughly blended add remainder of vinegar in same fashion. Keep refrigerated.

Bertha MacAusland

FRENCH DRESSING

2 cups sugar
1 pint vegetable oil
2 eggs
1½ teaspoons salt
pepper to taste

1 tablespoon Worcestershire
  sauce
2 tablespoons prepared mustard
1 bottle catsup (14 ounces)
1½ cups vinegar

Mix well in order given. Stores very well under refrigeration. Yield: 1½ to 2 quarts.

Robert Swain

FRENCH FRENCH DRESSING

2 teaspoons sugar
¼ teaspoon salt
¼ teaspoon paprika
¼ teaspoon dry mustard

6 tablespoons olive oil
2 tablespoons vinegar or lemon
  juice
1 clove garlic, peeled and sliced

Combine all ingredients in small bowl of electric mixer. Beat at high speed 4 minutes. **If a mixer is not used,** beat with fork or whisk ingredients with 1 tablespoon olive oil and 1 tablespoon vinegar. Then add: 2 tablespoons olive oil; beat. Add 1 tablespoon vinegar, 3 tablespoons olive oil. Dressing can keep almost indefinitely when refrigerated. Remove garlic after 6-7 days. Various additions: chopped olives, nuts, anchovies, etc. may be added just before serving. Yield: ¾ cup.

P. Lovell

FRUIT SALAD DRESSING

1 egg yolk
1 cup maple syrup

juice of ½ lemon
½ cup cream (whipped)

Beat egg yolk, add maple syrup; cook in double boiler until thick. Let cool. Then mix in lemon juice and cream. Serves: 4.

Natalie Norris

"HORIZONS" CREAMY GARLIC DRESSING

ORIGINAL RECIPE:

10 tablespoons grated garlic
1 teaspoon fresh ground black
  pepper
1 handful chopped scallions

1½ cups vinegar
¾ cup soy sauce
1 gallon mayonnaise

CUT DOWN TO FAMILY SIZE:

1 tablespoon grated garlic
dash fresh ground black pepper
1 tablespoon chopped scallions

2 tablespoons white vinegar
2 teaspoons soy sauce
1½ cups mayonnaise

Mix first five ingredients in processor or blender. Add mixture to mayonnaise. Use water to dilute to desired consistency. Serves: a party.

*This is served at Horizons Restaurant
on their famous mushroom salad*

LAMPLIGHTERS' SALAD DRESSING

3 ounces roquefort cheese
3 ounces blue cheese
8 ounces salad dressing
1 ounce evaporated milk
¼ teaspoon garlic salt

¼ teaspoon salt
¼ teaspoon Worcestershire sauce
1 medium onion, grated
2 tablespoons lemon juice
¼ cup whipped cream

Crumble cheese and mix thoroughly with other ingredients, except cream. Cheese should be gotten to the size of peas. Whip cream rather stiff and fold in. Keeps a week in refrigerator. Yield: 1-1½ cups.

Mrs. C. Crowell

POPPY SEED DRESSING

1½ cups sugar
onion juice or 1 small quartered
  onion
⅔ cup vinegar

2 cups oil
2 teaspoons dry mustard
3 tablespoons poppy seeds

Place sugar, vinegar, onions and mustard in blender. Mix and slowly add salad oil. Beat hard. Add poppy seed; give one short spurt. Yield: about 3¾ cups.

Christine Pope Gallagher

QUICK BLENDER MAYONNAISE

2 large eggs
½ teaspoon salt
½ teaspoon dry mustard

pinch of white pepper
2 tablespoons fresh lemon juice
1 cup salad oil

Place all ingredients except oil into blender. Blend ingredients at high speed for about 10 seconds. As blender continues to run, add oil in steady stream. Run blender for one minute more. You may have to stop blender a few times to scrape down sides with a rubber spatula. Yield: about 1½ cups. *P. Lovell*

SOUR CREAM DRESSING

3 egg yolks
1 teaspoon prepared mustard
1 scant teaspoon salt
2 rounded teaspoons sugar
dash cayenne pepper

2 teaspoons butter, melted
1 cup sour cream
¼ cup vinegar
3 egg whites, beaten

Put all ingredients except vinegar and egg whites into double boiler. Beat egg whites into soft peaks and fold into mixture. Cook, stirring, and drop vinegar in slowly; taste as you may need less than ¼ cup vinegar. Serves: 6.

Dorothy B. Lovell

WALNUTS AS SALAD CROUTONS

2 tablespoons butter or margarine
½ teaspoon salt or garlic salt

½ cup broken walnuts

Melt 2 tablespoons butter or margarine in skillet. Add ½ teaspoon salt or garlic salt. Brown ½ cup broken walnuts over medium heat, stirring constantly. Serve with tossed green salad.

FROZEN CRANBERRY SALAD

1 can cranberry jelly
2-3 tablespoons lemon juice
3 ounces softened cream cheese

½ pint heavy cream, whipped
½ cup mayonnaise
½ cup confectioners' sugar

Combine first two ingredients in bowl and freeze. Combine remainder of ingredients; spread on top of frozen mixture. Return to freezer. When ready to serve, remove from bowl — inverted. Very tasty with fowl and roast beef. Serves: 8.

Irene Thibodeau

FROZEN FRUIT SALAD

3 ounces cream cheese
½ cup salad dressing or
    mayonnaise
½ cup heavy cream, whipped
red food coloring

¼ cup chopped maraschino
    cherries, well drained
1¼ cups tiny marshmallows or
    12 large — cut up
1 #2 can fruit cocktail — drained

Soften cream cheese, blend with salad dressing. Fold in remaining ingredients. Add color for a delicate pink color. Pour into pan to freeze until firm. To serve, let stand out a few minutes. Serves: 6.

This is one of my favorite, do-ahead, company salads. If guests are few, cut in squares, wrap in plastic wrap and keep frozen for next batch of company!

Florence Eaton

EVERLASTING COLE SLAW

1 head cabbage
1 small onion
2 carrots
2 stalks celery
1 sweet pepper
½ cup sugar

⅔ cup vinegar
1 cup oil
1 teaspoon mustard
1 teaspoon celery seed
1 tablespoon salt

Shred cabbage fine, mince onion, grate carrots, dice celery thin, and dice pepper. Mix together and add sugar. Set aside in covered pot. In saucepan mix vinegar, oil, mustard and seasonings; bring to boil. Pour hot liquid over vegetables. Cover and refrigerate for 24 hours WITHOUT STIRRING. Will stay crisp and fresh for a week to ten days in refrigerator.   .

Muriel & Jack Raymond

WALDORF COLE SLAW

½ cup mayonnaise
1 tablespoon milk or cream
1 tablespoon vinegar or lemon
    juice
½ teaspoon sugar
pepper to taste

1 medium cabbage, grated
4/5 large carrots, grated
fresh herbs, fruit, nuts, dried figs
    other dried fruit, etc.
salt or substitute to taste

Mix well together. Serves: 4-6.

Jean Davis

CREAM CHEESE & SEAFOOD SALAD SPREAD

2 teaspoons unflavored gelatine
½ cup cold water
2 8-ounce packages cream cheese,
    softened
2 tablespoons cream or dry sherry
¾ teaspoon seasoned salt (or
    salt substitute)
¼ cup snipped parsley

1 6-ounce tin king crab meat,
    cut up
1 can tiny shrimp
1 can pitted black olives, halved
1/8 teaspoon ground black pepper
1 2-ounce jar pimentos sliced,
    drained and chopped

Sprinkle gelatine over water to soften; stir over hot water until dissolved. Beat into cream cheese until smooth. Stir in next four ingredients, plus black pepper and 2 tablespoons parsley. Pour into three-cup ring or other mold and refrigerate at least four hours, or until set. To serve, turn out on plate and press in shrimp and olives all around. Add parsley in center if a ring mold and around base. Serve with crackers. Serves: about 3 cups, for a party.

P. Lovell

CURRIED SHRIMP & MELON SALAD

4 pounds shrimp
1 cup mayonnaise
1½ tablespoons grated onion
2 tablespoons lemon juice
1½ cups chopped celery
1½ teaspoons salt

1½ tablespoons curry powder
6 tablespoons sour cream
1½ large honeydew melons
oil and lemon juice — French
   dressing
salad greens

ACCOMPANIMENTS:

chopped cashew nuts
chutney

coconut
1 egg, hard cooked & chopped

Cook shrimp. Make a sauce of mayonnaise, onion, lemon juice, celery, salt, curry powder and sour cream. Mix well with shrimp and chill. Halve the melon; remove seeds. Scoop out melon balls and marinate in French dressing. Scoop out remaining melon to within ½" of rind. Halve and chill the shells. Fill shells with shrimp mixture and place on greens. Garnish with melon balls and additional greens.

Serve accompaniments in separate bowls — chopped cashews, coconut, chutney and chopped egg. Serves: 6.

Connie Crowell

"DUMP" SALAD

1 pound cottage cheese
1 3-ounce package orange gelatin
1 8-12 ounce container cream
   topping

1 12-15 ounce can mandarin
   oranges
1 15-ounce can crushed pineapple

Drain crushed pineapple and oranges. Dump cottage cheese into bowl. Dump in dry gelatin and mix well. Refrigerate maximum of 15 minutes. Add pineapple and mandarin oranges. Mix well. Fold in cream topping. Serve on lettuce. Amount of cream topping depends on richness required. Serves: 6-8.

Edith Beers

Sandwich Glass Museum

BEET SALAD

1 package lemon gelatin	3 tablespoons vinegar
1 cup boiling water	½ teaspoon salt
¾ cup beet juice	2 teaspoons grated onion
1 cup chopped cooked beets	2 tablespoons horseradish
¾ cup diced celery	

Combine in order and pour into individual molds. Serve on lettuce with a sour cream dressing.

CINNAMON APPLE SALAD

¼ cup cinnamon candies (red, hot or other)	2 large apples, peeled and grated
1 cup water	1 3-ounce package lemon or orange gelatin

Boil cinnamon candies in water to dissolve; add gelatin and stir. Mix in grated apple and pour into mold*. Cool until set, in refrigerator. Serves: 4-6.

*I rub a little oil into the mold for easy removal.

Georgia Flagg

CRANBERRY SALAD

1 package raspberry gelatin	1 cup hot water
1 cup orange chunks	½ cup cold water
1 cup pineapple chunks	1 can cranberry sauce
1 cup chopped walnuts	(whole berry)

Dissolve raspberry gelatin in one cup hot water. Add ½ cup cold water. Chill until partially thickened. Add orange, pineapple, cranberry sauce and walnuts. Chill and serve. Serves: 4-6.

MOLDED CHICKEN & VEGETABLE SALAD

2 cups diced chicken, cooked	¼ teaspoon salt
1 cup carrots, sliced & cooked	¼ teaspoon pepper
1 cup cut celery	¼ cup sugar
1 cup peas, cooked slightly	¼ cup vinegar
2 cups stock or water	4 envelopes plain gelatin

Dissolve gelatin in cold stock; then heat and pour over chicken and vegetables. This is best molded in large bread pan. Serves: 10.

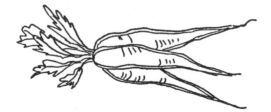

HUNGRY MAN'S SALAD AND DRESSING

GREENS:

1 large head romaine lettuce
½ to ¾ cup garlic croutons

¼ cup parmesan cheese, freshly
grated

DRESSING:

4 tablespoons olive oil
1 tablespoon wine or cider
vinegar
1 tablespoon Sushi Su vinegar

¼ teaspoon salt
1 clove garlic, thinly sliced
1 tablespoon oyster sauce
fresh ground pepper

Wash and separate romaine lettuce. Drain well. Break into bite-size pieces. Toss with a flourish, with dressing to cover lettuce. Add parmesan cheese and toss to distribute cheese. Add garlic croutons and toss lightly. Sequence of tossing is critical! Serve immediately.

Salad should be served on a dinner plate with a barbecued steak and baked potato, just prior to removal of medium rare steak from grill so that salad is half consumed before the steak and potato appear.

For a luncheon salad add 1 additional tablespoon vinegar and 1 cup crab meat or 1 cup crumbled poached fish — toss lightly with croutons.

Edward F. Roskowski

LIME HORSERADISH SALAD

1 package (3-ounces) lime gelatin
¾ cup boiling water
1 cup cottage cheese, small curd

½ cup condensed milk
½ cup mayonnaise
¼ teaspoon wet horseradish

Dissolve gelatin in boiling water and let cool. Add condensed milk, mayonnaise, cottage cheese and horseradish. Chill for one hour. Stir to foam up and chill again. Cut in squares and serve on lettuce.

Dorothy E. Siddall

PINEAPPLE MARSHMALLOW SALAD

1 cup water
1 3-ounce package lime or lemon
gelatin
1 cup whipped cream

1 cup crushed canned pineapple
1 cup small curd cottage cheese
1½ cups miniature
marshmallows

Combine water, gelatin, marshmallows in saucepan. Heat until marshmallows dissolve completely. Cool thoroughly. Add pineapple, cottage cheese and whipped cream. Pour into salad bowl and chill overnight. Serves: 4-6.

Mary C. Gleason

SPICED ORANGE MOLD

1 11-ounce can mandarin oranges
¼ teaspoon salt
6-inch stick cinnamon
½ teaspoon whole cloves

2 3-ounce packages orange gelatin
2 cups cold water
3 tablespoons lemon juice
½ cup broken pecans

Drain oranges, reserving syrup. Add water to make 1¾ cups. In saucepan mix syrup, salt and spices. Cover and simmer 10 minutes. Remove from heat and let stand 10 minutes. Remove spices. Dissolve gelatin in hot mixture. Add cold water and lemon juice. Chill until practically set. Stir in oranges and nuts. Chill until firm in quart mold. Serves: 6-8.

Connie Crowell

STRAWBERRY SALAD

3 3-ounce packages strawberry
  gelatin
1 cup boiling water
1 10-ounce package frozen
  strawberries

3 bananas, sliced
1 large can crushed pineapple
1 cup broken nuts
1 pint sour cream

Dissolve gelatin in water. Add thawed strawberries, bananas, crushed pineapple, and broken nuts to gelatin. Pour half into an 8″ by 11″ rectangular pan and chill to firm. Keep the other half at room temperature. When refrigerated gelatin is firm, pour sour cream over the mixture. Then pour remaining half on top and chill until firm. Serves: 6-8.

Flora Lovell

KRAUT SALAD OR RELISH

1 large can sauerkraut, rinsed
6 green onions, chopped
1 cup sugar
½ cup vinegar

½ cup salad oil
1 cup celery, cut up
½ green pepper, chopped
1 jar pimento, chopped

Mix together and refrigerate overnight.

Jean Denyer

ORANGE-ROMAINE SALAD

SALAD:

1 head romaine, in bite-size pieces	¼ cup sliced almonds
1 can drained mandarin oranges	1 tablespoon sugar

DRESSING:

½ teaspoon salt	2 tablespoons sugar
2 tablespoons red or white wine vinegar	½ cup salad oil
1 tablespoon snipped parsley	dash tabasco sauce

Stir fry almonds in tablespoon sugar until caramelized. Combine with romaine and oranges. Mix all the dressing components and shake well. Pour over salad. Serves: 6.

OVERNIGHT LAYERED SALAD

1 medium head iceberg lettuce, shredded	1 teaspoon seasoned salt
½ cup green onions and tops, thinly sliced	½ cup grated parmesan cheese
½ cup celery, thinly sliced	¼ teaspoon garlic powder
1 can (8 ounce) water chestnuts, sliced and drained	2 tablespoons sugar
1 package (10 ounce) frozen peas	½-¾ pound sliced bacon
	3 hard boiled eggs, chopped
	2 medium tomatoes, in wedges
	2 cups mayonnaise

Spread lettuce evenly in wide large salad bowl. Top with onions, celery, chestnuts, and peas. Spread mayonnaise evenly. Sprinkle with sugar, cheese, salt, and garlic powder. Cover and refrigerate overnight or for several hours. Cook bacon to crisp stage and crumble. Just before serving sprinkle with bacon bits and chopped egg and arrange tomato wedges on top.

To serve: Use a large spoon and fork to lift out servings, scooping down to bottom of dish to reach all layers. Serves: 8-10.   *Ruth Sisson*

WALDORF SALAD

2 cups pared apples	1 tablespoon sugar
1 cup 1-inch julienne celery sticks	½ teaspoon lemon juice
½ cup broken walnuts	dash of salt
¼ cup mayonnaise	½ cup whipping cream, whipped

Combine apples, celery and nuts. Blend mayonnaise, sugar, lemon juice and salt. Fold in whipped cream and chill. Serves: 6.   *Ina Ferguson*

Salads

WATERCRESS SALAD

2 bunches firm fresh watercress
1 tablespoon French mustard
2 tablespoons red wine vinegar
salt or salt substitute to taste
freshly ground pepper to taste
1 tablespoon chopped parsley

6 tablespoons salad oil
2 hard boiled eggs, sliced or
  chopped
2 tablespoons coarsely chopped
  red onion

Trim off tough watercress stems and discard. Rinse and pat dry. Put mustard, vinegar, salt and pepper into salad bowl and blend with wire whisk. Add oil while beating with whisk. Add watercress and sliced or chopped egg and chopped onion. Sprinkle with parsley and toss. Serves: 4.

If I should walk in Gully Lane
　　Think you that I would find
The boyhood lost so long ago —
　　The youth I left behind?

Are still the days so carefree there?
　　So filled with simple joy?
So heedless of the march of time
　　As when I was a boy?

Would clutching hands of bramble-bush
　　Still reach to hold me fast,
Or would they treat me as a ghost,
　　A specter from the past?

Would summer berries taste as sweet?
　　The wild grapes spice the air
With quite the winey fragrance that
　　In memory lingers there?

Ah me! So many years have fled,
　　So mingled joy with pain,
I fear to seek the boy who once
　　Did walk in Gully Lane.

　　　　　　— Thornton W. Burgess, 1939

But most of all I wonder at the Sandwich of today — at the way in which *you* have kept beautiful a beautiful inheritance to pass on to future generations.

Soups

Cape Cod ladies screening cranberries at Santuit Bog, Mashpee, 1889.

Digging clams for Cape Cod clam chowder.

DOWN ON PERCIVAL'S FARM

Benjamin Percival (1752-1817) of South Sandwich kept a vivid diary of family and town events over a long period. He was a careful and observant farmer, had ten children, served as Selectman for 19 years, taught winter school and was a Representative at Boston for six years. Here are typical entries over a composite year:

January — To Joseph Lawrence's charcoal pit and loaded up to carry to town tomorrow if it be weather/killing our hogs and cutting up pork/been for the last of our salt hay/Samuel Hilliard has been shoeing our sled/I have been mending shoes.

February — Sowed tobacco seed (in frames).

March — Carting dung and plowing/first robins and blackbirds/pruning our orchard.

April — To town to get plough irons sharpened/sowing oats and clearing a turnip yard/sowing flax.

May — Began to harrow for planting/planted 12 acres of corn/peach trees in bloom/planting potatoes/washed and sheared sheep/turned out 14 sheep in the woods/Apple trees in bloom and very thick.

June — Began to weed corn/turned cattle to the plains (fenced) to pasture/ setting out 320 tobacco plants/fired our charcoal pit.

July — Began to hill corn/hoeing tobacco/began to reap rye/50 folks here today a-cherrying.

August — Rain catched us with two acres of rye down/pulling flax/mowing oats/pair of oxen killed with the heat/putting flax in water/ground off new scythes.

September — Mowing (salt hay) at Lawrence Hole/carried home a load of hay from Lawrence Hole/winnowed 35 bushels of rye/cutting corn stalks/ a number have been here today to eat melons.

October — Harvesting beans/brought cattle from the plains and shut up hogs/cribbing corn/gathering winter apples/husking corn and twisting tobacco/pulling up potatoes/got up our sheep - 2 missing/bought 12 Greening apple trees, one dollar each/pulled up our Hanover turnips and put them in the ground (sand storage in protected area)/finished husking with assistance of some Indians/at Thomas Crocker's (Cotuit) to eat oysters.

November — Killing a sheep/making hay yard fences/secured our pompions (pumpkins)/Father has been to town with the turnips/calf died last night. I have skinned it/to beach for a load of thatch/A grand husking here this evening, 70 or 80 people husked 10 loads.

December — Carting split wood/killed our beef cow, 40 lbs. tallow, 465 lbs. meat, hide 58 lbs./work upon the shop chimney/cutting up our beef and salting it/School Master Tupper has come today to keep school/a large buck was found dead in Spectacle Pond and frozen in. The ponds are froze to bear.

BEAN SOUP

1 cup red onion, minced
1 cup celery, minced
¼ cup corn oil
3 cloves garlic
4 quarts water
½ cup dried chick peas
(garbanzo)
½ cup dried lima beans
½ cup dried pea beans
½ cup dried black beans

2 new potatoes, diced, unpeeled
½ cup carrots, diced
½ cup barley
1 cup tomato purée
3 tablespoons fresh parsley,
minced
2 tablespoons fresh dill, minced
1 teaspoon oregano
1 teaspoon rosemary
1 teaspoon celery seed

In a large saucepan sauté onion and celery in oil until soft. Add remaining ingredients, cover, bring to boil. Cook over low heat about 2 hours or until beans are tender, stirring occasionally. 257 calories per serving. Serves: 8 +

Jeanette Roderick

BROCCOLI CAULIFLOWER SOUP

1 package frozen cut up broccoli
(10 ounces)
1 package frozen cauliflower
(10 ounces)
1 can chicken broth (10 ounces)
½ teaspoon mustard seed
½ teaspoon dried dill weed
½ teaspoon mace

⅓ cup onion, finely chopped
¼ cup margarine or butter
2 tablespoons flour
½ teaspoon salt
pepper to taste
3½ cups milk
1 cup Swiss cheese, shredded

In 3-quart saucepan cook cauliflower, covered in ½ cup chicken broth until tender. In medium saucepan combine remaining chicken broth, broccoli, mustard seed and dill weed and cook until tender. Remove from heat, cover, and keep warm. Place cauliflower mix and mace in blender and blend until smooth. In 3-quart saucepan cook onion in margarine until tender. Stir in flour, salt, pepper. Add milk, heat and stir until thickened. Add cauliflower mix and shredded cheese to broccoli mix. Stir until cheese is melted. Add all ingredients to milk mixture and heat. Garnish, if desired, with pieces of broccoli. Serves: 4-6.

Jeanne Kelly

A TIME FOR HOT SOUP

The winter of 1875 was intensely cold. Seventy-five fishing vessels were rounding the Cape when fifty of them were caught in ice, blown into Barnstable Bay and frozen in. Volunteers pushed dories over the ice to Provincetown for provisions. Men walked from the vessels to Sandwich and Provincetown over the ice.

RUSSIAN BORSCHT

1 bunch beets	1 medium/large head cabbage
4 or 5 carrots	1 medium onion
5 or 6 potatoes	1 large can Italian tomatoes
½ head celery	pinch of pickling spice or
2 or 3 parsnips	fresh dill
2 green peppers	oil or butter for sautéing
bunch of green beans	sour cream or yogurt

Cut up coarsely beets, carrots, potatoes, celery, parsnips, one green pepper, green beans (and any other vegetables you wish; i.e. peas, squash, corn, etc.). Cover vegetables with water, season with salt and simmer until tender. Meanwhile, chop up cabbage, onion and second green pepper. Sauté in oil or butter, and add to soup. Add can of Italian tomatoes, and the pickling spice or fresh dill. Top with sour cream or yogurt just before serving. Very low in calories, depending on how much butter or oil is used for cooking cabbage. If thinner soup is preferred, add more water.

Janet Signorelli

CARROT SOUP

1 pound carrots, peeled and	2 quarts chicken broth
sliced thin	2 tablespoons chopped parsley
¼ pound butter	½ cup soup macaroni
4 onions, chopped	½ teaspoon chervil
1 teaspoon sugar	

Melt butter in large pot; stir in carrots, onions and sugar. Simmer until vegetables are soft (about 20 minutes). Add 1 quart chicken broth, stir in parsley and bring to boil. Reduce heat and simmer uncovered 30 minutes. Pour into blender, purée, and return to pot. Add remaining broth and simmer uncovered for 15 minutes. Cook pasta *al dente*; drain and add to broth and simmer for 3 minutes. Add chervil and serve.

Karen Olsen

THE FAUNCE DEMONSTRATION FARM

A remarkable and profitable farm operated between 1911 and 1916. This was built on land not previously cultivated and was established to prove that such a farm could be built anywhere on Cape Cod and could be operated at a profit if scientific principles of soil treatment, fertilization, land use, crop rotation, pruning, spraying and other exact procedures were followed. The farm had 150 fruit trees, 3,000 strawberry plants, 600 raspberry bushes, 1600 asparagus roots, a poultry plant, 8 varieties of grapes on south-facing slopes, potatoes as a cash crop, and feed corn and mangel beets for the chickens. Only two men worked here and the budget was minimal.

The Faunce Farm, including its beautiful main house at 111 Main Street, known as Uplands, had been turned over to trustees to serve the public interest on Cape Cod under the will of Mrs. Faunce who died in 1909.

CARROT LEEK BISQUE

2 pounds carrots
1 pound leeks
1 large can chicken broth
¼ pound butter

salt to taste
white pepper to taste
¼ teaspoon nutmeg

Peel and slice carrots thin. Peel and slice tender part of leeks thin. Sauté vegetables in butter until translucent. Add chicken broth and simmer 30 minutes. Purée while hot, until smooth. Add salt, pepper, and nutmeg to taste. Serve with parsley or croutons. Serves: 6-8.

Sherwood Landers

JOE'S CORN CHOWDER

⅓ pound bacon
4 medium onions, chopped fine
6 medium potatoes, cubed small
water

1 can cream-style corn (1 pound)
⅓ can milk (use can corn
  came in)
salt and pepper to taste

Cut bacon in small pieces and fry until crisp. Add chopped onions to bacon fat; continue frying until golden brown. Add potatoes to bacon and onions. Add water to cover. Bring to boil and simmer for at least 2 hours. Stir occasionally, and check the water. Uncover last 30 minutes, cooking until mixture is thick. Secret is the potatoes should be mushy. Add corn, milk, salt and pepper. Heat to simmer. Serve hot with crackers. Serves: 6-8.

Excellent to enjoy in front of a fire on a cold night. Recipe can be doubled or tripled successfully.

Joe Leis

GYPSY SOUP

3-4 tablespoons olive oil
2 cloves garlic, crushed
½ cup celery, chopped
1 cup fresh tomatoes, chopped
1½ cups chick peas (canned)
2 tablespoons paprika
1 teaspoon basil
dash cinnamon
1 bay leaf
1 tablespoon tamari

2 cups onions, chopped
2 cups sweet potatoes, chopped,
  peeled. or winter squash
¾ cup green pepper, chopped
3 cups soup stock or water
1 teaspoon turmeric
1 teaspoon salt
dash cayenne pepper or tabasco
  sauce

In large saucepan sauté onions, garlic, celery, potatoes (or squash) in olive oil for about 5 minutes. Add all seasoning except tamari. Add soup stock or water. Simmer covered 5 minutes. Add tomatoes, peppers and chick peas. Simmer another 10 minutes or so until vegetables are as tender as desired. Add tamari just before removing soup from heat.

Carol Colburn

Sow corn when the oak leaves are the size of a squirrel's ear.

American Indians

LEEK AND POTATO SOUP

2 fat leeks
1 cup celery
1 quart milk
2½ cups potatoes

5 tablespoons butter
2 tablespoons flour
salt and pepper
½ cup lobster (if available)

Cut leeks and celery into very thin slices, crosswise, and cook in 3 tablespoons butter, stirring constantly for 10 minutes. Add milk and cook in double boiler for 40 minutes. Cook and mash potatoes. Melt 2 tablespoons butter, stir in flour; add milk and vegetable mixture, and mashed potatoes. Stir to blend. A small quantity of lobster can be added at the end of cooking. Season with salt and pepper to taste. Serve with split, toasted and buttered common crackers if you can find them.

Shirley Cross

SPLIT PEA SOUP

1 pound dried green split peas
2 quarts water
1 meaty ham bone
1 cup onions, chopped
¼ teaspoon pepper

½ teaspoon garlic powder
½ teaspoon dried marjoram
1 cup celery, chopped
1 cup carrots, chopped

In large pot cover split peas with water. Soak overnight or bring to boil and boil gently for 2 minutes and soak 1 hour. Add ham bone, onion, garlic powder, pepper and marjoram. Simmer covered for 2 hours, stirring occasionally. Remove ham bone and cut off meat. Dice meat; add to soup with carrots and celery. Cook slowly for an additional 45 minutes. Serves: 10 +.

Claudette Powers

PEANUT BUTTER SOUP FOR CHILDREN AND GRANDMAS

1 tablespoon butter
3 tablespoons peanut butter
1 teaspoon onion salt

2 tablespoons flour
2 cups chicken stock (or broth)
1 cup milk

In top of double boiler heat butter, peanut butter, and onion salt. Stir in flour until smooth. Add chicken stock; stir well, and cook 20 minutes. Just before serving add milk and season to taste. Stir mixture well and serve. Serves: 2.

Marie Olander

Geraniums growing in an open window will prevent flies from entering the room.

CREAM OF TOMATO SOUP

1 medium sized can tomatoes
½ small onion
1 tablespoon sugar
½ teaspoon soda

1 quart milk
¼ cup flour
4 tablespoons butter, melted
⅓ teaspoon salt

Cook together tomatoes, onion, and sugar for 15 minutes. Blend in blender to purée. Add soda. Make cream sauce with melted butter, flour, and milk, adding milk slowly, stirring constantly, to avoid lumps. Heat until thickened. Combine cream sauce with tomato mixture. Heat, mixing ingredients well, and serve. Serves: 4.

Abigail Cullity

TURNIP AND PEA SOUP

1 pound white Cape Cod turnip,
  cut in chunks
1 large onion, chopped
3 cups seasoned water or stock
salt and pepper

2 tablespoons butter
2 cups peas, frozen or fresh
1 cup instant dry milk or can of
  evaporated milk

Cook turnip and onion in stock until soft. Cool slightly; blend in blender. Add dry milk (if using canned milk, add it last), 2 tablespoons butter and frozen peas, defrosted. Blend all together; season with salt and pepper. Heat and serve.

VICHYSSOISE

6 leeks or small onions
6 medium yellow onions
6 medium potatoes, peeled
¼ pound butter

1 pint chicken broth
1 pint cream
1 pint milk
1 tablespoon chives (to float)

Sauté leeks in butter until clear. Boil onions and potatoes until soft. Drain; reserve liquid and purée solids. Combine purée with liquids; chill 12 hours. Sprinkle chives on top before serving. Serves: 8.

Ruth Bergstrom

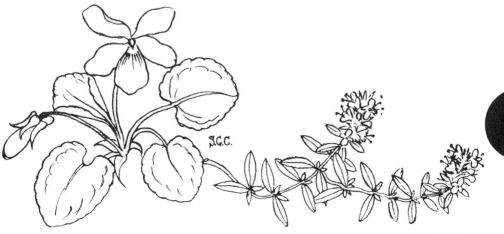

TURKEY VEGETABLE SOUP

roast turkey carcass
8 cups water
2 onions, peeled and chopped
2 bay leaves
1 cup celery, diced
1 tablespoon parsley
1 teaspoon salt
¼ teaspoon pepper
1 large can tomatoes, undrained,
   chopped

2 cups cooked turkey)
3 carrots, scraped and sliced
1 package frozen corn kernels
   (10 ounces)
½ teaspoon dried basil
2 cups tomato juice
1½ cups elbow macaroni
1 small green pepper, chopped
   (optional)

Remove stuffing from turkey carcass; break carcass up to fit in large saucepan. Add water, onions, bay leaves, celery, parsley, salt and pepper to pan and simmer for 2 hours. Remove from stove, cool slightly, remove bones. Cut any meat from bones into small chunks. Discard bones and return meat to pan. Add tomatoes, carrots, corn, basil, and tomato juice and simmer for 15 minutes more. Remove bay leaves. Add macaroni and green pepper and simmer until macaroni is tender, about 15 minutes.

This soup freezes well, but if you are freezing it, omit the macaroni and pepper until you are preparing to serve it. Serves: 8.

WINTER SQUASH SOUP

1 large butternut squash (about
   3 pounds)
3 tablespoons butter
2 large tart apples, peeled,
   cored, chopped
3 cups chicken broth
¼ teaspoon thyme
¼ teaspoon pepper
2 bay leaves

¼ teaspoon nutmeg
¼ teaspoon cinnamon
1 tablespoon brown sugar
   (optional)
1 cup light cream
3 tablespoons sherry (optional)
1 teaspoon salt
1/8 teaspoon white pepper
   (optional)

GARNISH:
2 tablespoons finely chopped nuts

Cut squash in half and scoop out seeds. Peel squash; cut into 2" chunks. Sauté onion in butter until limp, about three minutes. Stir in squash, apples and chicken broth. Add thyme, pepper, bay leaves, nutmeg, cinnamon, brown sugar to the squash-apple mixture. Simmer covered for 25-30 minutes, until squash is done. Cool slightly, remove bay leaves. Purée mixture, in small batches, in blender. Return purée to pot and add cream, sherry, salt, and white pepper. Reheat soup to hot but not boiling. Serve with chopped nuts as garnish. Serves: 6.

Pat Bryant

ZUCCHINI SOUP

3 large onions
2 green peppers
5 pounds zucchini, unpeeled
3 cloves garlic
1 cup fresh basil
   OR ½ teaspoon powdered basil
   OR ¼ cup dried basil
½ teaspoon pepper

6 tablespoons butter
½ cup water
2 teaspoons salt
milk (when served hot)
chicken stock (when served hot)
½ cup sour cream (when served
   cold)

Cut up onions, green peppers, and zucchini. Combine basil, water, salt, pepper, garlic, and butter with zucchini mixture and cook until vegetables are tender. Purée in food processor or blender. Cool. Freeze in portions. Serves: 6-8.

To serve: HOT: Add an equal portion of milk, chicken stock or any other stock. Mix well. COLD: Add sour cream to 1-quart base. Mix well.

Marcelia Berry

CHICKEN CHOWDER

2 tablespoons onion, minced
2 tablespoons margarine
1 cup potatoes, diced raw
½ cup celery, diced
1 cup chicken broth
1 cup peas
1 cup chopped cooked chicken
1 large can cream style corn

2 cups milk
½ teaspoon salt
1/8 teaspoon paprika
1/8 teaspoon pepper
¼ teaspoon curry powder
1 cup cooked noodles
1 tablespoon parsley, chopped

Sauté onion in margarine for 5 minutes. Add potatoes, celery, and broth. Cook 20 minutes. Add remaining ingredients and simmer 30 minutes. Serves: 8.

Peggy Wilson

FISH CHOWDER

1 pound haddock (or other
   white fish)
1 cup cold water
¼ cup salt pork, diced
2 cups potatoes, peeled and
   thinly sliced

3 tablespoons onion, chopped
½ cup water
3 cups milk
salt to taste
pepper to taste
butter

Bone fish and simmer in cup of cold water about 10 minutes. Remove fish and reserve stock. Peel off skin and discard it. Sauté diced salt pork until crisp. Put in saucepan with fish. Add potatoes, onions and ½ cup water. Cook, covered, for 10 minutes. Add this to fish stock and simmer mixture for 5 minutes. Add milk, salt, and pepper to mixture and bring to boiling but do not boil. Just before serving, add small amount of butter to each serving. Serves: 4-6.

Bertha MacAusland

NEW ENGLAND CLAM CHOWDER

3 cups clams, shucked
¼ pound salt pork, diced
3 medium potatoes, pared, diced
½ cup onions, chopped
1 cup water
2 cups milk

1 cup light cream
2 tablespoons flour (optional)
1 teaspoon salt
½ teaspoon pepper
2 tablespoons butter (optional)

Drain clams, reserving liquid. Add reserved liquid to water and boil potatoes until just barely soft. In frying pan, fry salt pork until crisp. Remove pork bits, add potatoes. Sauté onions in salt pork fat until soft. Combine onions and potato mixture. Add clams, milk, cream, salt and pepper to chowder mixture; heat to just below boiling. If you like thicker chowder, mix flour with a little water to form a thin paste and add to chowder, stirring until soup is slightly thickened. At serving time, a small amount of butter may be added to each serving, if desired. Quahogs or little neck clams make the best New England Chowder but canned minced clams may also be used. Serves: 6.

How thick clam chowder should be promotes many a discussion around the dinner table. The answer is probably, "however thick you like it". Serving salt crackers or biscuits to be crumbled up in the chowder seems to satisfy some "old salts" who insist that a soup spoon stand straight up in the bowl!

Pat Bryant

"Cape Cod Chowder should be served piping hot with old-fashioned big round thick crackers called pilot crackers. Some folk prefer the old-time smaller, round easily split, common crackers. In the old-time country store there was always a barrel of these and they were sold by the dozen, not by the pound. But I prefer the big flat pilots." Thornton W. Burgess, author.

DANIEL WEBSTER'S FISH CHOWDER

This, in his own words, is Daniel Webster's recipe for Fish Chowder. "Suitable," he said, "for a large fishing party."

"Take a cod of ten pounds, well cleaned, leaving on the skin. Cut into pieces 1½ pounds thick, preserving the head whole. Take 1½ pounds of clear, fat, salt pork, cut in thin slices. Do the same with 12 potatoes. Take the largest pot you have. Try out the pork first; then take out the pieces of pork, leaving in the drippings. Add to that three parts of water, a layer of fish, so as to cover the bottom of the pot; next, a layer of potatoes, then 2 tablespoons of salt, 1 tablespoon of pepper, then the pork, another layer of fish, and the remainder of the potatoes.

"Fill the pot with water to cover the ingredients. Put over a good fire, let the chowder boil 25 minutes. When this is done, have a quart of boiling milk ready, and ten hard crackers split and dipped in cold water. Add milk and crackers. Let the whole boil 5 minutes. The chowder is then ready and will be first rate if you have followed the directions. An onion may be added if you like the flavor."

LOBSTER CHOWDER

2 small lobsters, cooked
2 cups water
1 cup chicken stock or broth
¼ cup onions, chopped
2 celery stalks, chopped
2 carrots, cut up
1 bay leaf
4 peppercorns
2 tablespoons onion, finely
    chopped

1 cup potatoes, cooked, diced
3 cups milk
1 cup light cream
¼ cup butter
¼ cup flour
1 teaspoon salt
1/8 teaspoon pepper
¼ teaspoon nutmeg
paprika
parsley

Remove lobster meat from shell and cut into cubes. Save coral roe, if any. Cover broken up shell with water, chicken stock and mix in onions, celery, carrots, bay leaf, and peppercorns. Simmer about 20 minutes. Remove shells; strain stock through fine sieve or cheesecloth. Return stock to saucepan and add finely chopped onion and potatoes. Simmer until potatoes are tender. Force roe through a fine sieve; mix with butter and flour. Heat milk and gradually pour into roe mixture, stirring until milk is slightly thickened. Add roe-milk mixture with salt, pepper, and nutmeg to potato-lobster stock, constantly stirring. Heat to just below boiling point. Mix in light cream and lobster meat, stirring until everything is heated through. Serve with sprinkle of paprika and parsley in each bowl. Serves: 6.

OYSTER STEW

1 pint oysters (with liquid)
¼ cup butter
1 cup light cream, scalded
½ teaspoon paprika

3 cups milk, scalded
pepper
½ teaspoon salt

Pick over oysters; then cook in butter and oyster liquid until edges curl. Add cream and milk. Heat to boiling and season. Serve at once with crackers. Serves: 4.

In old New England a bowl of piping hot oyster stew formed the traditional Christmas Eve supper. Coming from the Merrie England of their ancestors, the custom of serving oysters on Christmas was quite natural in a country which had an abundance of delicately flavored oysters.

Union Oyster House, Boston, Mass., Established 1826

QUAHAUG CHOWDER

2 dozen medium-sized quahaugs
4 cups diced potatoes
1 quart milk

3 or 4 slices fat salt pork
3 medium onions, chopped

Grind quahaugs and save liquid. Add water to quahaug juice to make 1 quart. Boil 4 cups diced potatoes in the juice until nearly done. Dice 3 or 4 slices fat salt pork and fry until brown and crispy. Add 3 medium onions, chopped, and fry. Add to potatoes and quahaugs. Cook together until tender. Add 1 quart milk and heat until boiling. Serves: 4-5.

Jackie Staples

MYSTERY SOUP

This soup has no fixed recipe and as a result never turns out the same. However, it is a great way to use up leftover roasts and "veggies" that are looking a little tired.

Save the drippings in the roasting pan from a beef roast or chicken. Add two cups water to heated drippings and scrape pan. Pour this into container and cool until excess fat can be removed. Combine half cup (or so) of chopped onions and two crushed garlic cloves with butter or margarine in large saucepan and sauté for about three minutes. Add 6 cups water and 3 or 4 bouillon cubes (beef or chicken) and reserved drippings to saucepan; heat until the bouillon cubes dissolve. Add as much meat as you care to, cut in bite-size pieces (about 2 cups). Now you have your base or "stock".

Now comes the intriguing part. Look in your refrigerator and cupboards for inspiration. Just about any vegetable that holds its shape during cooking can go into your stock. Some possibilities are the following:

beans (any kind, fresh, frozen, canned)	celery, stalks, leaves	peppers (green or red)
	chard, spinach	potatoes
dried beans (soaked and softened first)	corn	pasta
broccoli	leeks, scallions	rice
cabbage	mushrooms	summer squash, zucchini
carrots	okra	tomatoes
cauliflower	peas, pea pods	turnips

Spices and herbs do wonders for enhancing flavors and making a dull soup a conversation piece. Here are some possibilities:

basil	thyme	rosemary
bay leaves	marjoram	pepper (black, white,
chili powder	nutmeg	cayenne)
ginger root	oregano	

Use your own judgment as to assortments and quantities of vegetables and flavorings to add. If your soup suffers from overcrowding, add more water and bouillon (1 cup to 1 cube). Tasting is the only way to go when you make this soup. If your product brings compliments, take a bow. If it turns out "so-so", don't let anyone know "who done it".

Pat Bryant

DANIEL WEBSTER 1782-1852

Webster, the famous orator, lawyer and statesman, and other business and political leaders from Boston enjoyed coming to Sandwich and Mashpee for hunting or fishing at various seasons, and always retained the services of a local guide called "John Trout". He was John Denson who lived on Main Street, Sandwich near Pine Street. Webster complained that after 1825 the new glassworkers took over many of his favorite spots for fishing or gunning. Nevertheless, he kept coming, and had a favorite room in the Fessenden Tavern, in the new section built in 1830 by General Sabin Smith. He was popular in the Tavern bar for standing drinks for all hands. He had a splendid house in Marshfield, where he is buried.

BERRY SOUP

2 cups strawberries, hulled and
halved
1 cup raspberries
⅓ cup sugar
1 tablespoon cornstarch

⅓ cup cold water
¼ cup fruit flavored liqueur or
brandy
½ teaspoon grated lemon peel
½ cup sweetened whipped cream

Heat strawberries, raspberries and sugar gently in saucepan to extract the juices. Set aside for 15 minutes. Mix cornstarch with cold water until smooth. Stir into berry mixture. Bring berry mixture to a gentle boil; stir constantly until soup is thickened. Remove from heat; add liqueur and lemon peel. Refrigerate several hours. Serve in dessert bowls with topping of whipped cream. Serves: 4-5.

BLUEBERRY SOUP

1 quart fresh blueberries
¼ cup fresh lemon juice
⅔ cup sugar
2 tablespoons cornstarch
¼ teaspoon cinnamon

1 cup water
1 cup dry white wine
½" thick lemon slice, seeds
removed
½ teaspoon vanilla

TOPPING:

⅔ cup plain yogurt
1 tablespoon sugar

½ teaspoon vanilla

Combine 2 cups blueberries and lemon juice in large saucepan; simmer, stirring, a few minutes, until berries become soft and release juices. Let mixture cool slightly and place in blender. Add sugar, cornstarch, and cinnamon to blender. Blend until mixture is well pureed. Strain purée through fine sieve into saucepan. Press purée to force all juice through strainer. Stir in water, wine and lemon slice. Boil mixture until it thickens slightly. Remove from heat; stir in vanilla. Cool to room temperature. Remove lemon slice; gently stir in remaining 2 cups blueberries; refrigerate 6-12 hours. At serving time, stir soup until blueberries are well blended and soup is smooth. Add generous topping of yogurt mixture to center of each serving.

Topping: Mix yogurt, sugar and vanilla together and refrigerate for several hours. Serves: 4-5.

Barbara Nolan

GREEK EGG AND LEMON SOUP

5 cups homemade chicken broth
⅓ cup rice, uncooked
3 egg yolks

3 tablespoons lemon juice
grated lemon rind

Cook rice in chicken broth 20-25 minutes. Rice should be very soft. Beat egg yolks until light and very thick. Add a little broth to egg yolks and blend well, then slowly add mixture to soup, stirring constantly over low heat until broth is slightly thickened. Remove from heat, and add lemon juice and rind. Allow to stand 5 minutes before serving.

Mardi Mauney

CHEDDAR CHEESE SOUP

2 carrots, scraped and sliced
2 cups potato, diced
¼ cup onion, chopped
1 cup water
3 tablespoons butter
salt to taste
1 cup cooked ham, diced
(optional)

3 tablespoons flour
2½ cups milk
1½ cups chicken stock or broth
1½ cups sharp cheddar cheese,
grated
cayenne pepper to taste
pepper to taste

Combine carrots, potato, onion, and water in large saucepan and simmer, covered, 20 minutes or until they are very tender. Cool mixture slightly, and purée it in blender until smooth. In another saucepan, mix butter, salt, pepper and flour; heat until it forms a smooth paste. Gradually add milk, stirring constantly. Add purée to milk mixture; stir until smooth. Add chicken stock, cheddar cheese and cayenne pepper. Keep heat very low and stir constantly until cheese is melted and soup is well blended. Add ham bits if desired, and reheat to just below boiling. Serves: 4-6.

BEEF STOCK

2 pounds lean beef, cut up
2 pounds beef bones, cracked
2 carrots, unpeeled
2 onions, unpeeled
2 stalks celery
1 garlic clove

½ teaspoon thyme
1 bay leaf
3 parsley sprigs
4 quarts cold water
2 tablespoons tomato paste
1 cup dry white wine

Place meat and bones in roasting pan and brown for 10 minutes. Add vegetables and lightly brown. Transfer to stock pot and add rest of ingredients. Bring very slowly to simmer; simmer for 4 hours. Remove any scum that surfaces while cooking. Slow cooking produces a clearer broth. When stock is reduced to good flavor, strain through a fine sieve or dampened cheese cloth. Do not season. Seasoning will depend on use. Use to flavor soups, stews, gravies, and sauces. Can be frozen in ice cube trays and stored in plastic bag in freezer.

CHICKEN STOCK

2 large carrots, sliced
2 celery stalks, sliced
3-4 pounds chicken necks, backs,
giblets (no livers) or 4 pounds
stewing fowl

2 large unpeeled onions, cut in
quarters
4 black peppercorns
4 cloves
4 quarts cold water

Put all in stock pot and bring very slowly to simmer. Simmer until stock is reduced and has a good flavor. Strain through a fine sieve or dampened cheese cloth. Can be frozen in ice cube trays and stored in plastic bag in freezer.

FISH STOCK

½ cup oil
½ cup carrots, chopped
2½ cups onions, chopped
2½ cups celery, chopped
4 sprigs parsley
4 black peppercorns

½ cup dry white wine
1½ quarts water
1 bay leaf
2½-3 pounds fish heads
 and bones

Heat oil and soften vegetables until they just begin to take on color. Add wine, water and fish. Bring to boil and skim. Add seasonings and simmer for 2 hours. Strain through fine sieve or dampened cheese cloth. Can be frozen in ice cube trays and put into plastic bag in freezer to be used when needed.

THE TAVERN AND ROAD NETWORK

Before the American Revolution, travel up-country was done on horseback. Goods could be moved by oxcart but only very slowly and not in the winter or spring. The only roads for passenger vehicles were in the immediate area of the cities. Every town had a tavern or public house where travelers could put up overnight and stable their horses. A record of such a trip is preserved in the diary of Benjamin Percival of South Sandwich, who in June 1795 journeyed to see his relations and friends who had established a new settlement in the Berkshires at Lee and Lenox. Many Cape Cod families moved there before and during the Revolution. Percival traveled on horseback with several friends. His record of the return trip from Lee to Sandwich is as follows:

Monday (June 29, 1795) Set out for home this morning. Got to Addams' Tavern in Becket by 9 o'clock. From there to Alexander's Tavern in Chester by 12 o'clock. Bailed (fed and watered) our horses, went to Park's Tavern in Russell, then to Douglas' Tavern in Westfield, then to Stebbins' Tavern in Westfield where we stayed all night.

Tuesday. From Stebbins' crossed (the Conn. River) at Springfield Ferry. Rode to Sikes' Tavern in Wilbraham before 8 o'clock. From there through Palmer, stopped at Powers' Tavern in Brimfield and bailed our horses. Rode through part of Weston to Rice's Tavern in Brookfield where we stopped, it being very hot. We came to Livemore's Tavern in Spencer where we stayed, having travelled 41 miles.

Wednesday. Came to Waite's Tavern in Leicester, got a glass of bitters, then came to Moore's Tavern in Worcester. Got shaved and got breakfast. Came to Grafton to Wood's Tavern, had some cider, came to Kingsley's Tavern in Upton, called at Amidon's in Mendon, to Penniman's in Milford to avoid a shower, and stayed at Thurston's Tavern in Franklin — 38 miles.

Thursday. Set off from Thurston's and rode to Gilbert's Tavern in Mansfield by 7 o'clock, from there to Crocker's Tavern in Taunton. Bailed our horses and came to Foster's Tavern in Middleboro — 36 miles.

Friday July 3. Arrived in town at Fessenden's about noon today.

After 1790, with sound currency and Federal encouragement, better public roads began to be built and even privately built turnpikes with toll stations, so that stage coaches could be operated on a regular schedule. Benjamin Percival rejoiced in sharing a weekly Boston newspaper with General Freeman and noted in 1800 "wagons and chaises are coming into general use for travel".

SHELLFISH STOCK

2½ cups water
2 whole cloves
6 black peppercorns
crushed shells from lobster,
  shrimp or crab

1 onion, chopped
4 stalks celery with leaves,
  chopped
2 packages instant chicken broth

Crush shells in blender. Simmer all together for ½ hour. Strain through fine sieve or dampened cheese cloth. Use to flavor sauces for seafood. Can be frozen in ice cube trays and stored in plastic bag in freezer.

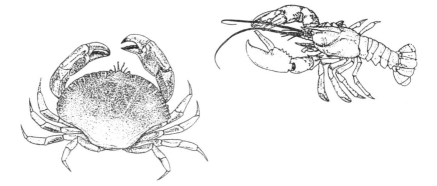

*A swarm of bees in May
Is worth a load of hay.
A swarm of bees in June
Is worth a silver spoon.
A swarm of bees in July
Is not worth a fly.*

Vegetables

CROW FARM, SANDWICH

The Almshouse was closed in 1901 and finally burned down in 1911. The property was bought by Henry A. Belcher of Boston, who had married a Nye girl of Sandwich and lived in the house at 127 Main St. at Tupper Road. Belcher reportedly intended to make the Charles St. property into a gentleman's farm, but gave up and sold it in 1916 to brothers David and Lincoln Crowell. It has been in successful operation since then as Crow Farm and continues to grow and sell fruits and vegetables through its own popular farm stand and other outlets. The farm is operated by David's son Howard, whose sisters, Carolyn Crowell and Eleanor (Mrs. John Winslow) occupy other houses on the property.

The illustration shows an earlier stand of about 1935.

167

ROBERT MAY'S COOKERY

This ancient classic is owned by a Burgess Society member in Sandwich. The author, Robert May, had worked for noble houses in England which could afford the game, shellfish and imported luxury foods and spices which are called for in the recipes. When the book was first written in 1664, May was rejoicing at the return of the Royal House under Charles II and the resumption of privileged entertaining by the upper classes after the rigors of the Puritan period under Cromwell.

The book suggests a bill of fare for each of the major holidays such as All Saints Nov. 1, when twenty main dishes were recommended including:

A capon in stewed broth with marrow bones
A goose stuffed, or two ducks
A grand salad
A shoulder of mutton with oysters
A roast chine of beef
Minced pies of capons, tongue, or veal
A swan or two roast geese

This set of dishes ended with a "double bordered custard." After a pause, a second course of another twenty dishes is listed, including a roast lamb, two herons, a potato pie, a pair of pheasants, a marinated fish such as pike, carp or bream, etc. A large number of guests would be served at such a feast, but still the quantities per person would be staggering by modern standards. It was an age of gluttony.

Full instructions are given for preparing each dish, involving much fat, much butter, much fruit and heavy sauces spread over each dish, so that the calories were beyond counting. Abundant spices from Asia as well as fruit from the Mediterranean were available to the rich, and were used lavishly.

168

FATHER'S BAKED BEANS

1 pound pea or yellow-eye beans
1 tablespoon sugar
1½ teaspoons salt
1 tablespoon dry mustard or
ginger

1 level teaspoon baking soda
⅓ cup molasses (dark)
1 large onion
chunk of salt pork 2"x1"
(½ pound)

Soak beans overnight. Bring to boil and simmer about an hour or until a few beans on spoon "blow back" (you can blow the skins back). Add other ingredients and put into casserole or bean pot. Add enough water to cover fully. Preheat oven to 300°. Cover pot tightly (you can use foil). Cook 4 to 6 hours. About every 2 hours, check to see if they need more water. Serves: 8.

To double recipe, add another tablespoon sugar and salt to taste and double molasses. Other ingredients remain the same.   *Russell Lovell*

LIMA BEAN CASSEROLE

1 package (1 pound) dried lima
beans
5 large stalks celery
3 large green peppers
3 medium onions
2 garlic cloves

3 cups chicken broth or bean
liquid
3 teaspoons salt — or less
1½ cups raisins
3 cups cheddar cheese, grated

Cover beans with water; boil until tender, about ½-¾ hour. Drain, saving liquid. Chop celery, green peppers, onions and garlic; sauté in vegetable oil until tender. Add to vegetables the chicken broth or bean liquid, salt, raisins, cheese and beans. Put into casserole and bake at 350° for one hour. Serves: 15.

Virginia Rockwell

SKILLET CABBAGE

4 cups cabbage, shredded
(½ head usually)
1 green pepper, diced
1½ cups celery, diced
1 tablespoon sugar

1 onion, chopped
2 tomatoes, chopped
2 tablespoons bacon drippings
(or other fat)

Combine in large skillet; cover and cook 10 minutes. Serves: 4.

Harriet Clark

A bayleaf placed on top of any flours, meal or grains which might become insect infested protects from bothersome pests.

COPPER PENNIES

2 pounds carrots, sliced, cooked
   until crisp, drained
1 large green pepper, chopped
1 large onion, chopped
1 can tomato soup

½ cup salad oil
1 cup sugar (or a little less)
¾ cup vinegar
salt and pepper to taste

In large bowl, combine onion, pepper and carrots. Bring remaining ingredients to boil. Pour over carrots and mix well. Cool and refrigerate. Best if made a day ahead. Drain excess liquid before serving. (I use the liquid on a tossed salad). Serves: 6.

Brooke Smith Nagtegaal
A similar recipe was submitted by Naomi White.

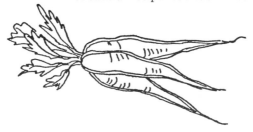

CARROT LOAF

2 cups carrots, cooked and
   mashed
¼ cup evaporated milk
2 eggs

½ teaspoon salt or to taste
1/8 teaspoon pepper or to taste
2 tablespoons sugar

Combine all ingredients. Place in greased casserole and bake uncovered in pan of hot water at 350° for about 45 minutes.

Gladys M. Burgess

TURMERIC CAULIFLOWER

1 tablespoon slivered fresh
   ginger
¼ teaspoon turmeric
1 small head cauliflower

3 tablespoons peanut or vegetable
   oil
¼ cup water

Break cauliflower into flowerets. Sauté ginger quickly in hot oil. Add cauliflower and stir fry. Add water, turmeric and stir. Cover and steam until just tender.

Brian Cullity

When the corn husks are thick, the winter will be a severe one.
Indian tribes of New England

CORN FRITTERS

1 cup canned corn
1 egg beaten
2 tablespoons oil or melted
  butter
1 tablespoon milk

½ cup flour
½ teaspoon baking powder
½ teaspoon salt
pepper to taste

Sift dry ingredients into bowl. Beat egg and add oil, milk and corn. Mix all together. Drop from spoon in hot fat in fry pan. Brown on both sides.

CORN PUDDING

2 cups whole corn
2 tablespoons flour
2 tablespoons sugar
3 tablespoons butter

1 teaspoon salt
3 eggs
1¾ cups milk

Combine first 5 ingredients in blender. Add eggs one at a time. Add milk and blend well. Pour into greased 1½-quart baking dish. Bake for 45 minutes at 325° or until knife inserted comes out clean. Serves: 6.

Louise Martens

CORN PUDDING II

1 can cream style corn
½ can (1 cup) milk
2 eggs
cheddar cheese, sliced thin

¼ cup green pepper
salt and pepper to taste
rolled cracker crumbs

Empty corn into greased baking dish. Measure milk into empty corn can and add eggs. Beat slightly with fork. Combine with corn, green pepper in baking dish; season to taste. Cover with rolled cracker crumbs and thin slices of cheddar cheese. Bake at 350° for 1 hour.

Corn-planting rhymes: —
One for the cut-worm,
One for the crow,
One for the blackbird,
And three to grow.

171

BLACK-EYED PEAS

1½ cups black-eyed peas	2 cloves garlic
3 cups water or stock	¼ teaspoon red pepper
1 medium onion, chopped	1 bay leaf
3 tablespoons raw rice	1 teaspoon salt
3 tablespoons oil	¼ teaspoon marjoram

Mix all together in pan and simmer 45 minutes or until tender. Serve with old-fashioned stewed tomatoes.

NEW POTATOES WITH SOUR CREAM AND DILL

12 small, red-skinned, new potatoes	½ cup sour cream
	2 tablespoons fresh dill

Leaving skins on, wash potatoes and put to boil in cold salted water; cook until tender. Peel or not, as desired. Toss in sour cream mixed with chopped dill.

FABULOUS FRIED ONION RINGS

1½ cups all-purpose flour	3 very large yellow onions (use Bermudas if you wish)
1½ cups beer, active or flat, cold or room temperature	3-4 cups shortening

Combine flour and beer in large bowl and blend thoroughly, using whisk. Cover bowl; allow to sit at room temperature for no less than 3 hours. Twenty minutes before ready to use batter, pre-heat oven to 200°. Place brown paper on cookie sheet. Peel onions carefully — and cut into ¼" thick slices. Separate slices and set aside. Melt shortening in skillet or deep fat fryer and heat to 375° (use thermometer if possible). Dip onion slices into batter with tongs — fry rings, turning once or twice until they are an even golden brown. Put on paper bags — and place in oven until all have been fried. Serves: 6.

These can be frozen — and packed in plastic bags. To reheat — arrange on cookie sheet and place in pre-heated oven 400° for 4-6 minutes.   *Polly Leis*

SAUTÉED CUCUMBERS

4 medium sized cucumbers
salt and pepper

4 tablespoons butter

Peel cucumbers, quarter lengthwise, and remove seeds. Cut into 2"x2½" pieces of equal length. Cook in kettle of rapidly boiling, salted water until barely tender. Drain, dip in cold water to stop cooking; drain. When ready to serve, heat quickly and gently in melted butter until heated through. Season to taste; serve immediately. Serves: 4.

Gloria K. Fox

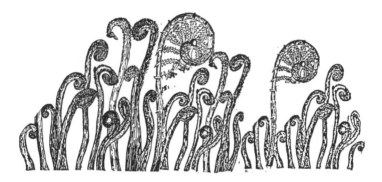

FIDDLEHEADS

The fiddlehead comes from the fiddlehead or ostrich fern. It is the soft, budding head of the plant which breaks through the ground in spring. It gets its name from its resemblance to the scrolling, curved head of a violin. Its flavor is described as a cross between that of asparagus and mushrooms. Pick only the ostrich fern.

TO PREPARE: Gently wash trimmed fiddleheads in several changes of cold water. Drain. Blanch the fiddleheads in a rapidly boiling kettle of salted water for one minute, then cool immediately. When ready to serve, heat quickly and gently in skillet with melted butter. Season to taste with salt and pepper.

Gloria K. Fox

Apart from the vegetables grown by cultivation, the forests and wilds provided a wealth of greens. Fiddleheads, an edible portion of the ostrich fern, were picked in the spring and served as a cooked vegetable, as were dandelion greens, sour dock, sheep's sorrel and lamb's quarters. Wild goose grass and other marsh grasses were used as much for a spring tonic as for a vegetable. Dulse, a type of seaweed which is harvested from the rocks at low tide and spread on the grass to dry, is even today a popular treat.

GLAZED ONIONS

16 small white onions
4 tablespoons sugar

6 tablespoons butter
salt

Peel onions and pierce root end with point of sharp knife. Boil in pan of cold, salted water. Cook until tender. Drain; pat dry with paper towels. Set aside. When ready to serve, melt butter in large skillet and add sugar. Cook slowly over moderate heat until mixture begins to caramelize. Add onions, and shake pan to coat onions with glaze. Watch carefully to insure mixture does not burn. When onions are coated and glazed, remove to serving dish. Serves: 4-6.

PARSNIP STEW

¼ pound salt pork, sliced
3 or 4 parsnips, sliced
4 or 5 small onions, sliced
1 cup water

4 or 5 potatoes, sliced
salt and pepper
parsley

Fry salt pork and leave in pot. Add vegetables, salt and about 1 cup of water. Simmer until vegetables are tender, add more water if necessary. When done it should be like gravy. Season to taste; add parsley. (I have made this stew with butter instead of salt pork, but it does not have as much flavor.)

This is an old Cape Cod recipe.

BROCCOLI/POTATO BAKE

3 cups hot mashed potato
1 3-ounce package cream cheese
¼ cup milk
1 egg
2 tablespoons butter

1 small can French fried onions
2 packages frozen broccoli spears,
    thawed — sliced lengthwise
1 cup shredded American cheese
salt and pepper to taste

Mix first five ingredients until smooth. Season to taste with salt and pepper. Fold in one-half can onions. Spread potato mixture in buttered 8"x12" pan (on bottom and up sides). Bake at 350° uncovered 25-30 minutes or until golden brown. Arrange broccoli on potato shell. Sprinkle with cheese and remaining onions. Bake uncovered for 5 minutes more. Serves: 6-8.

Amy Locherbie Ware

TO DRESS A POTATO

An old time Receipt Book states: To dress a potato, wash it well, but let there be no scraping. At the thickest end cut off a piece the size of a sixpence. This is the "safety valve" by which the steam, generated in the potato, escapes; and such escape prevents cracking. Pour all the water off, and let the skins be thoroughly dry before peeling.

POTATO BARGAIN OR STIFLE

6 or 8 thin slices salt pork
4 medium onions, sliced

8 potatoes, sliced thin
salt and pepper to taste

Fry salt pork in iron fry pan slowly; do not brown. Layer potatoes, onions and salt and pepper each layer. Barely cover with water, cover fry pan and simmer until potatoes are done and sauce has thickened, stirring occasionally. The amount of onions can vary according to taste. This is an old Cape Cod recipe for a single dish supper, more or less a hard times or depression meal.

Rosanna Cullity

POTATO BARGAIN VERSUS POMME DE TERRE ANNA

The King of Cape Dishes finds a rival in Paris. It was necessary to come to Paris to find the origin of our Cape Cod "Potato Bargain," otherwise known as "Stifle," "Smother" and "Sailor's Hurry."

Here in a hotel on the Champs Elysees one can get the very thing only in a French oven and under the name of Pomme de Terre Anna.

On Cape Cod we make ours by slicing eight raw potatoes quite thin and leaving them in water while we fry out in an iron frying pan some thin slices of salt pork, eight slices, two by four inches; fry slowly and do not brown. Put in part of the potatoes and slice an onion over them, a little salt and pepper, then another layer of potato, onion and seasoning, repeat, using four onions in all. There is usually water enough to cook them but it may be necessary to add a little. Cover the pan and cook slowly. Stir occasionally and at the last take off cover so the potatoes will be quite free from water when done.

Pomme de Terre Anna is started in the same way but before the potatoes are quite done they are put in a hot oven or under a broiler and browned on top. Without doubt, here in France they hold a red-hot iron over them to brown them. They have an iron on purpose for browning dishes, something like a thin stove lid with a long handle.

This Parisian rival is very delicious but would not satisfy a hungry fisherman as "Potato Bargain" does.

GOLDEN POTATO CASSEROLE

6 medium potatoes
10 ounces sharp cheese, grated
3 tablespoons milk
2 tablespoons melted butter
⅓ cup bread crumbs

1 pint sour cream
1 bunch green onions
1 teaspoon salt
1/8 teaspoon pepper

Boil potatoes, cool, peel and grate with coarse grater. Combine with sour cream, chopped green onions, milk and seasonings. Turn into a buttered 9"x13" dish. Smooth top with spatula. Combine melted butter and bread crumbs; sprinkle on top. Bake at 350° for 50 minutes. Serves: 8.

Pam Anderson

DORIS' SWEET AND SOUR YAMS AND PINEAPPLE

1 20-ounce can pineapple slices
1 tablespoon cornstarch
¼ teaspoon salt
3 tablespoons vinegar
1 tablespoon oil

4 green onions, diagonally sliced
½ cup celery, diagonally sliced
½ cup green pepper, chopped
2 16-ounce cans Louisiana yams, drained

Drain pineapple, reserving juice. Combine reserved juice, cornstarch and salt in saucepan and mix well. Continue stirring until sauce boils and thickens. Stir in vinegar. Add yams and pineapple slices; cover and simmer. Stir fry onions, celery and green pepper for 4 minutes. Combine with yams and pineapple. Serve immediately.

YAM SOUFFLÉ

6 egg whites
¼ cup sugar
¼ teaspoon mace
1 cup light cream

½ teaspoon salt
¼ teaspoon cinnamon
1 tablespoon grated orange peel
1 can, 24 ounces, yams, drained

In large bowl, let egg whites warm to room temperature. Pre-heat oven to 375°. Beat egg whites to soft peaks; gradually add sugar until stiff peaks form. In another bowl, combine yams, ¼ cup sugar, cinnamon, mace, and orange peel. Beat at high speed until smooth. Fold ⅓ of beaten egg whites into mixture, and blend thoroughly. Lightly fold in rest of egg whites. Gently turn into 1½ quart, straight-sided, buttered soufflé dish. Bake for 45 minutes until puffy and golden brown. Serve at once with butter.

RATATOUILLE NIÇOISE

⅓ cup olive oil
2 or more cloves garlic, chopped
1 large onion, sliced
2 medium zucchini, sliced
1 eggplant, peeled and cubed
1 or 2 tablespoons capers

3 tablespoons flour
2 green peppers, cut in strips
4 or 5 tomatoes, peeled and sliced
salt and pepper

In large skillet add garlic and onion to heated oil; cook until transparent. Combine squash and eggplant with flour, add this and green peppers to onion, cover and cook slowly about half an hour. Add tomatoes and simmer uncovered until mixture is thick. Season with salt and pepper. Add capers during last 15 minutes of cooking. Serve hot or cold.

NOTE: an interesting touch is added if sliced ripe olives are used as garnish.
Serves: 6.
Lib Andrews

JANE'S SPINACH PIE

10-16 ounces spinach, washed
   and cut up
1 or 2 medium onions, cut up
1 clove garlic, diced
¼ cup green pepper, diced

2 large eggs
2 cups milk
½ cup cubed cheese
pinch of sage
1 unbaked pie shell

Sauté garlic, onion and pepper in oil. Add spinach and pinch of sage. Stir fry until limp. Meanwhile beat eggs and add milk and cubed cheese. Mix with spinach. Pour into unbaked pie shell. Bake 350° about 35 minutes or until lightly browned.

SPINACH SQUARES

2 packages frozen chopped
   spinach
2 eggs, beaten
1 can cream of mushroom soup
1 cup mayonnaise

1 small onion, chopped
½ teaspoon salt
½ teaspoon pepper
1 cup cheese crackers, crushed
2 tablespoons butter, melted

Boil spinach in small amount of water until thawed; drain well. Mix eggs, soup, mayonnaise, onion and seasonings together. Stir in spinach and mix well. Spoon into buttered oblong baking dish; top with crushed crackers and butter and bake at 350° for 45 minutes. Cut into squares for serving. Serves: 6.

Evelyn Mora

SPINACH, RICE AND CHEESE CASSEROLE

3 cups rice, cooked
4 eggs, beaten
1 cup milk
1 tablespoon onion, grated
2 teaspoons salt
½ teaspoon rosemary

¼ cup butter, melted
1 pound cheddar cheese, grated
1 package cooked spinach,
   drained
½ teaspoon thyme

Mix, in order: butter, milk, onion, seasonings, eggs, cheese, rice and spinach. Bake 35 minutes at 350° in casserole dish. Serves: 4 to 6.

Nancy Barton

SQUASH-CRANBERRY CASSEROLE

4 8-ounce pieces Hubbard squash
½ cup light corn syrup
2 tablespoons butter
¼ teaspoon salt

½ cup sugar
1 tablespoon cornstarch
⅓ cup water
1½ cups cranberries

Peel and cut squash into serving-sized chunks. Arrange in cook-and-serve dish. Combine syrup, butter, and salt; heat to boiling. Pour over squash. Cover with foil and bake at 350° 45-55 minutes or until nearly tender. In saucepan combine sugar, cornstarch and water. Heat to boiling, stirring constantly. Add cranberries and cook 5 minutes. Pour over squash and continue to bake covered for 10 minutes. Serves: 8.

Mary Halverstadt

SQUASH SOUFFLÉ

2 cups milk
2 eggs, beaten
½ teaspoon salt
1-1½ teaspoons cinnamon
½ teaspoon nutmeg
1/8 stick margarine, melted
½ cup flour

⅓ cup sugar
½ teaspoon vanilla
2 cups winter squash (butternut,
  Hubbard, acorn) cooked and
  puréed (or 2 package frozen
  squash defrosted)

Mix flour, seasonings and sugar. Fold into milk, eggs, butter, vanilla and squash. Turn into greased baking dish and bake at 350° for 1 hour. Serve immediately.

Bob McMaster

SUMMER SQUASH CASSEROLE

2 pounds yellow summer squash,
  sliced (6 cups)
1 can condensed cream of
  chicken or mushroom soup
1 cup dairy sour cream

1 cup carrots, shredded
1 8-ounce package herb-seasoned
  stuffing mix
½ cup butter, melted
1 onion, chopped

In saucepan cook sliced squash and chopped onion in boiling salted water for 5 minutes; drain. Combine cream of chicken (or mushroom) soup and sour cream. Stir in shredded carrots; fold in drained squash and onion. Combine stuffing mix and butter. Spread half of stuffing mixture in bottom of 12"x7½"x2" baking dish. Spoon vegetable mixture atop. Sprinkle remaining stuffing over vegetables. Bake in 350° oven for 25-30 minutes. Serves: 6.

Catherine Kelleher

TOM SAWYER'S SUCCOTASH

2 pounds fresh shell beans (the
  kind with pink and white
  striped pods and beans),
  shelled
salt and butter to taste

1 dozen ears freshly picked corn,
  husked
1 piece salt pork about 2" square,
  scored down to rind

Cover beans with water, add salt pork. Cook, covered, until beans are tender. Fresh beans should take no longer than about 15 minutes. While beans are cooking, scrape raw kernels from corn cobs, reserving juice. Add corn and juice to beans and water; simmer only 2 or 3 minutes. Add dab of butter and salt to taste. Remove pork and serve at once in its delightful runny condition. Do not drain. Serves: 8 (generously).

Hope for leftovers: Tom considers it even better when heated up the next day. It freezes well. This is a taste that generations of New Englanders would almost lay down their lives for.

Helen Clark

We are indebted to the American Indians for this recipe. They ingeniously planted beans and corn in the same hill so that the climbing beans were supported by the sturdy corn stalks. When beans and corn were ripe, and so lovingly entwined; it seemed natural to cook them together. They called the dish succotash, and so it remains to this day.

OLD FASHIONED STEWED TOMATOES

4 medium tomatoes, peeled and
   diced (or canned tomatoes)
seasonings to taste: pinch of
   basil, thyme, oregano,
   marjoram, parsley, dill,
   caraway, onion flakes

2 teaspoons sugar
½ teaspoon salt
pepper to taste
butter to taste
2 slices bread, diced

Mix all ingredients in saucepan and bring to boil. Simmer for few minutes to meld the flavors. Alternate: pour all ingredients into baking dish and bake for 10 minutes at 350°. Dot the stewed tomatoes with butter just before serving.

GOLDEN VEGETABLE BAKE

2 tablespoons butter
2 tablespoons flour
1 cup milk, scalded
1 teaspoon salt
¾ teaspoon paprika
1/8 teaspoon pepper

2 eggs, beaten
1½ cups carrots, shredded
1 can cream style corn (1¾ cups)
⅓ cup green peppers, chopped
2 tablespoons onion

Melt butter, add flour and blend. Gradually add milk and seasonings. Stir a little hot mixture into eggs. Add egg mixture to sauce. Stir in vegetables. Pour into greased 1½-quart dish and bake at 350° for 50-60 minutes.

Mrs. Oscar Hollander, Jr.

VEGETABLE CASSEROLE

3-4 carrots, sliced
6-8 small onions, sliced
1 small zucchini squash, sliced
1 small summer squash, sliced
small amount of cauliflower

cheese, cubed or sliced
1 can celery soup
turkey or chicken dressing
   crumbs

In small amount of water cook together carrots, onions, zucchini, summer squash, and cauliflower until just tender. Drain. Put half of vegetables in a baking dish. Cover with ½ can of celery soup and half the cheese. Add remaining vegetables and another layer of cheese and soup. Top with turkey or chicken dressing crumbs. Bake at 350° for 20-25 minutes or until thoroughly heated.

Martha Gosse

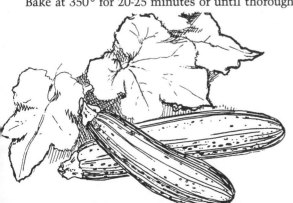

CURRIED VEGETABLES

1 medium onion, chopped
2 tablespoons oil
1 small head cauliflower broken
   into flowerets
1 medium eggplant, in 1" pieces
4 medium size carrots, ¼" slices
2 green peppers, ¼" strips
½ cup boiling water

½ pound green beans, broken
   in half
1 teaspoon chili powder
1 teaspoon cummin, ground
¾ teaspoon turmeric, ground
½ teaspoon cardamon, ground
1 bay leaf
½ cup tomato juice

Sauté onions in oil until yellow. Add vegetables, spices, bay leaf and cook about 5 minutes. Add boiling water and simmer 10 minutes. Add tomato juice and cook until vegetables are tender. Remove bay leaf and correct seasoning. Serves: 6-8.

Chris Mitchell

VEGETARIAN BURGERS

6 tablespoons butter or margarine
1 cup onion, finely chopped
1 cup celery, finely chopped
1 cup carrots, coarsely chopped
1 cup walnuts, finely chopped
2 eggs, slightly beaten

1 cup fine dry bread crumbs,
   Italian type
¾ teaspoon salt (can reduce
   if using salted butter or
   margarine)

Melt 4 tablespoons butter in large skillet over medium heat, add onion; sauté until tender. Stir in celery, carrots and walnuts; sauté 2 minutes longer. Remove from heat, stir in bread crumbs, eggs, salt. Form into patties and fry in remaining butter.

Good hot or cold with creamy dill dressing or catsup. Also can be done on an outdoor grill (instead of hot dogs and hamburgers). Try melted cheese on top and add different vegetables, i.e. raw zucchini.

Christina Murley

LENTIL STUFFED ZUCCHINI

¾ cups lentils, cooked with dash
   of soy sauce until tender
4 tablespoons ketchup
1 large onion, chopped
1 zucchini squash

fresh tomatoes to make thick
   mixture when combined with
   ketchup and lentils
1 green pepper, chopped

Sauté onion and pepper; add lentils, tomatoes and ketchup. Take center from zucchini and mix with other ingredients. Stuff into zucchini. Place in baking dish; cook at 350° for 45 minutes.

This is an English recipe calling for "Marrow" — a squash similar to our zucchini.

Judy Pease

Miscellaneous

Picking berries at Green Briar.

DINING AT THE ALMSHOUSE

The town voted in 1823 to reduce annual costs of support of the poor through establishment of a farm with a large residence building and professional keeper to quarter many of the persons who needed town support. The keeper's wife was cook and nurse. This farm was located on Charles Street in the present Crow Farm area. Its cost to the town was indeed minimal. Figures for 1843 show that it cost 88 cents per week to keep each resident, including food, supplies and keeper's salary. (Take-home pay for a Boston & Sandwich Glass Factory worker was on the order of 9 dollars per week.)

With inflation, costs rose to $2.29 per person per week at the Almshouse after the Civil War and there were demands for retrenchment and for obtaining useful work from the children of indigents. There were a great many vagrants on the road, some looking for work and all looking for hand-outs, which caused many householders to be nervous. Every night a number of tramps were allowed to eat and sleep at the Almshouse. This was considered generous, even when it was shown that the added cost to the town was only 12 cents per tramp per night. The history of the town of Wayland shows that the overseers of their Almshouse ordered that tramps should be fed on crackers and water only.

At the opposite end of the spectrum of generosity, Sandwich's benefactor, Jonathan Bourne of New Bedford, for whom the town of Bourne was named in 1884, provided a free turkey dinner for everyone at the Almshouse each Thanksgiving up to his death in 1889.

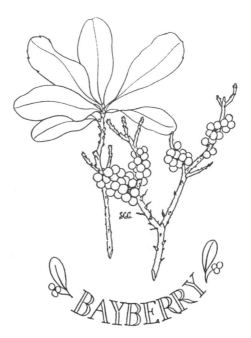

BAYBERRY

182

INSTRUCTIONS FOR BAYBERRY CANDLES

10 pounds of bayberries makes 1 pound of wax
1 pound wax makes 2 good size candles

Remove berries from twigs; pick them over to remove any leaves or twigs. Put a few berries in colander and shake back and forth to remove dust. Put berries in kettle filled with water. Use a large kettle so the wax will float to the top. Heat gently over medium heat for several hours. Remove from heat and place in a cool place, preferably out of doors, and wax will form in a solid cake.

Remove wax and brush off any sediment, and put it in a small kettle filled with water. Place over low heat until entirely melted and strain through cheesecloth. Repeat if necessary. Now your wax is ready for the molds, or to dip by hand. If you use a mold have the wicks longer than the molds, so you can pull out candles. Put wick in mold, and dip the tip of wick into warm wax and let harden. Then pour your wax into the mold. If you use a teapot, wax will be easier to handle. Hold the mold in upright position or tie to faucet. Let stand in cool place half a day. Then take a sharp pointed knife and loosen candles at the base and pull out. Here is where a long wick is handy. If candles do not come out easily, it is because your wax was not clean enough, and you will have to pour boiling water over the molds to loosen them.

CANDIED CRANBERRIES

A CAPE COD RECIPE:

½ cup firm cranberries   ½ cup sugar
½ cup water

Wash and dry berries and prick each with a needle. Boil sugar and water until syrup spins a thread (234°F.). Add berries and continue cooking until syrup forms a hard ball in cold water (250°F.). Lift berries from syrup, remove to wax paper and let stand until well dried. Roll in granulated sugar. Use like candied cherries.

The number and variety of things that were candied and used as sweet-meats is rather astonishing. Many types of flowers, such as violets, marigolds, cowslips and primroses were candied and scattered on salads, desserts and iced cakes.

CANDIED VIOLETS

1 cup sugar	¼ teaspoon rosewater
¼ cup water	OR ¼ teaspoon almond extract

Make a syrup of sugar and water and boil for awhile, stirring often. Add rosewater or almond extract and let syrup cool. Now take the violets which you have gathered and put some of them, a few at a time, into the syrup. Let them stay there for a minute or so, being sure they are treated all over. Then remove to wax paper with a skimmer or your fingers and put more in. If the syrup gets hard half-way through, cook up again adding a very little water. Place the candied violets to dry thoroughly before storing. Store between layers of wax paper in cardboard box.

Edna D. Ericksen

HOMEMADE SOAP

5 pounds lukewarm melted grease	½ cup cold water
1 cup (1 pound can) lye	3 tablespoons borax
1 quart cold water	¼ cup ammonia
	1 teaspoon salt

Dissolve lye in cold water and let stand until cool; add fat slowly, stirring constantly. Mix other ingredients together and add to first mixture. Stir whole until thick and light colored. Pour into pan lined with cloth. Mark into pieces of desired size before soap becomes hard. When hard, break pieces apart and pile in such a way as to insure free circulation of air in order that soap may dry out well before using.

Fats that are not fit for food and fat too dark to use for further deep fat frying may be made into soap at a saving of about 75 percent over an ordinary grade of commercial laundry soap.

SCRAP BOOK PASTE

2 tablespoons cornstarch   *1 cup cold water*

Mix together cornstarch and water. Bring to boil, stirring until it thickens and clarifies. Store in jar in refrigerator (or it molds). Does not darken paper as it ages. Some do. Non toxic! Non staining! and it sticks!

Betty Duquet

TO MAKE A ROSE POTPOURRI

First of all the roses should be just blown, of the sweetest smelling varieties and gathered as dry as possible. After each gathering spread the petals out upon a sheet of paper and leave until they are free from all moisture. Then place a layer of petals in your jar, sprinkling with very coarse salt, and so on, alternating layers of petals and sprinklings of salt until jar is almost filled. Leave for a few days until a froth is formed, then mix thoroughly, adding more petals and salt and repeat mixing operation daily for a week.

The next step is the addition of various aromatic gums and spices, such as benzoin, cassia buds, cinnamon, cloves, cardamon and vanilla beans, all of which may be obtained at any drug store. Five cents each of benzoin, cassia buds (or ½ teaspoon ground cinnamon) and 5 cents worth cardamon beans will be sufficient for an ordinary jar. Cloves should be used sparingly, probably half dozen whole ones bruised in a mortar, or not more than a half a teaspoon of the ground spice. One vanilla bean will suffice.

After these have been added, mix again and leave for a few days more when you may add the essential oils. Those of the jasmin, violet, tuberose and attar of rose are best, with just a hint of ambergris and musk, and all of these must be procured from a perfumer, although a druggist could get them for you if he chose to. Ten cents worth of each of these is enough, with the exception of attar of roses, these drops being so exceptionally pleasing for a rose jar that twice the amount may be used.

Mix the oils in thoroughly and keep covered except when you wish to perfume your room.

If these directions are followed carefully, you will have a rose jar which will be a joy forever.

JEFFERSON'S TWO RULES

Two rules of Jefferson are very applicable to the times:
— "Never spend your money before you get it;" and
"Never buy what you do not want because it is cheap."

— from an 1852 Family Receipt Book

DANDELION GREENS

Remove the brown leaves and roots of the dandelions and wash in at least three waters. Let soak overnight in cold water. Cook in a small amount of boiling salted water, to which a pinch of baking soda is added when the boiling point is reached. Simmer greens about 1 hour, then drain well and serve with lemon juice, vinegar, or the fat from fried salt pork.

Dandelions were considered to be a natural spring tonic and were dug up in the spring before the buds had opened.

COOKING IS COMFORTING

Cooking is comforting, and so
When everything goes awry
It's wise to stop our worrying
And make an apple pie.
When unexpected sorrow comes
To make our poor hearts ache,
There's nothing helps us more than work
So bake a luscious cake.
For, as the body wants good food
To keep it strong and whole,
Perhaps it's work the spirit needs
To make a healthy soul.
A simple task can calm our mind,
And consolation bring;
A job well done allays our grief —
Cooking IS comforting.

HELP OUT

Ready on my pantry shelves
Are cans both great and small,
Just to help me fix a lunch
When friends make me a call.

In the corners of my heart
I store the joys I've had,
To cheer me up with memories
When else I might grow sad.

New Mode of Washing Materials

Half a pound of Soap, half a pound of Soda and a quarter of a pound of quick lime

Preparation

Cut up the Soap and dissolve it in ½ a gal. of boiling Water, pour ½ a gal. of boiling Water over the ½ lb. of Soda and a sufficient quantity of boiling Water over the ¼ lb. of Lime to cover it, the Lime must be quick and fresh, if quick it will bubble up on pouring the boiling Water over it. Each of the three must be prepared in separate vessels, then put the dissolved lime and Soda together and boil them twenty min. after which pour them in a Jar to settle.

A SPIDER!!

A "spider" is a black iron frying pan that earlier had legs for use on the hearth. The legs are no longer necessary, but the spider continues to be a popular utensil whether used in the oven or on top of the stove.

ROSEMARY

Before Route 6A by-pass was built there was a house on Brady's Island. The Brady family had to walk the railroad tracks to reach town. Access to the railroad tracks was over a small foot bridge behind where the police station is now.

The chocolate plant is known to botanists as THEOBROMA CACAO, meaning FOOD OF THE GODS. The tree grows to the average height of thirteen feet, and from five to eight inches in diameter. It requires an average temperature of 80 degrees F for proper development. The seeds are removed from the fully ripened pods and cured before being processed.

The Nye Homestead on Old County Road, an historic preservation project of the Nye family of America Association, was built by Benjamin Nye, one of the first fifty men to settle Sandwich. In 1669 he built one of the first grist mills in the country, and shortly thereafter started his home nearby. The mill no longer exists, but the lovely colonial home shows ample evidence to trace the many changes through the years from the original small peaked roof central chimney building, through first floor additions, to the final addition of the complete second floor. The house, now open to the public, stands in its original setting, a reminder of days past in the history of Sandwich.

HAVE YOU TRIED ADDING:

Chopped chives and parsley to diced buttered carrots or summer squash?

Onions chopped fine to beets or string beans when served with French dressing as a salad?

Brown buttered bread crumbs sprinkled over string beans?

A few capers to chicken salad and to drawn butter sauce for fish or lamb?

A tablespoon of sherry to prepared halves of grapefruit or to a fruit cup?

A cube of mint jelly to prepared grapefruit halves?

A little cheese to cream sauce for creamed fish, potatoes or cauliflower?

Hoxie 1680 House

Town meeting records for 15 May 1690 state: "The Towne hath given Lodwick Hawkse a quarter of an acre of land to set his hous upon for convenience for water", but it was not the Hoxie House we know today. Sandwich's Hoxie House, which is reputed to be the oldest dwelling on Cape Cod, was owned by descendents of Rev. John Smith who came to Sandwich in 1675. The house now bears the name Hoxie after the family who lived there in the mid-1800's. The house still has its original foundation for the fireplace, and many of its original timbers. A window of the period was used to reproduce the casements. The Hoxie House, on its original site overlooking Shawme Pond, helps preserve the true feeling of earlier times in Sandwich.

THE HERB GARDEN

Parsley and thyme and mint and sage,
Tarragon, chives and rue,
Basil and borage and bay and dill,
All had their work to do.
Different powers in different herbs,
Everyone knew were hiding,
So Grandma put rosemary in her shoe
When Grandpa took her riding.
What was the magical spell it cast
To bind two lives together,
Tight in a love that should live and last
Through cloudy and sunny weather!
Grandma, of course, was supposed to be shy
And wait, till he spoke of his fancies,
But Grandma put rosemary in her shoe,
She wasn't taking chances.

1959 marked the completion of the beautification of the Town's artesian well area. At the suggestion of the Woman's Club of Sandwich, a Committee under the capable leadership of Winnifred Coe, supervised the town-funded masonry work. The fountain, with its over-look at the Grist Mill, is now one of the most popular stopping points in Sandwich.

Observations of a long time Sandwich resident — written in 1940's:

"A cranberry bog looks rather like a rice paddy, the product of hands and spades, but it is a nest of elaborate machinery for digging, pumping, dusting, spraying, plowing, burning and many other things. Nearly every grower is a graduate gadgetologist. His powerful pumps may be made of Buick rear-ends and discarded tug-boat propellers, but they run as sweetly as if they were Pratt and Whitney."

"The most entertaining piece of equipment is the separator which guards the cranberry sauce from inferior berries. The principle is simple. The berries are dropped automatically against a "bounce board" set at a 45 degree angle. If they bounce high enough, they leap over another board rejoicing. It they do not, they have to try again. This process is repeated several times and eliminates almost all the unworthy berries. The only ones it cannot reject are the green ones which are pinky-white. These are removed by hand."

There is a gingko tree on Jarves Street. This tree is a descendant of an ice age tree. It grows to about 100 feet tall and has fan shaped leaves. These leaves turn yellow in the fall and drop to the ground in a very short time.

ATAVISM

Agatha Jane was a barnyard cat
Born on a tussock of hay,
One of a family of six, and so
Her mistress gave her away.
And we brought her home to the city,
To our wee little two by four,
Where there's never a sight of a meadow,
And cement comes up to the door.
And we buy her the best of cat meat,
And give her the top of the milk,
And all our friends admire her,
As she lies on her cushion of silk.

DID YOU KNOW THAT:

Some of the piling groups that can be seen on the Scorton Marsh are the founda-
tions for platforms, called staddles, that the salt marsh hay was piled on after
harvest. When the ground in the marsh firmed in the fall, the farmer would bring
the hay to the farm to be used in the winter. The availability of the hay was one
of the reasons the first settlers came here.

TABLE OF EQUIVALENTS

Volumes of Liquids
3 teaspoons is 1 tablespoon
2 tablespoons is 1 ounce or ⅛ cup
5 tablespoons plus 1 teaspoon is ⅓ cup
1 pony is 1 ounce
1 jigger is 1½ ounces
1 large jigger is 2 ounces
1 wineglass is 4 ounces, which is ½ cup or 1 gill
8 ounces is 1 cup
16 ounces is 2 cups or 1 pint
32 ounces is 4 cups or 1 quart
128 ounces is 4 quarts or 1 gallon
25.6 ounces is 1 fifth (a fifth of a gallon or 4/5 of a quart)
40 ounces is an imperial quart
24 ounces is a typical wine bottle (champagne is 26 ounces)
1 liter (1000 milliliters) is 1.0567 quarts or 33.8 ounces.
1.75 liters is 1.85 quarts or 59.2 ounces
3.785 liters is 1 gallon

Weight of solids (dry)
1 pound is 16 ounces or 454 grams
1 kilogram is 1,000 grams or 2.2 pounds
1 bushel is 64 pounds or 4 pecks
1 peck is 16 pounds or 8 quarts
4 quarts is 8 pounds
1 quart is 2 pounds
1 pint is 1 pound or 2 cups of standard measuring size (level full)
Some foods will equal 2 cups to a pound, including butter, cottage cheese, oil, and granulated sugar.
Others are lighter: cocoa, bread flour, chopped nuts, grated cheese are 4 cups to the pound.

Other equivalents
5 whole eggs are 1 cup
8 egg whites are 1 cup
16 egg yolks are 1 cup
2⅓ cups raw rice is 1 pound
1 cup raw rice is 3 to 4 cups cooked
4 cups chopped walnuts is 2½ pounds unshelled
juice of 1 lemon is 2 to 3 tablespoons
juice of 1 orange is 6 to 8 tablespoons

FRUIT IN THE SUN COOKER

The unique sun-cooking operation at the Green Briar Jam Kitchen may be viewed during the summer months.

A NOTE ON GLASSES FOR DRINKS

Both size and shape of the glass are important to a satisfying drink — not as critical as the contents, but not to be ignored. A thirsty soul is restive at being offered something in a little four ounce cup, and a person who cannot face a huge drink should not be offered anything in a twelve-ounce tumbler, even ginger ale or iced tea.

A standard size is eight ounces (one cup). This comes in many shapes, of which a favorite is a squat, solid double-old-fashioned glass; the same volume occupies a modest tall tumbler. Taller glass tumblers come in nine, ten, and twelve-ounce sizes.

Twelve ounces is about the capacity of the usual coffee/cocoa mug, and beer steins are usually of sixteen ounces. The importance of shape is seen in the nearly spherical brandy breather glass, of which the standard size holds no less than twenty ounces. Beside a little brandy and lots of fumes, this glass looks and feels right holding Irish coffee with lots of whipped cream.

British glasses come in Imperial measures such as beer pints of twenty ounces. The yard glass of coaching days is thirty-six inches long and holds when full (no foam) an imperial quart of 40 ounces.

Finally, pretty stemmed glasses with a shallow bowl for strained (straight up) cocktails have three faults: they are too small, too spilly, and warm up too fast. The more compact the shape the more efficient on all these counts.

FRIENDS

They are kind to each other's hopes . . .
they cherish each other's dreams.

— Thoreau

THORNTON W. BURGESS

An imaginative naturalist of international reputation, Thornton W. Burgess produced more than 170 books and 15,000 stories in a writing career which spanned five decades. In print and on the radio, his Mother West Wind and Peter Rabbit stories have provided not only beloved bedtime companions but animal "teachers" as well.

Burgess was born in 1874 in the Cape Cod town of Sandwich. Later he drew on childhood memories to create charming bedtime stories for his own young son. Animal characters came alive in habitats such as the Old Briar Patch, Smiling Pool, and Crooked Little Path.

Through his books and stories Burgess' own definition of the word 'conservation' is kept alive today . . . "to re-establish and maintain nature's fine balance among all living things and to hold as a sacred trust the obligation to make only the best possible use of natural resources, to the end that the inheritance we of today have received from the past may be passed on unimpaired, even improved, to future generations.

In 1974, on the 100th anniversary of the birth of Thornton W. Burgess, a museum was established in his name. The museum, located on Water Street in the historic village of Sandwich, contains the largest collection of Thornton W. Burgess material known.

In 1979, the landmark Green Briar Jam Kitchen on Discovery Hill Road was purchased by the Society. This property is adjacent to the Briar Patch, preserved as conservation land, home to Peter Rabbit and friends, and is now the Green Briar Nature Center.

AVOIDING COOKING DISASTERS

Read your recipe thoroughly, often enough to understand it. • Assemble all ingredients, and have the necessary tools at hand. • Use the right sized pot or pan for your particular recipe. Too large a pot causes too much evaporation; too small a pot, too little. • The wrong temperature is probably responsible for more cooking failures than any other single factor. • Always check your oven. Power fluctuations, surges and drops, can alter the temperature by 50 to 100 degrees. • Use recommended temperature for deep fat frying. Your food will absorb less fat. • Invest in some good thermometers: oven, deep fat, instant probe for meats. • Top of the stove sautéing, using high heat, is best done in a cast iron skillet. • Too high a temperature used in top of the stove cooking usually results in ruined food, ruined pan, and in some cases may even be grounds for divorce. • If the salt is left out of some baked products, the recipe will fail. Salt produces a necessary chemical reaction with the other ingredients. • You cannot make a butter cookie with margarine and produce a butter cookie. BUTTER IS BUTTER!

MY MOTHER'S ADVICE TO THE BRIDE: Always try out a new recipe before your husband comes home. If it fails, you have sufficient time to throw it away and prepare his favorite quick dish.

R.C.

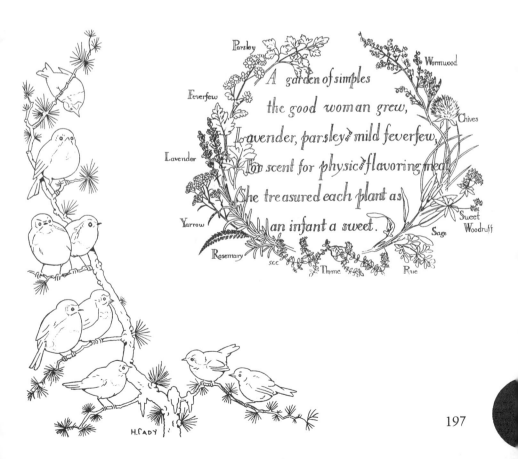

A garden of simples the good woman grew,
Lavender, parsley & mild feverfew,
For scent for physic & flavoring meat
She treasured each plant as an infant a sweet.

Parsley Wormwood Feverfew Chives Lavender Yarrow Sweet Woodruff Sage Rosemary Thyme Rue

H. CADY

COCKTAILS

In 1842 Charles Dickens wrote of his visit to a Boston hotel:

"The bar is a large room with a stone floor, and there people stand and smoke and lounge about, all the evening; dropping in and out as the humour takes them. There too the stranger is initiated into the mysteries of Gin-sling, Cocktail, Sangaree, Mint Julep, Sherry Cobbler, Timber Doodle and other rare drinks."

This seems to be a very early reference to the cocktail. In the History of Cape Cod, Frederick Freeman says in his comments on Timothy Ruggles of the Newcomb Tavern, on Grove Street in Sandwich: "He personally attends both bar and stable, equally expert whether in currying a horse, mixing a cocktail, impressing his guests with the extent of his varied lore . . ."

Ruggles was a host at the Tavern in Sandwich from 1736 to 1753, but we expect that the word "cocktail" was becoming current in the 1850's, and that Freeman used it as a popular word rather than from actual description of Ruggles' bar. The dictionary now says that cocktails were invented in the Prohibition period to cover the taste of poor liquor.

COMPLAINT AGAINST SILAS BLUSH

Sandwich Dec 17 - 1803

 Mr. Nye - Sir there is one Silas Blush in this place with his wife Cloey, and four or five children who live intirely by Pilfering & stealing he took Ground to till this year where-on he had forty or fifty bushels of corn & two Lazy to Gather it. Sold it all standing & has no other way to Get Corn but by stealing as he will not work. Esq. Bacon told me he would bind him, wife & children out when ever the Town of Sandwich had a mind to send them should have done it before if he had not Gon of.   *Your hu^m Svt*
   John Freeman

 To the Selectmen of the Town of Sandwich - I hereby enter my complaint to you against Silas Blush as a Topper, he continually pilforing and makes a great disturbance in the neighborhood, therefore pray you would take immediate measures to send him back to his Town of Boston where he belongs.
  Sandwich Dec 20 1803   *John Freeman*

Index

Gathering hay on the salt marsh.

The great marsh at Sandy Neck showing salt marsh hay "staddles".

SALT MARSHES OF GREAT VALUE

Salt marshes along the northern shores of Bourne, Sandwich, and Barnstable were considered of great value by early settlers. The settlers agreed the marsh was to belong to cattle owners. They cut their own proportional part of the hay, stacked it on "staddles" formed on the marsh and took it ashore as needed.

The contiguous marshes of Sandwich and adjoining Barnstable form the largest salt marsh in the state of Massachusetts.

Yesteryears Doll Museum

PHOTO CREDITS

Rosanna Cullity: Two lady berry-pickers, Picking berries at Green Briar, Cows at Hilliard Farm, Cranberries at Beaton's Bog.

Eleanor Hill: Great Marsh with "staddles", Cows at Sandy Neck.

Beverly Overstreet: Chickens in coop, Sam Jillson digging clams.

William P. Quinn: Rum runner Annie L. Spindler.

Edward C. Robinson: Cranberry separators, Digging clams, Family on porch, Grandma making pie, Harvesting cranberries, Mowing salt marsh hay.

Sandwich Archives: Croquet game, Ice cutting.

Sandwich Historical Society: Daniel Webster Inn (Old Central House).

Titcomb's Bookshop: F. H. Burgess calendar, Ice cream broadside.

Yarmouth Historical Society: Salt works.

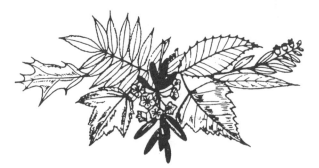

Index

Index

Index

Index

Index

ORDER FORM

"FLAVORS OF CAPE COD" Recipe Collection.
Thornton W. Burgess Society, Inc.
6 Discovery Hill Road, East Sandwich, Massachusetts 02537

Please send me _____ copies of your book at $9.95 per copy, plus $2.25 each for shipping and handling. Massachusetts residents please add 5% Sales Tax (50 cents per copy). Enclosed is my check or money order for total of $_____.
Make checks payable to The T. W. Burgess Society.

Name..

Address...

City/State/Zip..

All proceeds from the sale of the Recipe Collection book support the programs of the non-profit educational Thornton W. Burgess Society. The purpose of the Society is to promote: REVERENCE FOR WILDLIFE AND CONCERN FOR THE NATURAL ENVIRONMENT.

ORDER FORM

"FLAVORS OF CAPE COD" Recipe Collection.
Thornton W. Burgess Society, Inc.
6 Discovery Hill Road, East Sandwich, Massachusetts 02537

Please send me _____ copies of your book at $9.95 per copy, plus $2.25 each for shipping and handling. Massachusetts residents please add 5% Sales Tax (50 cents per copy). Enclosed is my check or money order for total of $_____.
Make checks payable to The T. W. Burgess Society.

Name..

Address...

City/State/Zip..

All proceeds from the sale of the Recipe Collection book support the programs of the non-profit educational Thornton W. Burgess Society. The purpose of the Society is to promote: REVERENCE FOR WILDLIFE AND CONCERN FOR THE NATURAL ENVIRONMENT.

ORDER FORM

"FLAVORS OF CAPE COD" Recipe Collection.
Thornton W. Burgess Society, Inc.
6 Discovery Hill Road, East Sandwich, Massachusetts 02537

Please send me _____ copies of your book at $9.95 per copy, plus $2.25 each for shipping and handling. Massachusetts residents please add 5% Sales Tax (50 cents per copy). Enclosed is my check or money order for total of $_____.
Make checks payable to The T. W. Burgess Society.

Name..

Address...

City/State/Zip..

All proceeds from the sale of the Recipe Collection book support the programs of the non-profit educational Thornton W. Burgess Society. The purpose of the Society is to promote: REVERENCE FOR WILDLIFE AND CONCERN FOR THE NATURAL ENVIRONMENT.

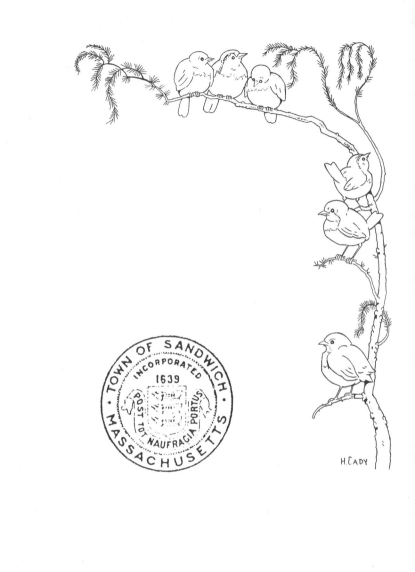

TOWN OF SANDWICH · MASSACHUSETTS
INCORPORATED 1639
POST TOT NAUFRAGIA PORTUS

H. CADY

Dexter Gristmill 1640